The Ismaili Imams

The Ismaili Imams
A Biographical History

by
Farhad Daftary

I.B.TAURIS
in association with
THE INSTITUTE OF ISMAILI STUDIES
LONDON, 2020

I.B. TAURIS
Bloomsbury Publishing Plc
50 Bedford Square, London, WC1B 3DP, UK
1385 Broadway, New York, NY 10018, USA
29 Earlsfort Terrace, Dublin 2, Ireland

In association with
The Institute of Ismaili Studies
Aga Khan Centre, 10 Handyside Street, London N1C 4DN
www.iis.ac.uk

BLOOMSBURY, I.B. TAURIS and the I.B. Tauris logo are trademarks of Bloomsbury Publishing Plc

First published in Great Britain 2020
Reprinted 2020

Cover design: www.paulsmithdesign.com
Cover image © Nour Foundation. Courtesy of the Khalili Family Trust

ISBN: HB: 978-0-7556-1798-2

Typeset by RefineCatch Limited, Bungay, Suffolk
Printed and bound in Great Britain

To find out more about our authors and books visit www.bloomsbury.com
and sign up for our newsletters.

The Institute of Ismaili Studies

The Institute of Ismaili Studies was established in 1977 with the object of promoting scholarship and learning on Islam, in the historical as well as contemporary contexts, and a better understanding of its relationship with other societies and faiths.

The Institute's programmes encourage a perspective which is not confined to the theological and religious heritage of Islam, but seeks to explore the relationship of religious ideas to broader dimensions of society and culture. The programmes thus encourage an interdisciplinary approach to the materials of Islamic history and thought. Particular attention is also given to issues of modernity that arise as Muslims seek to relate their heritage to the contemporary situation.

Within the Islamic tradition, the Institute's programmes promote research on those areas which have, to date, received relatively little attention from scholars. These include the intellectual and literary expressions of Shi'ism in general, and Ismailism in particular.

In the context of Islamic societies, the Institute's programmes are informed by the full range and diversity of cultures in which Islam is practised today, from the Middle East, South and Central Asia, and Africa to the industrialised societies of the West, thus taking into consideration the variety of contexts which shape the ideals, beliefs and practices of the faith.

These objectives are realised through concrete programmes and activities organised and implemented by various departments of the Institute. The Institute also collaborates periodically, on a programme-specific basis, with other institutions of learning in the United Kingdom and abroad.

The Institute's academic publications fall into a number of inter-related categories:

1 Occasional papers or essays addressing broad themes of the relationship between religion and society, with special reference to Islam.

2 Monographs exploring specific aspects of Islamic faith and culture, or the contributions of individual Muslim thinkers or writers.

3 Editions or translations of significant primary or secondary texts.

4 Translations of poetic or literary texts which illustrate the rich heritage of spiritual, devotional and symbolic expressions in Muslim history.

5 Works on Ismaili history and thought, and the relationship of the Ismailis to other traditions, communities and schools of thought in Islam.

6 Proceedings of conferences and seminars sponsored by the Institute.

7 Bibliographical works and catalogues which document manuscripts, printed texts and other source materials.

This book falls into category five listed above.

In facilitating these and other publications, the Institute's sole aim is to encourage original research and analysis of relevant issues. While every effort is made to ensure that the publications are of a high academic standard, there is naturally bound to be a diversity of views, ideas and interpretations. As such, the opinions expressed in these publications must be understood as belonging to their authors alone.

Contents

Tables and Maps

Tables

Maps

Preface

An important Shiʿi Muslim community, the Ismailis have been grossly misunderstood and misrepresented until recent times. This is mainly due to the fact that the rich literature produced by the Ismailis remained inaccessible to 'outsiders'. In the event, the Ismailis were studied and evaluated almost exclusively on the basis of evidence collected, or fabricated, by their detractors. With the recovery and study of genuine Ismaili texts on a large scale, modern scholarship in the field has increasingly painted a completely different picture of Ismaili history and thought – a picture as fascinating as the myths and legends rooted in the animosity or imaginative ignorance of the earlier generations, but one that is rooted in serious scholarship. That the present biographical history of the Ismaili Imams can now be compiled itself attests to the modern progress in Ismaili studies.

The Ismailis are the only Shiʿi Muslim community with a present and living hereditary Imam, who traces his ancestry to ʿAli, the first Shiʿi Imam. This book offers, for the first time, a connected biographical history of all the Ismaili Imams, numbering forty-nine. The Ismailis, who have always remained unwaveringly devoted to their Imams, have had a very long and complex history, dating back to the formative era of Islam when different communities of interpretation were articulating their doctrinal positions.

The Ismailis have experienced many ups and downs in the course of their history. As religious minorities they were frequently obliged to struggle for their survival in many of the lands where they lived. However, at other times they possessed their own caliphate and empire, and their Imams ruled as Fatimid caliphs, in rivalry with the Sunni Abbasid caliphs of Baghdad. At other periods of their history, they were obliged to take refuge in their mountain fortresses and defend themselves passionately against formidable adversaries like the Saljuq Turks, who dispatched large military expeditions against their strongholds in Persia. Against all odds and vicissitudes, including the devastating onslaught of the Mongols, the Ismailis retained their cohesion and religious identity, revolving around the guidance and teachings (*ta'lim*) of their Imams. In due course, they emerged as a progressive and modernised Muslim community, thanks to the enlightened leadership of the last two Ismaili Imams, known internationally as the Aga Khans.

The Ismaili Imams, whose brief biographies are presented here, have lived in many lands. These, in chronological order, have included the Hijaz, the birthplace of Islam, Iraq, Syria, Ifriqiya (today's Tunisia), Egypt, Persia, India and finally Europe. Of all these regions, the Imams' residence in Persia, lasting more than seven centuries until 1841, was the longest continuous period. The members of the Ismaili community, or Jamat, too, have been scattered in many countries and regions, and today may be found on almost every continent, with the majority in Asia, the Middle East, Africa and certain Western countries. They hail from a diversity of ethnicities, speak a variety of languages and represent a plurality of cultural backgrounds. However, all Ismailis are united in their unwavering devotion to their 'Imam of the time'.

The sources of information on Ismaili Imams, too, are diverse and varied in genre and language. For some Imams, notably those who ruled as Fatimid caliphs, the information is abundant. In fact, several monographs have been written on some Fatimid Imam-caliphs. At the other end of the spectrum there are the so-called concealed Imams, who made every effort to guard secretly their identity and other biographical details. This is reflected in the fact that some entries in this book contain considerable details which are absent in certain other biographies. In fact, in a few cases, due to a dearth of information, we have been obliged to treat two or three Imams as a group rather than separately and individually.

This book draws on a wide range of historical and other types of source materials. The author also draws extensively on the results of his own research on Ismaili history, accumulated over more than five decades since the 1960s, and presented in his book *The Isma'ilis: Their History and Doctrines* and other works cited here in the select bibliography. As noted, the modern scholarship in Ismaili studies is a relatively new field of Islamic studies, and with continuous progress in this field doubtless the missing details of at least some of the biographies of the Ismaili Imams may in due course be filled.

It remains for me to extend my deepest gratitude to a number of colleagues at The Institute of Ismaili Studies who contributed significantly to the completion of this biographical project. In particular, Isabel Miller and Tara Woolnough provided invaluable editorial help and Russell Harris assisted greatly in identifying and obtaining images in addition to producing the maps and genealogical tables. I would also like to thank Wafi Momin and his colleagues at the Ismaili Special Collections Unit of the Institute for providing some of the images related to the Alamut period of Ismaili history. I also benefitted from Alnoor Merchant's vast knowledge of Ismaili numismatics, for which I remain indebted to him. Finally, special thanks are due to Fayaz Alibhai, who initiated an earlier version of this project in connection with his inputs into the Ismaili Heritage Project of the Institute.

FD
May 2020

Part One

The Ismaili Imamate in History

The Ismailis represent the second largest Shi'i Muslim community, after the Twelver (or Ithna'ashari) Shi'is, and today they are scattered as religious minorities throughout more than thirty countries of Asia, the Middle East, Africa, Europe and North America. The Ismailis have had their own complex and highly eventful history dating back to the formative period of Islam, when different communities of interpretation elaborated their distinctive doctrinal positions. One of these early Shi'i communities, the Imamis, propounded a doctrine of the Imamate that subsequently served as the central teaching of the Ismailis who, together with the Twelvers, evolved out of the early Imami Shi'i community.

The Shi'i doctrine of the Imamate was based on the belief in the permanent need of humankind for a divinely guided, sinless and infallible Imam who, after the Prophet Muhammad, would act as the authoritative teacher and guide of men in all their spiritual affairs. This Imam would be entitled to temporal leadership as much as to religious authority. However, his mandate would not depend on his actual rule over any portion of the Muslim society (*umma*). This doctrine further taught that the Prophet himself had designated his cousin and son-in-law, 'Ali b. Abi Talib, as his legatee (*wasi*) and successor, by an explicit designation (*nass*) under divine command. After 'Ali, the

Imamate would be transmitted from father to son by the rule of *nass*, or designation, among the descendants of 'Ali and his spouse Fatima, the Prophet's daughter. And after his son Husayn b. 'Ali, it would continue in the Husaynid 'Alid line until the end of time. Indeed, the Prophet himself is reported to have said: 'Verily I am leaving among you two weighty things, and if you hold on to them you will not go astray after me: the book of God and my progeny.'

This 'Alid Imam belonging to the *ahl al-bayt*, or the Prophet's family, is the sole legitimate Imam at any time. Indeed, the world could not exist for a moment without such an Imam who is the 'proof of God' (*hujjat Allah*) on earth. The Imam's existence in the terrestrial world was viewed as so essential that the recognition of the 'Imam of the time' and obedience to him were made the absolute duty of every believer (*mu'min*). This book is the first attempt of its kind to compile brief biographies of all the Imams acknowledged by the Ismailis throughout the course of their history.

The Ismailis share their earliest history with the Twelvers, and some other Shi'i groups who are no longer in existence. This period, from 'Ali b. Abi Talib (d. 661) to his great-great-grandson Ja'far al-Sadiq (d. 765), coincided with the early history of Imami Shi'ism when the doctrine of the Imamate was also formulated. It was in the aftermath of Imam al-Sadiq's death that the consolidated Imami Shi'is, then concentrated in southern Iraq, split into a number of groupings each one recognising a different one of his sons as their new Imam. Under the circumstances, the Ismailis recognised Isma'il, Imam al-Sadiq's original heir-designate, and separated from the rest of the Imami Shi'is. Named after Isma'il, the Ismailis then commenced their independent existence as a distinct Imami Shi'i community.

The opening phase of Ismaili history, lasting until the foundation of the Fatimid caliphate in 909, remains rather obscure as we do not have any reliable sources from this period when the Ismaili Imams remained in concealment to protect themselves against the Abbasids' rampant persecution of the 'Alids. Indeed, during this *dawr al-satr* or period of concealment in early Ismaili history, the Imams made every effort to hide their true identity and places of residence, also adopting a variety of pseudonyms, all as *taqiyya* or precautionary dissimulation tactics. However, it is known with certainty that the early Ismaili Imams successfully organised a revolutionary, dynamic movement designated as *al-da'wa al-hadiya*, 'the rightly guiding mission', or simply as the *da'wa*, 'mission'. The religio-political message of the pre-Fatimid Ismaili *da'wa* revolved around uprooting the Abbasids, who had usurped the legitimate rights of the 'Alids, and installing the Ismaili Imam to a new Shi'i caliphate. This message was disseminated by a network of *da'is*, or summoners. The secret central headquarters of the *da'wa* organisation were eventually located in Salamiyya, Syria. By shortly after the middle of the ninth century, Ismaili *da'is* were active in almost every important region of the Muslim lands, from Central Asia to North Africa.

The success of the early Ismaili *da'wa* culminated in the establishment of the Fatimid caliphate in 909 in North Africa, in a region then known as Ifriqiya (now covering Tunisia and eastern Algeria). The establishment of the Fatimid caliphate represented not only a great success for the Ismailis, who now for the first time possessed an important state (*dawla*) under the leadership of their Imam, but for the entire Shi'a as well. Not since the time of 'Ali had the Shi'i Muslims witnessed the succession of an 'Alid from the *ahl al-bayt* to the actual leadership of a major Muslim state. The Fatimid victory, thus, heralded the fulfilment of a long-awaited Shi'i ideal.

The ground had been meticulously prepared for Fatimid rule in North Africa by the *da'i* Abu 'Abd Allah al-Shi'i, who had been active amongst the Kutama Berbers of Ifriqiya since 893. He converted the bulk of the Kutama tribal confederation and transformed them into a disciplined army. It was with the help of his Kutama tribal warriors that Abu 'Abd Allah achieved his speedy conquest of Ifriqiya, which was then ruled by the Sunni Aghlabids on behalf of the Abbasids. Meanwhile, after a long and eventful journey from Salamiyya, which commenced in 902, the contemporary Ismaili Imam, 'Abd Allah al-Mahdi (d. 934) had settled in the remote trading town of Sijilmasa (in today's south-eastern Morocco). In 909, the *da'i* Abu 'Abd Allah handed over the reins of power to his Imam in Sijilmasa.

On 4 January 910, 'Abd Allah al-Mahdi made his triumphant entry into Qayrawan, the capital of Ifriqiya, and was proclaimed caliph. The new Shi'i dynasty came to be known as Fatimid, derived from the name of the Prophet's daughter Fatima, to whom al-Mahdi and his successors traced their Husaynid 'Alid ancestry. An important aspect of the Fatimid caliphate was the recognition of the Fatimid caliphs as Ismaili Imams also, though after 1094 not by the entire Ismaili community. The Fatimids were, indeed, Imam-caliphs.

'Abd Allah al-Mahdi and his next three successors ruling from Ifriqiya, al-Qa'im (r. 934–946), al-Mansur (r. 946–953) and al-Mu'izz (r. 953–975), encountered numerous internal and external difficulties while they were consolidating their power in that remote part of the Muslim world. In addition to the persistent hostility of the Abbasids and of the Umayyads of Spain (al-Andalus), the Fatimids had intermittent military encounters with the Byzantines in Sicily and elsewhere in the Mediterranean. Soon, the early Fatimids also confronted internal dissent and animosity from the indigenous Khariji Berbers and the Sunni Arab inhabitants of the cities of Ifriqiya led by their influential jurists, who mainly followed the Maliki school of jurisprudence.

Fatimid rule was consolidated firmly only under the fourth member of the dynasty, al-Mu'izz, who succeeded in transforming the Fatimid caliphate from a regional state into a flourishing empire. He was also the first Fatimid Imam-caliph to concern himself distinctly with the propagation of the Ismaili *da'wa* outside the Fatimid dominions. Unlike the Abbasids, the Fatimid Imam-caliphs had not abandoned their *da'wa* activities on assuming power.

After subduing the entire Maghrib, al-Mu'izz started making meticulous plans for the conquest of Egypt, an important objective in the Fatimid policy of eastern expansion. It fell to Jawhar to successfully lead the Egyptian expedition on behalf of al-Mu'izz. Jawhar, one of the ablest of Fatimid commanders, entered Fustat in 969, and declared a general amnesty for the Egyptians, also tolerating religious freedom, a general attribute of Fatimid rule. Jawhar immediately proceeded to build a new capital city, later named al-Qahira al-Mu'izziyya (the Victorious One of al-Mu'izz), and al-Qahira (Cairo) for short. He also built two royal palaces there, for the Fatimid Imam-caliph and his heir-designate, separated by a broad open space, later used for public ceremonies and parades, all in accordance with plans drawn up by al-Mu'izz himself. Shortly afterwards, Jawhar laid the foundations of al-Azhar. In 988, this mosque also became an academic institution. Under the Fatimids, al-Azhar played a key role in disseminating knowledge and Ismaili doctrines, with a variety of students and scholars participating in its lecture sessions. On the demise of the Fatimids, this institution of teaching and learning, too, lost much of its earlier academic standing and impact.

In 973, the Fatimid Imam-caliph al-Mu'izz arrived in Cairo and took up residence in his new capital city. It was also in al-Mu'izz's reign that an Ismaili school of jurisprudence (*madhhab*) was finally established. This came about mainly through the work of al-Qadi al-Nu'man (d. 974), the foremost Fatimid jurist. His efforts in preparing legal compendia culminated in the compilation of the *Da'a'im al-Islam* (The Pillars of Islam), which was endorsed by al-Mu'izz as the official code of the Fatimid state. Ismaili law accorded special importance to the central Imami Shi'i doctrine of the Imamate. Indeed, the authority of the infallible 'Alid Imam and his teachings became the third and most decisive principal source of Ismaili law, alongside the Qur'an and the *sunna* of the Prophet, which are accepted as the first two sources by all Muslims.

In 975, al-Mu'izz was succeeded by his son al-'Aziz, who became the first Fatimid Imam-caliph to commence his reign in Egypt. By the end of al-'Aziz's reign in 996, the Fatimid empire had attained its greatest extent, with its suzerainty acknowledged from the Atlantic to the Red Sea, the Hijaz, Yemen and Palestine. At the same time, the Fatimid *da'is* continued to be active in Syria, Iraq, Persia and other eastern regions beyond the frontiers of the Fatimid state. Countless individuals in these regions now recognised the Fatimid caliph as the rightful 'Imam of the time'. In 977, al-'Aziz made Ibn Killis, a Fatimid administrator, his vizier, and as such he was the first of the Fatimid viziers. Originally a Jew, Ibn Killis was noted for his patronage of scholars and poets. Later, al-'Aziz appointed a Coptic Christian, 'Isa b. Nasturus, as vizier. He was the first of several Christians to occupy the vizierate under the Fatimids. The policy of assigning high administrative posts to Christians and Jews, as well as Sunni Muslims, in a Shi'i state was basically in line with the religious tolerance and meritocracy practised by the Fatimids.

Al-'Aziz was succeeded by his son al-Hakim bi-Amr Allah, who was only eleven years old at the time of his accession in 996. One of his most important achievements was the foundation of the Dar al-'Ilm (House of Knowledge), sometimes also called the Dar al-Hikma (House of Wisdom), which was set up in 1005 in a section of the Fatimid palace. A wide range of religious and other subjects were taught at this institution of learning, which was also equipped with a major library. Many Ismaili *da'is* received at least part of their training there.

The Ismaili *da'wa* was greatly expanded under al-Hakim, acquiring the distinctive features of its organisation. It now became particularly active in Iraq and Persia, where Hamid al-Din al-Kirmani (d. after 1020), among many others, was operating as a *da'i*. An eminent philosopher, al-Kirmani was perhaps the most learned theologian of the entire Fatimid period. He produced several theological treatises on the doctrine of the Imamate. Additionally, similarly to earlier *da'is* of the Iranian lands, such as Abu Ya'qub al-Sijistani (d. after 971), he amalgamated his theology with Neoplatonism and other philosophical traditions. These Ismaili *da'is* of the Iranian world, in fact, elaborated the distinct Ismaili intellectual tradition of philosophical theology. Nasir-i Khusraw (d. after 1070), the Central Asian *da'i*, was the last great member of this 'Iranian school of Ismailism'.

The Ismaili *da'wa* activities, especially outside the Fatimid dominions, reached their peak in the long reign of the eighth Fatimid Imam-caliph al-Mustansir (r. 1036–1094), even after the Sunni Saljuqs replaced the Shi'i Buyids as overlords of the weakened Abbasid caliphs in 1055. The Fatimid *da'is* won many converts in Iraq, Persia and Central Asia as well as in Yemen, where the Sulayhids ruled as vassals of the Fatimids from 1047 until 1138. The most prominent *da'i* of al-Mustansir's period was al-Mu'ayyad fi'l-Din al-Shirazi, who had originally succeeded his Persian father as the chief *da'i* of Fars in southern Persia. In due course, he converted Abu Kalijar Marzuban (r. 1024–1048), the Buyid ruler of Fars and Khuzistan in Persia. Fleeing from Abbasid persecution, in 1047 al-Mu'ayyad fi'l-Din arrived in Cairo and played an active part in the affairs of the Fatimid state and *da'wa*.

In 1058, al-Mustansir appointed al-Mu'ayyad as chief *da'i* (*da'i al-du'at*), a post he held for twenty years until shortly before his death in 1078. In this capacity, al-Mu'ayyad established close relations with the *da'wa* leadership in both Yemen and Badakhshan. The latter region was then in the general charge of Nasir-i Khusraw, another eminent *da'i* of al-Mustansir's reign. A learned theologian, philosopher, traveller and renowned poet of the Persian language, Nasir arrived in Cairo in 1047, the same year as al-Mu'ayyad. After training as a *da'i* for three years in Cairo, Nasir returned to his native Badakhshan and began his career as the chief *da'i* or *hujja* of Khurasan. Later, he sought refuge from persecution in the remote valley of Yumgan in the midst of the Pamir mountains. Nasir remained in contact with the *da'wa* headquarters in Cairo and the chief *da'i* al-Mu'ayyad, who remained his mentor. It was mostly during his long period of exile in Yumgan that Nasir-i Khusraw extended the *da'wa* throughout Badakhshan, nowadays divided between Tajikistan and Afghanistan.

Meanwhile, the Ismaili *da'wa* had continued in many parts of Persia, then incorporated into the Saljuq sultanate. By the early 1070s, the Persian Ismailis of the Saljuq dominions were under the authority of a single *da'i*, 'Abd al-Malik b. 'Attash, with secret headquarters in Isfahan, the main Saljuq capital. This learned *da'i* was also responsible for launching the career of Hasan-i Sabbah, the future founder of the Nizari Ismaili state and *da'wa* in Persia.

By the final decades of al-Mustansir's reign, the Fatimid caliphate had already embarked on its decline. Racial rivalries in the Fatimid armies continuously provided a major source of unrest in Fatimid Egypt. Matters came to a head in 1062 when open warfare broke out near Cairo between Turkish regiments, aided by Berber soldiers, and black regiments. The victorious commander of the Turks rebelled against al-Mustansir in 1070 and had the *khutba* pronounced in the name of the Abbasids in Alexandria and elsewhere. At the same time, Egypt was plagued by a serious economic crisis marked by famine caused by the low level of the Nile for seven consecutive years (1065–1072). The atrocities of the Turkish troops eventually led to a complete breakdown of law and order.

It was under such circumstances that al-Mustansir finally appealed for help to Badr al-Jamali, an Armenian general in the service of the Fatimids in Syria. In 1074, Badr arrived in Cairo with his Armenian troops, quickly subduing the rebellious Turkish troops, and then restoring relative peace and stability to the Fatimid state. Badr al-Jamali acquired all the highest positions in the Fatimid state, also becoming the first person to be designated as the 'vizier of the pen and the sword', with full delegated powers, in addition to being the supreme commander of the armies (*amir al-juyush*), his best-known title. Henceforth, it was viziers, who were often military commanders, who were the effective authority in the Fatimid state. By the end of al-Mustansir's rule, of the Fatimid possessions in Syria and Palestine only Ascalon and a few coastal towns such as Acre and Tyre still remained intact, while in North Africa the Fatimid dominions were practically reduced to Egypt proper.

The eighth Fatimid Imam-caliph, Abu Tamim Maʿadd al-Mustansir biʾllah, died in 1094. The dispute over his succession led to a permanent split in the Ismaili *daʿwa* and community with lasting consequences. Al-Mustansir had initially designated one of his eldest sons Abu Mansur Nizar (1045–1095) as his successor by the rule of *nass* or designation. However, al-Afdal, who a few months earlier had succeeded his own father Badr al-Jamali as the all-powerful vizier and 'commander of the armies' had his own designs. Accordingly, he deprived Nizar of his succession rights and placed his much younger half-brother Ahmad on the Fatimid throne with the caliphal title al-Mustaʿli biʾllah. The new caliph, who was, furthermore, married to al-Afdal's sister, would be entirely dependent on his vizier. Supported by the Fatimid armies, al-Afdal quickly obtained for al-Mustaʿli the allegiance of the leading figures of the Fatimid court and the Ismaili *daʿwa* in Cairo. Nizar refused to endorse al-Afdal's designs and fled to Alexandria, where he led a revolt. There, he was declared caliph with the title al-Mustafa li-Din Allah. This declaration is attested to in a gold dinar minted in Alexandria on that occasion, and currently preserved at The Institute of Ismaili Studies. Nizar was initially successful in his confrontations with the Fatimid forces. However, by the end of 1095, he was obliged to surrender. He was taken to Cairo and executed there.

This succession dispute permanently split the Ismailis into two rival factions, later designated as Nizari and Mustaʿlian, named after al-Mustansir's sons who had claimed his heritage. The Imamate of al-Mustaʿli, installed to the Fatimid caliphate, was acknowledged by the official *daʿwa* establishment in Cairo, as well as the Ismaili communities of Egypt, Yemen and western India. These communities, which depended on the Fatimid regime and later traced their Imamate in the progeny of al-Mustaʿli, maintained their relations with Cairo, henceforth serving as the headquarters of the Mustaʿlian Ismaili *daʿwa*. On the other hand, the Persian Ismailis, who were already under the leadership of Hasan-i Sabbah (d. 1124), upheld Nizar's right to the Imamate. In fact, Hasan now founded the independent Nizari Ismaili *daʿwa*, and severed relations with the Fatimid regime. In the rest of this introduction we shall discuss the subsequent history of the Nizari Ismailis, who may generally be referred to simply as the Ismailis.

Hasan-i Sabbah's seizure of the fortress of Alamut in the Alburz mountains of northern Persia in 1090 had marked the foundation of what would become the Ismaili state of Persia and Syria. As the undisputed leader of the Persian Ismailis, Hasan was already following an independent policy against the Saljuq Turks when the Fatimid Imam-caliph al-Mustansir died in 1094. As noted, he readily upheld the cause of Nizar and severed his ties with the Fatimid regime. Hasan had thus founded the independent Nizari Ismaili *daʿwa* on behalf of the Nizari Imam, who was then inaccessible.

The Ismaili state, centred at Alamut with a network of fortresses and territories scattered in different regions of Persia and Syria, usually though not always in remote mountain localities, lasted some 166 years until its demise in 1256 under the onslaught of the Mongol hordes. This initial Alamut phase in Nizari Ismaili history was marked by numerous political vicissitudes. Hasan-i Sabbah designed a strategy against the Saljuqs, whose alien rule was detested throughout Persia. He aimed to defeat them locality by locality from numerous impregnable fortresses. He did not realise his objective of uprooting Saljuq rule, nor did the Saljuqs, despite their much greater military strength, succeed in dislodging the Ismailis from their mountain strongholds. By his final years, a stalemate had developed between the Ismailis and the Saljuqs, and despite the incessant hostilities of the Saljuqs and their successors, the Ismaili state survived until 1256. Meanwhile, the *daʿis* dispatched from Alamut to Syria had organised an expanding Ismaili community there. The Syrian Ismailis, too, acquired a network of castles while pursuing policies of both defensive struggle and diplomacy towards various Muslim rulers and the Crusaders, who made them famous in Europe in their imaginary tales as the Assassins.

After Nizar's execution in Cairo in 1095, the name of his successor was not divulged by Hasan-i Sabbah. The early Nizari Ismailis were thus left without an accessible Imam in another *dawr al-satr*, or period of concealment, as had occurred in the pre-Fatimid period in Ismaili history. The concealed Ismaili Imam was now once again represented in the community by a *hujja*, his chief representative. Indeed, Hasan and his next two successors at Alamut ruled as *hujjas* of the inaccessible Imams. Numismatic evidence from this period indicates that Nizar's own name and caliphal title (al-Mustafa li-Din Allah) continued to be mentioned on coins minted at Alamut for about seventy years after his death. On these coins, Nizar's progeny are blessed anonymously.

Nonetheless, it is a historical fact that Nizar did have male progeny, and some of them even launched abortive revolts in Fatimid Egypt. And some of his descendants sought refuge in Persia, as related in a recently recovered manuscript of Hasan-i Muhmud-i Katib's *Haft bab*, written a few decades after the declaration of *qiyama* at

Alamut in 1164. At the same time, already in Hasan-i Sabbah's time many Nizari Ismailis believed that a son or grandson of Nizar had been brought secretly from Egypt to Persia. This Fatimid would become the progenitor of the line of the Nizari Imams, who initially remained inaccessible, but eventually emerged openly at Alamut, starting with the fourth lord of Alamut, Hasan 'ala dhikrihi'l-salam (r. 1162–1166), and took charge of the affairs of their *da'wa* and state. Hasan 'ala dhikrihi'l-salam declared the *qiyama* or Resurrection in 1164, initiating a new era in the history of the Nizari Ismailis. Relying on expounding Ismaili *ta'wil*, or esoteric exegesis, however, he interpreted this long-awaited Last Day symbolically and spiritually for his community. Accordingly, *qiyama* meant the manifestation of unveiled truth (*haqiqa*) in the person of the 'Imam of the time'; and this was a spiritual resurrection only for those who acknowledged the rightful Imam and were thus capable of comprehending the esoteric, immutable essence of Islam. It was in this sense that Paradise was actualised for the Nizari Ismailis in this world, while the outsiders were rendered spiritually non-existent.

Muhammad, son and successor of Hasan 'ala dhikrihi'l-salam, devoted his long reign (1166–1210) to a systematic elaboration of the *qiyama* in terms of a doctrine. The exaltation of the autonomous teaching authority of the current Imam, which had already been explained according to Hasan-i Sabbah's doctrine of *ta'lim*, now became the central feature of Ismaili thought. And the *qiyama* came to imply a complete personal transformation of the Ismailis who were expected to fully apprehend their Imam in his true spiritual reality.

The sixth lord of Alamut, Muhammad's son and successor Jalal al-Din Hasan (r. 1210–1221), who had become particularly concerned with the isolation of his community from the larger Muslim world, attempted a daring rapprochement with the Sunni Muslims. He repudiated the doctrine of the *qiyama* and instructed his community to observe the *shari'a* in its Sunni form. Henceforth, the rights of Jalal al-Din Hasan to Ismaili territories in Persia and Syria were officially recognised by the Abbasids and other Sunni rulers. The Ismailis evidently interpreted their Imam's new policies as the re-imposition of *taqiyya*, which had been lifted in the *qiyama* times. The observance of *taqiyya* could, indeed, imply any type of accommodation to the outside world as deemed necessary by the infallible 'Imam of the time'. The rapprochement with Sunni Muslims had obvious advantages for the Ismaili community, who had been marginalised as 'heretics' (*malahida*) for a long time. Above all, the Imam had now achieved the peace and security that his community and state much needed.

In the long reign of Jalal al-Din Hasan's son and successor, 'Ala al-Din Muhammad (r. 1221–1255), the observation of the Sunni form of the *shari'a*, which had been adopted previously for *taqiyya* purposes, was gradually relaxed within the community and the traditions associated with *qiyama* were once again revived. The Ismaili leadership now also made systematic efforts to explain the different religious policies of the earlier lords of Alamut, setting them within a coherent theological framework. In this connection, it is mainly through the Ismaili works written or supervised by the eminent Shi'i philosopher and theologian Nasir al-Din al-Tusi (d. 1274) that we have a clear exposition of the Ismaili thought of the Alamut period. Foremost among the scholars who were then fleeing before the Mongol invasions, al-Tusi had sought refuge in the Ismaili fortresses of Persia and, in fact, converted to Ismailism in the course of the three decades or so that he spent in their fortress communities. Be that as it may, the Ismaili teachings of the Alamut period brought them even closer to the esoteric traditions more widely associated with Sufism, also enabling them to maintain a distinct identity and spiritual independence under changing circumstances.

The Persian Ismailis, who had successfully struggled against too many formidable adversaries and for so long, were finally overwhelmed by the all-conquering Mongol armies led by Hülegü himself. Subsequently, the Mongols uprooted the Abbasid caliphate while continuing to massacre large numbers of the local inhabitants of their conquered territories. Meanwhile, the surrender of the chief Ismaili stronghold of Alamut to the Mongols in 1256 had sealed the fate of the Ismaili state of Persia, although some individual castles, like Lamasar and Girdkuh, held out against the Mongols for a while longer. A year later, Rukn al-Din Khurshah, the Ismaili Imam and the last lord of Alamut who had ruled for exactly one year, was murdered in Mongolia, where he had been taken to see the Great Khan. The Mongols massacred large numbers of Ismailis in Persia. Many of the survivors then migrated to Central Asia, Afghanistan and Sind, where Ismaili communities already existed. But in Syria, the Ismailis attained the peak of their power and glory in the second half of the twelfth century under their most eminent *da'i*, Rashid al-Din Sinan (d. 1193), who successfully led them for three decades. The Syrian Ismailis were spared the Mongol debacle, but by 1273 all their castles had fallen into the hands of the Mamluks, then ruling over Egypt and Syria. The Syrian Ismailis were permitted to live in their traditional abodes as loyal subjects of the Mamluks, and then of their Ottoman successors.

In the early centuries after the demise of the Ismaili state in 1256, the various Ismaili communities, scattered from Persia to Central Asia and South Asia as well as in Syria, elaborated a diversity of religious and literary traditions in different languages. Many aspects of Ismaili history during these early post-Alamut centuries are still shrouded in obscurity due to a scarcity of primary sources. Additional difficulties in research stem from the widespread application of *taqiyya* adopted by the Ismailis to safeguard themselves against rampant persecution. The Ismailis now resorted to Sunni, Sufi and Twelver Shi'i guises, while guarding their literary heritage secretly.

So for several centuries, when the Ismailis of various regions were effectively deprived of ready access to an organised central leadership, the Ismaili communities continued to develop independently under the local leadership of their *da'i*s, *pir*s, *khalifa*s and *shaykh*s, who often established their own hereditary dynasties. Meanwhile, a group of Ismaili dignitaries had managed to hide Imam Rukn al-Din Khurshah's young son, Shams al-Din Muhammad (d. *c.* 1310), who had succeeded to the Imamate in 1257. He was taken to Adharbayjan, in northwestern Persia, where he and his immediate successors to the Imamate lived secretly.

During the early post-Alamut centuries, the Persian Ismailis disguised themselves particularly under the mantle of Sufism, without establishing formal affiliations with any of the Sufi orders (*tariqa*s) then spreading throughout Persia and Central Asia. This practice soon gained wide currency among the Ismaili communities of Central Asia and Sind as well. Indeed, by the middle of the fifteenth century, Ismaili-Sufi relations had become well established in the Iranian world. A type of coalescence had now emerged between Persian Sufism and Nizari Ismailism, two esoteric traditions in Islam that had close doctrinal affinities. This also explains why the Persian-speaking Ismailis have regarded several of the great mystic poets of Persia, such as Farid al-Din 'Attar (d. *c.* 1221) and Jalal al-Din Rumi (d. 1273), as their co-religionists. Soon, the dissimulating Persian Ismailis adopted even more visible aspects of the Sufi way of life. Thus, the Imams appeared to outsiders as Sufi masters or *pir*s, while their followers adopted the common Sufi appellation of disciple or *murid*.

By the middle of the fifteenth century, the Ismaili Imams had emerged in the village of Anjudan, near Qum and Mahallat, in central Persia, initiating the so-called Anjudan revival in their *da'wa* activities. Mustansir bi'llah, who succeeded to the Ismaili Imamate around 1463 and died in 1480, may have been the first Imam to have definitely established his residence in Anjudan. Carrying the Sufi name of Shah Qalandar, his mausoleum is still preserved in Anjudan, together with two other mausolea that contain the graves of several other Imams with their invaluable epigraphic inscriptions. The Ismaili Imams now successfully reorganised their *da'wa* activities to win over new converts and reassert their authority over various Ismaili communities, especially in Central Asia and India. The Anjudan revival in Ismaili history, lasting until the closing decades of the seventeenth century, also witnessed a revival in literary activities. In the context of the Ismaili–Sufi relations of the period, valuable details are preserved in a book titled *Pandiyat-i javanmardi*, containing religious and chivalrous admonitions of Imam Mustansir bi'llah. Other doctrinal works of the Anjudan period were written by Khayrkhwah-i Harati (d. after 1553), and other *da'is*.

The advent of the Safawids and the adoption of Twelver Shi'ism as their state religion in 1501 promised more favourable opportunities for the activities of the Ismailis. However, this optimism was short-lived, as the Safawids and their jurists soon suppressed all popular forms of Sufism and those Shi'i groups that fell outside the boundaries of Twelver Shi'ism. As a result, by the time of Shah 'Abbas I (r. 1587–1629), the greatest of the Safawid monarchs who established his capital at Isfahan, the Persian Ismailis had adopted Twelver Shi'ism, the then 'politically correct' form of Shi'ism, as their prevalent form of disguise. Particularly in Persia, the Ismailis and their Imams were quite successful in dissimulating as Twelver Shi'is. This is clearly attested to in an epigraphic decree issued by Shah 'Abbas I in 1627, in which the contemporary Imam and his community in Anjudan, are referred to as Ithna'asharis. As a result of the long-term observance of this *taqiyya* practice, countless Persian Ismailis might, in fact, have become integrated and fully assimilated into the dominant Twelver communities of their surroundings. Be that as it may, it is likely that Shah Khalil Allah 'Ali was the last Ismaili Imam to reside in Anjudan. According to his gravestone, he died in 1680.

The Ismaili *da'wa* now achieved particular success also in India, where *da'is* dispatched from Persia organised and led the community. These *da'is*, more commonly designated as *pir*s in the Indian context, converted large numbers of Hindus, first of all in Sind and later in many parts of the Indian subcontinent, who became generally known as Khojas. The Ismailis of the Indian subcontinent developed a distinctive religious tradition known as Satpanth or the 'true path' (to salvation), as well as a devotional literature, the *ginan*s, derived from a Sanskrit word (*jñana*) meaning sacred knowledge or wisdom. Composed in a number of Indic languages and dialects of Sind, Punjab and Gujarat, these hymn-like poems were initially transmitted orally for several centuries before they were recorded, mainly in the Khojki script developed in Sind within the Khoja community.

The authorship of the greatest number of *ginan*s is traditionally attributed to a few early *pir*s, such as Shams al-Din and Sadr al-Din. Pir Sadr al-Din is also credited with building the first *jamat-khana* in Sind for the religious and communal activities of the Khojas. From early on, the *pir*s attempted to maximise the popular appeal of their preaching in a Hindu ambience. Therefore, in addition to using Indian vernaculars rather than Arabic or Persian, they used Hindu idioms and mythology. Be that as it may, in time the Satpanth tradition of the Ismaili Khojas developed its own set of themes and theological concepts, similarly to a number of other traditions developed in the Indo-Muslim context of the Indian subcontinent.

Imam Shah Khalil Allah, the thirty-ninth Imam, was succeeded by his son Shah Nizar. Sometime during the earliest decades of his Imamate (1680–1722), Shah Nizar transferred his residence and the headquarters of the *da'wa* from Anjudan to the nearby village of Kahak, ending the Anjudan phase of Ismaili history. Shah Nizar, the fortieth Imam, and his immediate successors lived in Kahak, which was later abandoned in favour of various localities in the province of Kirman. However, the Imams maintained a foothold in Kahak at least until the opening decades of the nineteenth century. Imam Shah Nizar died in 1722, according to his gravestone, shortly before the Afghan invasion of Persia and the demise of the Safawid dynasty. Shah Nizar's mausoleum is still preserved in Kahak. This necropolis also contains several graves with Khojki inscriptions, attesting to the pilgrimage of Ismaili Khojas from India to see their Imam. Kahak is indeed cited in some *ginan*s as the abode of the Ismaili Imams. By that time, close relations had developed between the Imams and their Khoja followers in India.

By the middle of the eighteenth century, the Imams had moved their residence to Shahr-i Babak in the province of Kirman. The forty-second Imam, Sayyid Hasan 'Ali, acquired extensive properties in that locality as well as in the city of Kirman. It was during his Imamate that Nadir Shah Afshar expelled the Afghan invaders from Persia, overthrew the Safawids and proclaimed himself king, founding the Afsharid dynasty of Persia. Sayyid Hasan 'Ali was also the first Ismaili Imam to abandon the traditional *taqiyya* practices that had been almost uninterruptedly maintained since the Mongol invasions. He became actively involved in the affairs of Kirman, establishing close relations with the province's Afsharid ruler, Shah Rukh (r. 1747–1759).

The forty-fourth Imam, Abu'l-Hasan 'Ali, also known as Sayyid Abu'l-Hasan Kahaki, was appointed around 1756 to the governorship of Kirman by Karim Khan Zand (r. 1751–1779), founder of another short-lived Persian dynasty that succeeded the Afsharids. This Imam, whose career is recorded extensively in the chronicles of Kirman, played a key role in that province's political life in the turbulent years when Agha Muhammad Khan (r. 1779–1797), the founder of the Qajar dynasty, challenged Zand rule in various regions of Persia. Imam Abu'l-Hasan 'Ali, who was a popular governor of Kirman, ruled autonomously over the province, even after Karim Khan Zand's death in 1779. It was also in his time that the Ni'mat Allahi Sufi order was revived in Persia by its contemporary master, Rida 'Ali Shah (d. 1796), who like his predecessors resided in the Deccan, India. This Sufi order spread rapidly in Kirman, where the shrine of their eponymous founder Shah Niʿmat Allah Wali (d. 1431) is preserved in Mahan. The arrival of several prominent Niʿmat Allahi Sufis in Kirman also served to renew the ties between this order and the Ismaili Imams. Indeed, Imam Abu'l-Hasan ʿAli, who died in 1792, developed close connections with the Niʿmat Allahis.

Imam Abu'l-Hasan ʿAli was succeeded in the Ismaili Imamate by his eldest son Shah Khalil Allah. Soon after his accession in 1792, Shah Khalil Allah married Bibi Sarkara, daughter of Muhammad Sadiq Mahallati, who bore the next Imam, Hasan ʿAli Shah Aga Khan I, in 1804 in Kahak. Muhammad Sadiq Mahallati (d. 1815), himself a relative of the Imams, was also a Niʿmat Allahi Sufi. Bibi Sarkara's brother Muhammad ʿAli, better known by his Sufi *tariqa* name of ʿIzzat ʿAli Shah, was another prominent Niʿmat Allahi dervish. This maternal uncle of Aga Khan I developed close relations with Zayn al-ʿAbidin Shirvani (d. 1837), who became the master of the chief branch of the Niʿmat Allahi order. Thus, by the early decades of the nineteenth century very close ties had developed in Persia between the family of the Ismaili Imams and the Niʿmat Allahi Sufi order, ties that later created difficulties for Aga Khan I.

In 1815, Shah Khalil Allah moved to Yazd, situated between Kirman and Isfahan on the route to Baluchistan and Sind, a decision which seems to have been motivated by the Imam's desire to be yet closer to his Khoja followers, who continued to embark on the perilous journey for seeing (*didar*) their Imam in Persia. It was at Yazd in 1817 that this Imam became a victim of anti-Ismaili instigations by some local Twelver *mulla*s, and lost his life in the course of a dispute between his followers and some local shopkeepers. In the event, the Imam and several of his followers, including a Khoja *murid*, were murdered.

Muhammad Hasan al-Husayni, also known as Hasan ʿAli Shah, was only thirteen years old when he succeeded his father Shah Khalil Allah as the forty-sixth Ismaili Imam. Soon after, the youthful Imam's mother Bibi Sarkara went to the Qajar court in Tehran seeking justice for her murdered husband and her son. The instigators of the murder were punished after a fashion. In addition, the second Qajar monarch, Fath ʿAli Shah (r. 1797–1834), appointed the Imam to the governorship of Qum, also giving him properties in nearby Mahallat. At the same time, the Qajar monarch gave one of his daughters, Sarv-i Jahan Khanum, in marriage to the Imam, and bestowed upon him the honorific title (*laqab*) of Agha Khan (or Aqa Khan), meaning lord and master. Henceforth, Hasan ʿAli Shah became known in Persia as Agha Khan Mahallati, because of his royal title and the family's deep roots in the Mahallat area. This title, inherited by Hasan ʿAli Shah's successors, was in due course simplified in Europe to Aga Khan.

Aga Khan I now led a tranquil life in Persia, enjoying honour and respect at the Qajar court in Tehran. Then in 1835, Fath ʿAli Shah's grandson and successor, Muhammad Shah Qajar (r. 1834–1848), appointed the Imam to the governorship of Kirman. This region was in constant turmoil due to incessant raids by bands of Afghans and Baluchis. Aga Khan I soon restored law and order to the province with the help of the local Khurasani and ʿAta Allahi tribesmen who were his followers. However, in 1837 he was dismissed abruptly, due to the machinations of a new powerful chief minister, Hajji Mirza Aqasi.

The Aga Khan's dismissal seems to have been related to ongoing rivalries over the leadership of the Niʿmat Allahi Sufi order in Persia. Zayn al-ʿAbidin Shirvani, better known as Mast ʿAli Shah, who had already been recognised as the master of the order by the majority of the Niʿmat Allahis, was supported also by Aga Khan I. On the other hand, the chief minister, a Niʿmat Allahi Sufi himself, aspired to that same position. In the circumstances, Mast ʿAli Shah was banished from the court and Aga Khan I aroused the enmity of Hajji Mirza Aqasi who persistently intrigued against him. Be that as it may, the Aga Khan's dismissal led to prolonged confrontations between the Ismaili Imam and the Qajar regime, culminating in a series of military encounters in 1840. The details of these confrontations are vividly recounted in the Aga Khan's memoirs, *ʿIbrat-afza*, written subsequently in Bombay. The Imam's forces were eventually defeated decisively in 1841, obliging him to seek refuge in Afghanistan. This marked the end of the Persian period of the Ismaili Imamate, which had lasted some seven centuries since the Alamut times.

Henceforth, a close association developed between the Aga Khan and the British Raj. In 1842, the Aga Khan proceeded to Sind to the excitement of his Khoja followers, most of whom were now seeing their Imam for the first time. Subsequently, the Imam stayed for various periods in Gujarat, Bombay and Calcutta, while the British authorities attempted persistently, but to no avail, to arrange for his safe return to his ancestral home. In 1848, the Imam finally decided to settle permanently in Bombay, marking the commencement of the modern period in the history of the Ismaili Imamate.

As the spiritual leader of a Muslim community Aga Khan I received the valuable protection of the British establishment in India, which stabilised his position to the benefit of his Khoja followers there. Nevertheless, he encountered some challenges to his religious authority. Matters came to a head in 1866, when a group of dissident Khojas, denying their Ismaili identity, brought their case before the Bombay High Court. In connection with this so-called 'Aga Khan Case', a detailed judgment was finally rendered against the plaintiffs and in favour of the Ismaili Imam on all counts.

This judgment legally established in British India the status of the Aga Khan's followers as a community of 'Shia Imami Ismailis', also recognising the Aga Khan as the spiritual head of that community and heir in lineal descent to the Ismaili Imams of the Alamut period. The authority of the Aga Khan was never again seriously challenged in India or anywhere else. The forty-sixth Imam indeed devoted much time and energy to delineating and defining the religious identity of his followers, who had been practising *taqiyya* in India and elsewhere under different guises with harmful effects on their true religious identity. Similar efforts were made successfully in subsequent times by later Ismaili Imams.

After an eventful Imamate of sixty-four years, Aga Khan I died in 1881. He was succeeded by his eldest son Agha 'Ali Shah, his only son by his Qajar spouse. The forty-seventh Imam was born in 1830 in Mahallat, where he spent his youth. He eventually arrived in Bombay in 1853 and regularly visited different Khoja communities in Gujarat and Sind. Agha 'Ali Shah led the Ismailis for a brief period (1881–1885), during which time he concentrated mainly on improving the educational and welfare standards of his community.

Agha 'Ali Shah was succeeded in 1885 by his sole surviving son, Sultan Muhammad (Mahomed) Shah, Aga Khan III, who led the Ismailis as their forty-eighth Imam for seventy-two years, perhaps longer than any of his predecessors. Born in Karachi in 1877, he was only eight years old when he was installed to the Imamate in 1885. Aga Khan III became well known also as a Muslim reformer and statesman due to his prominent role in Indo-Muslim as well as international affairs. His life and career are, therefore, amply documented, in addition to his autobiography published in 1954.

Aga Khan III grew up under the tutelage of his capable mother, Shams al-Muluk (d. 1938), a granddaughter of Fath 'Ali Shah Qajar, while his paternal uncle Aqa Jangi Shah (d. 1896) was his nominal guardian. In 1898, he paid his first visit to Europe, where he later established permanent residences. Aga Khan III maintained friendly relations with the British throughout his life, which brought immense benefits to his followers in India and Africa who lived under British imperial rule.

From early on, Aga Khan III concerned himself also with the affairs of the Muslims of India, in addition to those of his own community of followers, especially in the Indian subcontinent and East Africa. Like his grandfather, he devoted much energy to defining and delineating the specific religious identity of his Ismaili followers, especially seeking to distinguish them from the Twelver Shi'is who had provided a protective shield for them for several centuries. This identity was elaborated in the constitutions that the Imam promulgated periodically for his followers in different regions, starting with the first one issued in Zanzibar in 1905. He also guided his community through his directives or *farman*s.

At the same time, Aga Khan III increasingly adopted socio-economic reform policies that would benefit his followers. The development of a new communal organisation for the Ismailis, in order to implement his reforms, was another priority for this Imam. Consequently, Aga Khan III developed an elaborate administrative system of councils. Indeed, he worked vigorously for consolidating and reorganising his followers into a modern Muslim community with high standards of education, health and social welfare. He paid particular attention to the emancipation of women and their education and participation in communal affairs. He founded and maintained a large number of schools, hospitals and dispensaries in East Africa, the Indo-Pakistan subcontinent and elsewhere.

Aga Khan III died in his villa near Geneva in 1957, and was later buried in a permanent mausoleum at Aswan, Egypt, the land of his Fatimid ancestors. In accordance with his last will and testament, Aga Khan III was succeeded by his grandson, Prince Karim, the son of Prince Aly Khan. Mawlana Hazir Imam Shah Karim al-Husayni, as he is addressed by his followers, is the forty-ninth and present Imam of the Ismailis. He is internationally known as His Highness Prince Karim Aga Khan IV. Born in 1936 in Geneva, he was educated at Le Rosey, an exclusive private school in Switzerland, and Harvard University.

The present Ismaili Imam has continued and substantially expanded the modernisation policies of his grandfather, also developing a multitude of new initiatives and institutions of his own for the benefit of his community. At the same time, Aga Khan IV has concerned himself with a wide range of social, economic, cultural and environmental issues, which are of broader interest to Muslims and the developing countries in general. For this he has created a complex institutional network, generally referred to as the Aga Khan Development Network (AKDN). Implementing projects in a variety of fields, the AKDN now disburses annually close to one billion dollars on its activities.

In the area of social development, Aga Khan IV's network has been particularly active in East Africa, Central Asia, Pakistan and India in projects related to health, education and housing services, as well as rural development. Many of these projects are promoted or financed through the Aga Khan Foundation (AKF), established in 1967 in Geneva with branches in several countries. The AKF collaborates with a multitude of national and international organisations for implementing a variety of programmes in developing countries.

The present Imam of the Ismailis has been particularly concerned with the education of his followers and Muslims in general. He has launched a series of programmes for the religious education of Ismaili children and young adults with specially designed primary and secondary curricula materials. In the field of higher education, his major initiatives include The Institute of Ismaili Studies, founded in London in 1977 for the promotion of general Islamic studies as well as Shi'i and Ismaili studies; the Aga Khan University, set up in Karachi in 1985 with faculties in medicine, nursing and education as well as its Institute for the Study of Muslim Civilisations set up in London in 2002, and other faculties in East Africa; the University of Central Asia, established in 2000, with campuses in Tajikistan and other Central Asia countries, to address the specific educational needs of the region's mountain-based societies. More recently, he founded the Global Centre for Pluralism in Ottawa, Canada, to promote pluralistic values and practices in culturally diverse societies worldwide.

As a progressive Muslim leader, Aga Khan IV has allocated a good proportion of his resources to promoting a better understanding of Islam, not merely as a major religion with multiple expressions and interpretations, but also as a world civilisation with its plurality of social, intellectual and cultural traditions. In pursuit of these aims, he has initiated a number of innovative programmes for the preservation and regeneration of the cultural heritage of Muslim societies. The apex institution here is the Aga Khan Trust for Culture (AKTC), set up in Geneva in 1988 for promoting an awareness of the importance of the built environment in both historical and contemporary contexts, and for pursuing excellence in architecture. The AKTC's mandate now covers the Aga Khan Award for Architecture; the Aga Khan Historic Cities Programme; and the Aga Khan Museum, established in Toronto.

Aga Khan IV takes a personal interest in the operations of all his institutions. By 2017, when the Ismailis celebrated the sixtieth anniversary (Diamond Jubilee) of his Imamate, he had established an impressive record of achievement not only as an Ismaili Imam but also as a Muslim leader deeply aware of the demands of modernity. Indeed the last two Ismaili Imams have successfully responded to the challenges of a rapidly changing world, making it possible over the last 135 years for their Ismaili followers globally to evolve into a progressive Shi'i Muslim community with a distinctive Islamic identity. In 2015, the Portuguese government welcomed the establishment of the 'seat of the Ismaili Imamat' in Lisbon, in recognition of its supra-national nature and the capacity to enter into national and international treatises.

The present Ismaili Imam has also transformed the historical Ismaili Imamate into a modern-day institution capable of adapting to changing circumstances, a great achievement in and of itself. The Ismaili community in turn, has responded by continuously reaffirming the bond that has historically existed between the Ismaili Imams and their community of followers. All this has enabled the Ismailis to enjoy the unique distinction of being today the only Shiʿi Muslim community with a living and present Imam, with high standards of education and well-being.

Part Two

The Early Imams

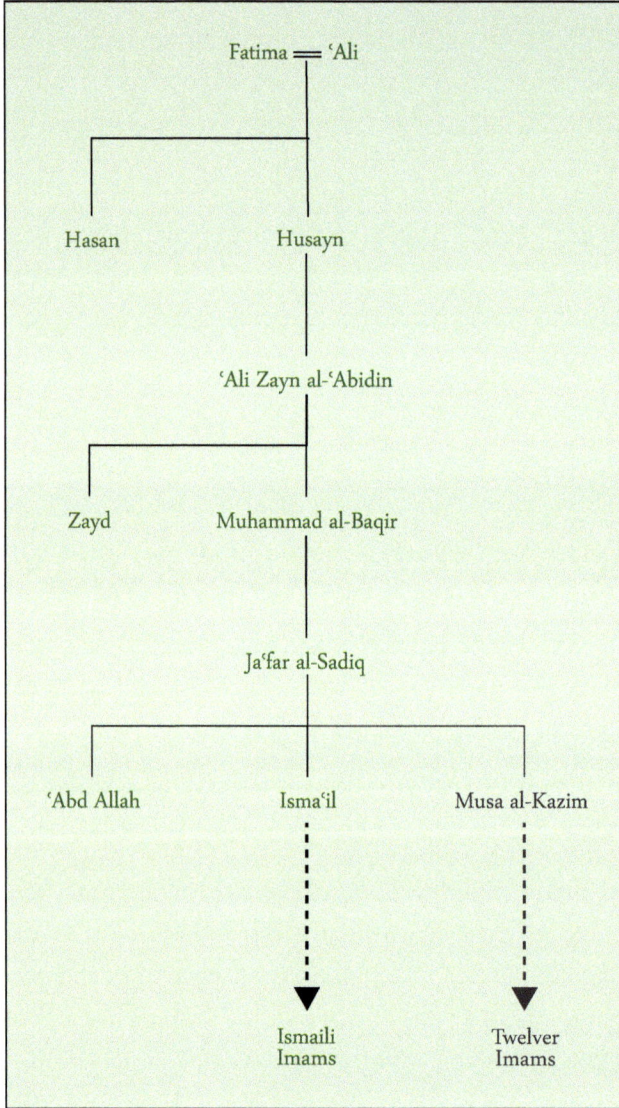

The early Imams

1

ʿAli b. Abi Talib (d. 661)

Born around 600 in Mecca, ʿAli was the first cousin and son-in-law of the Prophet Muhammad, married to his daughter Fatima. He was also the first Shiʿi Imam; the very term 'Shiʿa' is derived from the designation *shiʿat ʿAli* or the 'Party of ʿAli'. He is, furthermore, considered by all Muslims as the fourth of the early caliphs, known as the 'rightly guided caliphs' (*al-khulafa al-rashidun*). The caliphal title *amir al-muʾminin*, or 'commander of the faithful', is used by the Shiʿa exclusively in reference to ʿAli.

ʿAli's father, Abu Talib, son of ʿAbd al-Muttalib b. Hashim, was the chief of the Banu Hashim, the Prophet's clan of the influential Meccan tribe of Quraysh; ʿAli's mother was Fatima bint Asad. When ʿAli's father became impoverished, ʿAli was taken into the Prophet's household. Some five years later in 610, when Muhammad commenced his prophetic mission, ʿAli was one of the earliest converts to Islam being around ten years old.

In 622, the Prophet Muhammad was obliged to emigrate from Mecca to Medina, then known as Yathrib, to escape the Meccan persecution of the nascent Muslim *umma*. This emigration (*hijra*) marked the beginning of the Islamic calendar. On the night of the Prophet's flight to Medina, ʿAli risked his life by sleeping in the Prophet's bed as a decoy. Subsequently, ʿAli also emigrated to Medina and participated in almost all the military expeditions against the various enemies of the early Muslim community. ʿAli's bravery in these early Islamic battles (*maghazi*) became legendary. In particular, after the battle of Khaybar in 629, ʿAli gained a reputation as an invincible warrior with a supernatural strength. In Medina, where shortly after his arrival he married the Prophet's daughter Fatima, ʿAli distinguished himself both as a close Companion of the Prophet, and for his extensive knowledge of the Qurʾan.

According to all Shi'i Muslims, the Prophet Muhammad had nominated 'Ali under divine command as his successor when he halted at Ghadir Khumm on the return from his 'farewell pilgrimage' to Mecca. Sunni Muslims reject this designation (*nass*), maintaining that the Prophet died without designating a successor. At any rate, on the Prophet's death, or shortly afterwards, in 632, a dispute arose within the nascent Muslim community over the question of succession to the Prophet. This succession dispute permanently split the unified Muslim community of the Prophet's time into two rival factions that eventually became known as Sunni and Shi'i. An early group, originally comprised of 'Ali's friends and supporters, believed that he was better qualified than any other Companion to succeed the Prophet as the leader of the Muslim community, also holding that he had been designated as such by the Prophet. 'Ali himself was firmly convinced of the legitimacy of his own claim to Muhammad's succession, based on his close kindship and association with him and his intimate knowledge of Islam, as well as his early merits in the cause of Islam.

However, after much debate, Abu Bakr, one of the earliest converts to Islam and another trusted Companion of the Prophet, was elected by a group of leading Muslim notables as the successor. He took the title of *khalifat rasul Allah* or 'successor to the Messenger of God', a title that was soon simplified to *khalifa* (whence the word 'caliph' in Western languages). 'Ali withheld his own oath of allegiance (*bay'a*) to Abu Bakr for about six months, until after the death of Fatima. It has been related that 'Ali refrained from actively asserting his own right to succession because he did not want to throw the Muslim community into strife. Subsequently, 'Ali remained aloof from communal activities during the caliphates of Abu Bakr (r. 632–634) and his next two successors, 'Umar (r. 634–644) and 'Uthman (r. 644–656).

From early on, the Shi'a also held a particular conception of religious authority that set them apart from other Muslims. They believed that Islam contained inner truths that could not be grasped solely through human reason. Thus, they recognised the need for a religiously authoritative guide, or Imam, as the Shi'a have traditionally preferred to designate their spiritual leader. In addition to being the guardian of the Islamic revelation and leader of the community, the successor to the Prophet was seen by the Shi'a to have a key spiritual responsibility connected with the elucidation and interpretation of the Islamic message. For the Shi'a, the Prophet's family, or the *ahl al-bayt*, provided the sole authoritative channel for elucidating the teachings of Islam. Indeed, 'Ali, the foremost member of the *ahl al-bayt* (originally together with his father-in-law Muhammad, wife Fatima and their sons, Hasan and Husayn, also known as the *panj tan*), made it clear in his speeches and letters that he himself considered the *ahl al-bayt* to be entitled to the

1.1 The Kufans swear allegiance to Imam ʿAli. The youth on the left, possibly Bilal, holds Imam ʿAli's sword, Dhu'l-Faqar. This miniature is from a late 16th–early 17th century copy of the *Maqtal-i Husayn* by the celebrated Ottoman Sufi author, Lamiʿi Čelebi (1473–1532).

1.2 Khaybar: The Conquering Palm of ʿAli, a reference to ʿAli's chivalric prowess, reversed in the original, from the *Ahmed I Falnama*, dated *c.* 1580s.

1.3 Cutwork paper calligraphy in the form of a lion (Arabic, *asad*), one of the symbols of Imam ʿAli, by Mir ʿAli Haravi, mid-16th century.

leadership of the Muslims as long as there remained a single one of them who recited the Qurʾan, knew the *sunna* and adhered to the religion of the truth.

In the chaotic aftermath of ʿUthman's murder, ʿAli was declared caliph in 656. In the event, the Islamic community had then become greatly divided over the question of ʿUthman's blameworthiness that had led to a widespread rebellion against him. From the start of his rule, ʿAli was confronted with a variety of difficulties that eventually escalated into the first civil war, or *fitna*, in Islam, lasting throughout his short-lived caliphate (656–661). ʿAli's caliphal authority was particularly challenged by Muʿawiya b. Abi Sufyan, the powerful governor of Syria and cousin of ʿUthman, who found the call for avenging ʿUthman's murder a suitable pretext for challenging ʿAli. Following the controversial battle between their armies at Siffin, Muʿawiya prepared the ground for installing his own clan of the Banu Umayya to the leadership of the Muslim community.

Meanwhile, ʿAli, whose political position had been greatly undermined, retreated to Kufa, his temporary capital. By the end of 660, ʿAli had lost much of his earlier support, through especially the desertion of various groups from his army – the seceders being later designated as the *khawarij*, or Kharijis, who were to become opposed to both Sunnis and Shiʿis. ʿAli was murdered in Kufa in January 661 by a Khariji and was buried near Kufa. Much later, a shrine was built over his tomb, around which the town of Najaf developed gradually. Of 'Ali's fourteen sons, Hasan, Husayn and Muhammad b. al-Hanafiyya, acknowledged as Imams by different Shi'i communities, are well known in history.

'Ali is highly revered by the Ismailis and other Shi'i Muslims as the *wali Allah*, or the 'friend of God', and as the Prophet's *wasi*, or legatee. It is through *walaya*, or devotion to 'Ali (and subsequent Imams), that true knowledge of Islam in all its exoteric (*zahir*) and esoteric (*batin*) dimensions can be acquired. The Prophet Muhammad had brought the revelation (*tanzil*) while 'Ali, the repository of the Prophet's knowledge ('*ilm*), provided its interpretation (*ta'wil*). He was held to be divinely guided and infallible (*ma'sum*). He would intercede with God on the Day of Judgment on behalf of his followers, like the succeeding Imams. Some extremist Shi'is (*ghulat*) even proclaimed 'Ali's divinity. 'Ali also enjoys an esteemed status amongst the Sufis. Indeed, most Sufi spiritual chains of authority (with the notable exception of the Naqshbandiyya) are traced back to the Prophet through 'Ali. He was a profoundly pious and religious man, unwaveringly devoted to the cause of Islam and the rule of justice in accordance with the Qur'an and the *sunna*. 'Ali's sermons, letters and sayings were subsequently collected by Sharif al-Radi (d. 1015) in a work entitled *Nahj al-balagha* (The Way of Eloquence), with a multitude of commentaries on it by Shi'i as well as Sunni scholars.

The early Shi'a represented a unified group centred in Kufa, southern Iraq. These partisans of 'Ali survived his murder and numerous subsequent tragic events. After 'Ali, his partisans in Kufa remained convinced that only a member of the Prophet's family could legitimately succeed him, and they now recognised 'Ali's eldest son Hasan, born in 625, as his successor to the caliphate. However, Hasan abdicated a few months later under obscure circumstances in favour of Mu'awiya, who had already effectively established his authority. Thus, Mu'awiya founded the first ruling dynasty in Islam, the Umayyads, who stayed in power for nearly a century.

Meanwhile, following his peace treaty with Mu'awiya, Hasan b. 'Ali retired to Medina and refrained from any political activity until his death in 669. However, the Shi'a continued to regard him as their Imam after 'Ali, while the 'Alids considered him as the head of their family. It may be noted here that in subsequent centuries Hasan was removed from the list of the Imams acknowledged by the Nizari Ismailis, who came to regard him as a temporary or trustee (*mustawda'*) Imam, as distinct from the permanent (*mustaqarr*) Imams. The latter category of Imams was reserved for Hasan's younger brother Husayn and the succeeding Imams in his Husaynid 'Alid progeny.

2

Husayn b. ʿAli (d. 680)

The second surviving grandson of the Prophet Muhammad through his daughter Fatima and ʿAli b. Abi Talib was born in Medina in 626. He is one of the early Shiʿi Imams, counted as the second one for the Ismailis of all branches. Husayn was initially brought up, together with his elder brother Hasan, in the Prophet's household. There are many accounts of the Prophet's treatment of these grandsons and his great love for them. Husayn inherited his father's fighting spirit and intense family pride. He was originally opposed to his brother's peace treaty with Muʿawiya, but eventually accepted it and respected the truce as long as Muʿawiya was still alive.

Like his father, Husayn was firmly convinced that the Prophet's family (*ahl al-bayt*) was divinely chosen to lead the Muslim community. He, therefore, refused to accord his oath of allegiance (*bayʿa*) to Muʿawiya's son Yazid, who succeeded his father in the Umayyad dynasty in 680, contrary to the terms of the peace treaty agreed between Muʿawiya and Hasan b. ʿAli. Meanwhile, on Hasan's death in 669, the Shiʿis of Kufa had revived their aspirations for restoring the caliphate to the Prophet's family. They had now recognised Husayn as their new Imam. In the aftermath of Muʿawiya's death in 680 and the succession of his son Yazid, the leaders of the Kufan Shiʿis once again wrote to Husayn and offered him their support against the Umayyads. Meanwhile, Husayn had already refused to accord his *bayʿa* to Yazid and had taken refuge in Mecca.

Husayn finally decided to respond to the Kufan summons. However, he thought it prudent to assess the situation in Kufa before embarking on his fateful journey to Iraq. He dispatched his cousin, Muslim b. ʿAqil b. Abi Talib, on a fact-finding mission to Kufa. Muslim collected thousands of pledges of support and, thus assured of the conditions in Kufa, advised Husayn to assume the active leadership of the Shiʿis and their Iraqi

2.1 Imam Husayn addressing the Umayyad army at Karbala, from a manuscript of *Hadiqat al-su'ada* by Mahmud b. Sulayman Fuzuli, produced in Baghdad around 1600.

2.2 A painting by Kamal al-Mulk, dated 1892, depicting a *ta'ziya* performance in the building called the Takiya Dawlat. This was an immense Husayniyya hall built in 1868 by Nasir al-Din Shah Qajar in Tehran near the Golestan Palace.

sympathisers in Kufa. Thus Husayn set out from the Hijaz for Kufa with a small band of relatives and companions. Meanwhile, the situation had changed drastically in Kufa upon the appointment of a new strong governor by Yazid. He took over the city, arresting and executing Muslim b. 'Aqil, and also enacting severe intimidating measures against the Kufans and their tribal leaders who had pledged their support to Husayn.

On reaching the plain of Karbala, near Kufa, Husayn's small party was intercepted by an Umayyad army of 4,000 men. Refusing for a final time to yield to Yazid, Husayn and his company of seventy-two men were attacked and brutally massacred on 10 Muharram 61/10 October 680. Only women and some children were spared. 'Ali b. Husayn (Zayn al-'Abidin), who was acknowledged as the next Imam by the Imami Shi'is, was one of the survivors. The Shi'is have particular reverence for these martyrs (*shuhada*), reserving the title of *sayyid al-shuhada*, Lord of the Martyrs, for Imam Husayn himself. Thus concluded the most tragic episode in the early history of Shi'i Islam.

2.3 A standard or *ʿalam* made in Persia in the 16th century. The central field features a pierced floral scroll decoration and the phrases 'Ya Allah', 'Ya Muhammad' and 'Ya ʿAli'.

The heroic martyrdom of the Prophet's grandson, together with that of numerous other members of the *ahl al-bayt*, infused a new religious fervour in the Shiʿa. The event, solidly establishing the Shiʿi martyrology, would play a crucial role in the consolidation of the Shiʿi ethos and identity. Subsequently, public rites of remembrance and penitence for Husayn's martyrdom developed in different regions. The Shiʿi Buyids officially initiated the commemoration of this event on the tenth of Muharram, referred to as ʿAshura, in Baghdad. Such commemorations were also encouraged in Fatimid Egypt, from the time of the Fatimid Imam-caliphs al-Muʿizz (r. 953–975) and al-ʿAziz (r. 975–996). The ceremonies reached their culmination under the Twelver Shiʿi dynasty of the Safawids (1501–1722) in Iran. ʿAshura is also commemorated in elaborate mourning rituals and popular plays known as *taʿziya*. In certain Shiʿi Muslim communities, the event is observed annually in special buildings known as Husayniyyas. Husayn's tomb in Karbala, located in due course, has served as a major pilgrimage site for different Shiʿi communities.

3

'Ali b. Husayn Zayn al-'Abidin (d. 714)

'Ali b. Husayn was born in Medina around 658. He was present at the massacre of his family at Karbala in 680, but did not participate in the fighting because he was ill at the time. He was taken, together with other survivors, to the Umayyad caliph Yazid in Damascus. Subsequently, 'Ali retired to Medina, and led a pious life, which earned him the honorifics Zayn al-'Abidin ('Ornament of the Worshippers') and al-Sajjad ('He who Constantly Prostrates'). He also acquired a widespread reputation for generosity, giving alms and food to the poor. 'Ali adopted a quiescent attitude towards the Umayyads and the Zubayrid anti-caliphate (ended in 692), remaining aloof throughout his life from all political activity.

During its first half-century, Shi'i Islam had remained unified and maintained an almost exclusively Arab composition, with a limited appeal to non-Arab Muslims or the so-called *mawali*. These features changed with the Shi'i movement of al-Mukhtar, which arose in the aftermath of the martyrdom of Imam Husayn. Al-Mukhtar's successful Shi'i campaign, with a general call to avenge Husayn's murder, was launched on behalf of Imam 'Ali b. Abi Talib's then only surviving son, known as Muhammad b. al-Hanafiyya after his mother who hailed from the Banu Hanifa. Al-Mukhtar succeeded in attracting large numbers of the *mawali*, comprised of Aramaeans, Persians and other non-Arabs, to his movement. He briefly led a revolt in Kufa before being defeated and killed by a coalition of Arab tribal leaders in 687. However, al-Mukhtar's movement survived in Kufa and elsewhere. The sixty-odd years intervening between al-Mukhtar's movement and the victory of the Abbasids over the Umayyads in 750 represent the

3.1 Imam Zayn al-ʿAbidin preaching in defence of his father, Imam Husayn, in the presence of the Umayyad caliph, Yazid. Ottoman, late 16th century. The text in Ottoman Turkish includes a quotation in Arabic from *Surat al-Israʾ*.

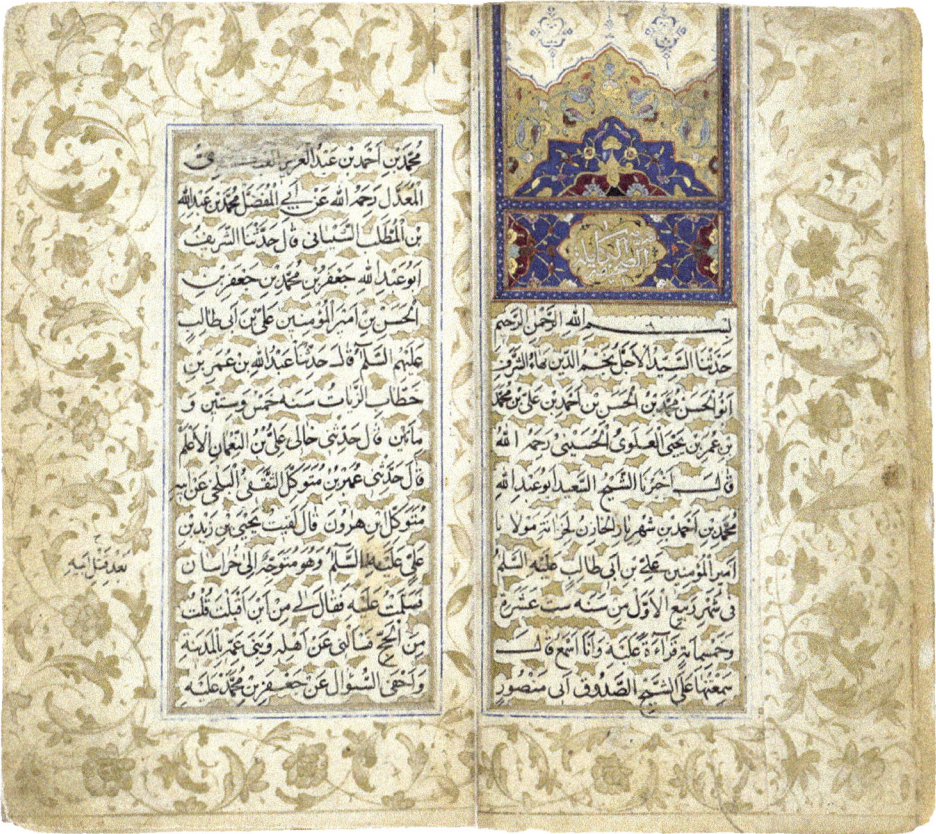

3.2 Title page of a manuscript of the *Sahifa al-sajjadiyya*, copied by the calligrapher Muhammad Qasim, dated Rajab 1068/April 1658.

second phase in the formative period of Shiʿi Islam, when different Shiʿi groups, consisting of both Arabs and *mawali*, coexisted. In this fluid setting, Shiʿism developed in terms of two main branches or factions, the Kaysaniyya and the Imamiyya, each with its own internal divisions and Imams. The Kaysaniyya, a radical branch in terms of both doctrine and policy, evolved out of al-Mukhtar's movement and accounted for the majority of the Shiʿis until shortly after the Abbasid revolution. Meanwhile, there had also appeared the Imamiyya, the common heritage of the Ismailis and the Ithnaʿasharis or Twelvers. The Imami Shiʿis recognised a particular line of the Husaynid ʿAlid Imams. The early Imamis, who like other Shiʿis of the Umayyad times were centred in Kufa, adopted a quiescent stance in the political domain while developing their doctrinal position.

The Imamis traced their Imamate through ʿAli b. Husayn Zayn al-ʿAbidin, the progenitor of the Husaynid line of the ʿAlid Imams. ʿAli b. Husayn had also adopted a quiescent attitude towards al-Mukhtar and his movement. However, after the death of his uncle Muhammad b. al-Hanafiyya in 700, Imam Zayn al-'Abidin as the eldest Husaynid 'Alid enjoyed an influential position also within the broader 'Alid family. In addition, due to his renowned piety, he gradually came to be held in great esteem in the pious circles of Medina. By the closing years of his life, he had indeed gathered around himself a Shi'i following as well as an entourage of 'Alid relatives and pious Muslims.

Imam Zayn al-'Abidin transmitted *hadith* from his father Husayn, his uncle Hasan and his distant cousin 'Abd Allah b. 'Abbas, among others. Shi'i tradition ascribes to him a number of shorts texts as well as a collection of prayers for various occasions, known as *al-Sahifa al-sajjadiyya*, on which there are numerous commentaries. Having survived his father by some thirty-odd years, Imam 'Ali b. Husayn Zayn al-'Abidin died in 714 and was buried next to his uncle Hasan in the cemetery of Baqi' in Medina.

4

Muhammad al-Baqir (d. c. 732)

Abu Ja'far Muhammad b. 'Ali al-Baqir was born in Medina in 677. Al-Baqir's mother was Fatima, a daughter of Hasan b. 'Ali b. Abi Talib, making him a grandson of both Hasan and Husayn. He was popularly known as al-Baqir, short for *baqir al-'ilm*, meaning 'he who splits open knowledge', reflecting his erudition in religious learning.

Upon the death of his father Imam Zayn al-'Abidin around 714, al-Baqir became the Imam of the Imami Shi'is and maintained the former's quiescent policy. He spent his entire life in Medina and refused to lend his support to any of the anti-Umayyad revolts then organised by various Shi'i groups in Iraq. Nevertheless, al-Baqir's relations with the ruling Umayyads were at times uneasy. According to Shi'i reports, Imam al-Baqir was summoned to Damascus by the Umayyad caliph Hisham b. 'Abd al-Malik (r. 724–743) on several occasions and was briefly imprisoned during one of these visits.

Imam al-Baqir's reputation as a scholar spread beyond the confines of his own Shi'i following. Indeed, Sunni and Shi'i sources are in agreement in describing him as a defining scholar of the religious sciences, such as *hadith*, *fiqh* and *tafsir* or Qur'an commentaries, which were then in the early stages of their development and to which he contributed significantly. He has been mentioned as a reporter of *hadith*, particularly of those supporting the Shi'i cause and derived from Imam 'Ali. It should be noted that in Shi'i Islam, *hadith*s are reported on the authority of the Imams and include the sayings of the Imams in addition to the Prophetic traditions. In fact, Imam al-Baqir is considered a trustworthy transmitter of *hadith* even by the Sunni experts, in addition to being named among the early legal scholars (*fuqaha*) of Medina. Many of his own numerous sayings on the subject of *zuhd* were also transmitted in Sufi circles. Imam al-Baqir's Qur'an commentary (*tafsir*) has been partially preserved.

In the Shi'i tradition, Imam al-Baqir is held to have initiated the theological and legal teachings that were further elaborated by his son and successor Imam Ja'far al-Sadiq, forming the doctrinal basis of Imami Shi'ism. Indeed Imami Shi'ism, the common heritage of the Ismaili and Ithna'ashari communities, with its distinctive identity in terms of doctrine and ritual, crystalised around the teachings of Imams al-Baqir and al-Sadiq. Above all, Imam al-Baqir seems to have concerned himself with the spiritual authority of the Imams who possessed what was considered to be a divinely inspired knowledge (*'ilm*). He taught that the world was in permanent need of such an Imam. He is also credited with introducing the principle of *taqiyya*, the precautionary dissimulation of one's true religious belief and practice, that was to protect the Imam and his followers under adverse circumstances. This principle was later adopted by the Ismaili and Twelver Shi'is, although it did not find any prominence in Zaydi Shi'i teachings.

Imam al-Baqir's legal and ritual teachings comprised many of the features that were later regarded as distinctive aspects of Imami Shi'i law. Among these, mention may be made of the prohibition on the wiping of the soles of one's footwear (*mash 'ala'l-khuffayn*) in the ritual ablution, and the permitting of *mut'a*, or temporary marriage, which was upheld later by the Twelvers but rejected by the Ismailis and the Zaydis, founded by followers of his half-brother Zayd.

Imam al-Baqir was the first Imam of the Husaynid 'Alid line to attract some extremist Shi'i theorists (*ghulat*) to his side. The most prominent of these Shi'i *ghulat* in his following were al-Mughira b. Sa'id (d. 737) and Abu Mansur al-'Ijli (d. 742) who claimed to have derived their authority and teachings from al-Baqir. It has been reported that al-Baqir, in line with his own teachings, disavowed both al-Mughira and Abu Mansur, who went on to found their own groups of followers in Kufa. In this context it may be added in passing that Imam al-Baqir occupies a central position in an enigmatic text entitled *Umm al-kitab*, which has been preserved by t he Ismailis of Central Asia. This book, extant only in archaic Persian, contains the discourses of Imam al-Baqir in response to questions raised by an anachronistic group of disciples, including the extremist Jabir al-Ju'fi (d. *c.* 745). Modern scholarship has shown that the *Umm al-kitab* was apparently composed in the middle of the eighth century within a Kufan *ghulat* group known as the Mukhammisa or Pentadists, who existed on the fringe of Imami Shi'ism and believed in a divine pentad comprising Muhammad, Fatima, 'Ali, Hasan and Husayn.

4.1 Imam Muhammad al-Baqir teaching in Medina, by the artist Qasim ʿAli, dated *c.* 1525, from the *Ahsan al-kibar* of Varamini, written in the mid-14th century.

In spite of many difficulties, Imam al-Baqir succeeded during his Imamate of some twenty years in expanding his Imami Shiʻi following and acquiring an esteemed position among the Shiʻi circles of Kufa. He did indeed acquire a number of adherents from amongst the eminent traditionists and jurists of Kufa, such as Zurara b. Aʻyan (d. 767). The renowned poet al-Kumayt b. Zayd al-Asadi (d. 743) was another follower of Imam al-Baqir. His relations with his activist brother Zayd, the eponymous founder of the Zaydi branch of Shiʻism, remained cordial. Having taken important steps towards establishing the identity of Imami Shiʻism, Imam al-Baqir died around 732, the date given in most Shiʻi sources, one century after the death of the Prophet. He was buried in the Baqiʻ cemetery in Medina.

5

Ja'far al-Sadiq (d. 765)

Abu 'Abd Allah Ja'far b. Muhammad al-Sadiq was the eldest son of Imam Muhammad al-Baqir. His mother, Umm Farwa, was a great-granddaughter of the caliph Abu Bakr. He was born in Medina in 702, the year mentioned in most sources. Imam Ja'far, who later in life acquired the honorific al-Sadiq (the Trustworthy), succeeded to the Imamate of the bulk of the Imami Shi'is upon the death of his father, Muhammad al-Baqir, around 732. He was held to have been designated as his father's successor by the latter's *nass* or explicit designation. Imam al-Sadiq is the last of the early Imami Imams recognised by both the Ismailis and the Twelvers, being the fifth for the former and the sixth for the latter.

Imam al-Sadiq's long Imamate of some thirty-odd years coincided with a most turbulent period in early Islamic history when numerous Shi'i revolts took place and the Abbasids finally uprooted the Umayyads and established their own dynasty. Throughout this period, Imam al-Sadiq maintained the politically quiescent tradition established by his grandfather and father. Consequently, he refused to become involved in the revolt of his uncle Zayd, which unfolded in Kufa in 740 and evolved into the Zaydi branch of Shi'i Islam. Later, he refused to be drawn into the anti-Umayyad movement of the Abbasids that capitalised on Shi'i sentiments and the sanctity of the *ahl al-bayt*. Finally, he did not offer any support to the anti-Abbasid uprising of his distant Hasanid 'Alid cousin, Muhammad b. 'Abd Allah al-Nafs al-Zakiyya in 762. Imam Ja'far al-Sadiq was clearly not prepared to accept the claims of any other 'Alid, or Abbasid, because he considered himself as the sole rightful Imam of the time designated by the previous Imam.

The Imami Shi'is expanded significantly and became a major religious community with a distinctive identity during the eventful Imamate of Ja'far al-Sadiq. However,

Imam al-Sadiq's rise to eminence occurred gradually during his Imamate, while the Imami Shi'is remained overshadowed by the Kaysanis and other radical Shi'is until shortly after the accession of the Abbasids in 750. Imam al-Sadiq, who spent his entire life in Medina, had gradually acquired a widespread reputation as a religious scholar. He was a reporter of *hadith*, and was later cited as such even in the chain of authorities (*isnad*) accepted by Sunni Muslims. He also taught jurisprudence (*fiqh*) and, building on the work of his father, has been credited with founding the Imami Shi'i school of religious law (*madhhab*), named Ja'fari after him. For the Imami Shi'is, including the later Ismailis and Twelvers, Imam al-Sadiq, like other Imams, is considered as infallible and sinless (*ma'sum*) and his own sayings and deeds have been recorded in their various works of *hadith* and jurisprudence. The foremost Ismaili jurist of the Fatimid period, al-Qadi al-Nu'man (d. 974), preserved numerous *hadith* and legal opinions reported from Imam al-Sadiq. For the Imami Shi'is, Imam al-Sadiq's legal opinions indeed represent authoritative expositions of Islamic law.

Imam al-Sadiq was accepted as a teaching authority not only by his Imami Shi'i partisans but by a wider circle that included many of the pious-minded Muslims of Medina and Kufa, where the bulk of the Imami Shi'is had continued to be located. He

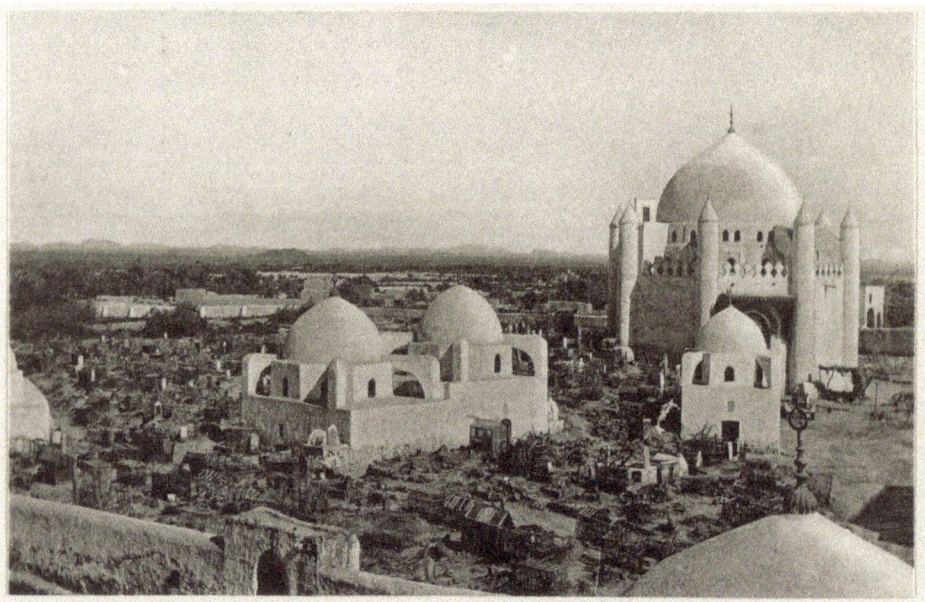

5.1 A photograph of the cemetery of al-Baqi' in Medina, published in 1916 by the German archaeologist and orientalist Bernhard Moritz (1859–1939). The large mausoleum held the tomb of Imam Ja'far al-Sadiq.

5.2 Imam Jaʿfar al-Sadiq and the Abbasid caliph al-Mansur. From a dispersed manuscript of the *Rawdat al-safaʾ*, a universal chronicle written by the Persian historian Mirkhwand (d. 1498).

also had scholarly relations with Abu Hanifa (d. 767) and Malik b. Anas (d. 795), eponyms of the Hanafi and Maliki Sunni schools of jurisprudence. Furthermore, over time Imam al-Sadiq surrounded himself with a noteworthy group of scholars comprising some of the most eminent contemporary jurist-traditionists and theologians, such as Hisham b. al-Hakam (d. 795), the foremost exponent of Imami scholastic theology (*kalam*). Indeed, the Imami Shiʿis now came to possess a distinctive body of ritual as well as theological and legal doctrines. Foremost among such Imami doctrines was the basic conception of the doctrine of the Imamate, elaborated during Imam al-Sadiq's Imamate. This central Shi'i doctrine was essentially retained by the later Ismailis and the Twelvers.

The doctrine of the Imamate was founded on belief in the permanent need of humankind for a divinely guided, sinless and infallible (*ma'sum*) Imam who, after the Prophet Muhammad, would act as the authoritative teacher and guide of humankind in all their spiritual affairs. The doctrine further taught that the Prophet himself had designated 'Ali as his legatee (*wasi*) and successor, by an explicit designation (*nass*) under divine command. After 'Ali, the Imamate would be transmitted from father to son by the rule of the *nass*, among the descendants of 'Ali and Fatima, and after Husayn b. 'Ali, it would continue in the Husaynid 'Alid line until the end of time. This 'Alid Imam, the sole legitimate Imam at any time, is deemed to be in possession of special knowledge (*'ilm*). Indeed, the world could not exist for a moment without such an Imam who is the proof of God (*hujjat Allah*) on earth. In line with his passivity and prudence, Imam al-Sadiq also refined the principle of *taqiyya*, or precautionary dissimulation, and made it an absolute article of Shi'i faith.

Like his father, Imam al-Sadiq too attracted a number of *ghulat* thinkers to his circle of associates, but he kept their speculations within tolerable bounds by imposing a certain doctrinal discipline. As a result, such extremist ideas were kept in check. The foremost radical theorist in Imam al-Sadiq's following was Abu'l-Khattab al-Asadi, the most renowned of all the early Shi'i *ghulat*. Abu'l-Khattab propagated a number of extremist ideas and acquired many followers of his own, the Khattabiyya, also adopting a revolutionary policy in conflict with the Imam al-Sadiq's quiescent stance. Eventually Imam al-Sadiq was obliged to refute and denounce Abu'l-Khattab. Soon afterwards, in 755, Abu'l-Khattab and a group of his supporters, who had gathered in the Mosque of Kufa with rebellious intent, were attacked and killed by the forces of the city's Abbasid governor.

Having established a solid doctrinal basis for Imami Shi'ism, Imam Ja'far al-Sadiq died in Medina in 765 during the caliphate of the Abbasid al-Mansur (r. 754–775). He was buried in the Baqi' cemetery next to his father and grandfather, whose tombs were destroyed by the Wahhabi regime in Saudi Arabia in modern times. The dispute over Imam al-Sadiq's succession to the Imamate caused historic divisions in Imami Shi'ism, leading to the formation of independent Ismaili and Ithnáashari (Twelver) communities.

6

Isma'il b. Ja'far al-Sadiq

Abu Muhammad Isma'il was the second eldest son of Imam Ja'far al-Sadiq. He is the eponym of the Ismailis and is counted as their sixth Imam. Isma'il also carried the epithet of al-Mubarak (The Blessed One). Isma'il's mother was Fatima, Imam al-Sadiq's first wife, a granddaughter of Hasan b. 'Ali b. Abi Talib. Isma'il was the full-brother of 'Abd Allah al-Aftah, later acknowledged as the Imam of a short-lived Shi'i group called Aftahiyya or Fathiyya. It is related that Imam al-Sadiq did not take a second wife as long as Fatima was alive. As a result, there was a significant age difference between Isma'il and 'Abd Allah, on the one hand, and Musa, from a slave concubine called Hamida, on the other. Indeed, Isma'il was some twenty-five years older than his half-brother Musa, later called al-Kazim, who would be acknowledged as the seventh Imam of the Twelvers. As Musa was born in 745, Isma'il's birth was in all probability sometime around 720.

Few biographical details are available on Isma'il. The Ismaili sources contain little historical information on him or on the opening phase of Ismaili history. On the other hand, the Twelver sources, including their earliest heresiographies, which are better informed than the Sunni ones regarding the Shi'i groups and their Imams, are generally hostile towards Isma'il and the claims raised on his behalf. Clearly, the Twelvers, who recognised Musa al-Kazim as their Imam after Ja'far al-Sadiq, were interested in upholding his rights against Isma'il.

Isma'il had evidently established contacts and relations with certain activist Shi'is in his father's following. These radical Shi'is, such as al-Mufaddal al-Ju'fi, were not generally satisfied with the quiescent policies of Imam al-Sadiq and his predecessors. In this context, it is reported that Isma'il was involved in at least one anti-Abbasid plot in 755, in collaboration with several others, including Bassam al-Sayrafi, a radical Shi'i engaged in moneylending in Kufa. The reigning Abbasid caliph al-Mansur summoned Isma'il along with his father and Bassam to his administrative capital at Hira near Kufa. He had Bassam executed but spared Isma'il out of respect for Imam al-Sadiq. Isma'il may also have collaborated with Abu'l-Khattab al-Asadi (d. 755), the most renowned of the early Shi'i *ghulat* on the margins of Imam al-Sadiq's following and the eponym of the Khattabis. Indeed, some Twelver sources identify the Khattabis, one of the most radical early Shi'i groups, with the nascent Isma'iliyya. However, the nature of any connections that may have existed between Isma'il and Abu'l-Khattab, on the one hand, and between the earliest Ismailis and the Khattabis, on the other, are shrouded in obscurity. Abu'l-Khattab, as is known, was denounced and refuted by Imam al-Sadiq for his extremist ideas, such as attributing divinity to the Imams. And the later Ismailis regarded Abu'l-Khattab as a 'heretic' and condemned the beliefs of his followers, the Khattabis.

Few other details are available on Isma'il. It is a fact that Imam al-Sadiq had originally designated Isma'il as his successor to the Imamate by the rule of the *nass*. There can be no doubt about the authenticity of this designation, which forms the basis of the claims of the Ismailis and which should have settled the question of al-Sadiq's succession in due course. However, Isma'il was not present at the time of his father's death in 765, when three other sons ('Abd Allah, Musa and Muhammad) simultaneously claimed the succession. As a result, Imam al-Sadiq's Imami Shi'i partisans now split into several groups, some of which evolved into the Ismaili and Twelver branches of Shi'i Islam.

The exact date and the circumstances of Isma'il's death also remain unknown. According to the Ismaili tradition, he survived his father and succeeded him in due course. However, the majority of the sources report that Isma'il predeceased his father in Medina and was buried in the Baqi' cemetery there. Many Ismaili and non-Ismaili sources repeat that during Isma'il's funeral procession, Imam al-Sadiq made deliberate attempts to show the face of his son to witnesses, though some of the same sources also report that Isma'il was seen in Basra soon afterwards. In accounts of Isma'il's death and burial, al-Mansur (r. 754–775) is named as the ruling Abbasid caliph. Isma'il's grave in the Baqi' cemetery was visited by the Bohra scholar Hasan b. Nuh al-Bharuchi (d. 1533) in 1498, and it still existed in 1885, before being destroyed in modern times, along with other graves there, by the Wahhabis.

On the death of Imam al-Sadiq in 765, among a number of other splinter groups two Kufan-based groups, supporting the claims of Isma'il b. Ja'far and his son Muhammad, separated from the deceased Imam's Shi'i following. These two groups may be identified with the earliest Ismailis. One group, denying that Isma'il had died in his father's lifetime, maintained that he was the true Imam after Ja'far al-Sadiq. Furthermore, they held that he would return imminently as the Mahdi. These Shi'i partisans of Isma'il, designated by the later Twelver heresiographers as *al-Isma'iliyya al-khalisa*, or the Pure Ismailis, believed that Imam al-Sadiq had announced Isma'il's death merely as a ruse to protect his son, whom he had hidden because he feared for his safety.

A second group of the earliest Ismailis, affirming that Isma'il died during the lifetime of his father, now recognised Muhammad b. Isma'il as their next Imam. They held that Muhammad was the rightful successor to his father and that Imam al-Sadiq had personally designated him as such. The Twelver heresiographers call this group the Mubarakiyya, named after Isma'il's epithet al-Mubarak. Thus, it seems likely that the Mubarakiyya were initially the upholders of Isma'il's Imamate, and subsequently they traced their Imamate to Isma'il's son Muhammad. At any rate, it is certain that Mubarakiyya was one of the earliest designations of the nascent Isma'iliyya. Later, a faction of the Mubarakiyya persisted in maintaining continuity in the Imamate and later also acknowledged the Fatimid caliphs as their Imams. The Ismailis of the Fatimid times, who upheld continuity in the Ismaili Imamate in the progeny of Isma'il, acknowledged Isma'il himself as their sixth Imam. This enumeration was subsequently retained by the various branches of Ismaili Shi'ism.

7

Muhammad b. Ismaʿil al-Maymun

Muhammad b. Ismaʿil, the seventh Imam of the Ismailis, was the eldest son of Ismaʿil b. Jaʿfar al-Sadiq. He was also the eldest grandson of Imam al-Sadiq. Born around 738, he was twenty-six years old at the time of al-Sadiq's death in 765. Soon afterwards, on the death of his uncle ʿAbd Allah in 766, Muhammad became the eldest member of Imam al-Sadiq's family; he was older than his other uncle Musa al-Kazim by about eight years. As such, he enjoyed a certain degree of esteem and seniority in this Husaynid Fatimid branch of the ʿAlid family. Muhammad b. Ismaʿil bore the epithet of al-Maymun (The Fortunate One).

On the death of Imam al-Sadiq in 765, his Imami Shiʿi following split into several groups. One group acknowledged Ismaʿil, who had been designated as his successor by the rule of the *nass*, as their next Imam. However, Ismaʿil was not present in Kufa or Medina at the time of his father's death; and, the majority of the sources relate that he had in fact predeceased his father, though some of them add that he was seen later in Basra. Be that as it may, another group of the Imami Shiʿis, affirming that Ismaʿil had died in the lifetime of his father, now recognised his son Muhammad as their Imam. These Shiʿis, later designated as the Mubarakiyya (after Ismaʿil's epithet al-Mubarak), further held that al-Sadiq had personally designated his grandson, Muhammad, as his successor upon Ismaʿil's death. At any rate, the Mubarakiyya were one of the early Ismaili groups. These partisans of Muhammad b. Ismaʿil were initially referred to also as the Maymuniyya, after his own epithet.

Soon after 766, Muhammad b. Isma'il permanently left Medina, the residence of the 'Alids, for the East, going into hiding to avoid Abbasid persecution. This initiated the *dawr al-satr*, or 'period of concealment', in early Ismaili history, which lasted until the establishment of the Fatimid caliphate in 909. Henceforth, Muhammad b. Isma'il acquired the additional epithet al-Maktum (The Hidden One).

Muhammad b. Isma'il maintained his secret contacts with his Mubaraki followers who, like most other Shi'i groups of the time, were centred in Kufa. He evidently spent the later part of his life in Khuzistan, in southwestern Persia, where he had some followers and from where he dispatched *da'i*s to adjoining areas in southern Iraq. The exact date of Muhammad's death remains unknown. However, it is certain that he died during the caliphate of the celebrated Abbasid Harun al-Rashid (r. 786–809), not long after 795. Muhammad b. Isma'il had at least two sons, Isma'il and Ja'far, when he lived openly in Medina. After his emigration, he had four more sons, including 'Abd Allah, who, according to the later Ismailis, was his rightful successor to the Imamate.

On the death of Muhammad b. Isma'il, his Shi'i following (the Mubarakiyya) split into two groups. One small group traced the Imamate in his progeny. Subsequently, belief in continuity in the Ismaili Imamate was adopted as the formal doctrine of the Ismailis who acknowledge the Fatimid caliphs as their Imams. However, the bulk of the Mubarakiyya denied Muhammad's death and awaited his reappearance as the Mahdi, or its equivalent *qa'im*. For these earliest Ismailis, Muhammad b. Isma'il was their seventh and final Imam. This also explains why the Isma'iliyya later acquired the additional denomination of the Sab'iyya, or Seveners, referring to those who acknowledged only one heptad of Imams. Drawing on their cyclical view of the sacred history of humankind, these earliest Ismailis also considered Muhammad b. Isma'il as their seventh and the last of the speakers (*natiqs*). On his return, he would initiate the final era (*dawr*) of history, fully revealing the hitherto hidden esoteric truths (*haqa'iq*) of all the preceding revelations. Muhammad b. Isma'il would rule the world in justice during that eschatological age of pure spiritual knowledge before the physical world came to an end. In this sense, Muhammad b. Isma'il would acquire the cosmological designation of the *qa'im al-qiyama*, or the 'Lord of the Resurrection'.

Part Three

The Concealed Imams

It is certain that for almost a century after the death of Muhammad b. Isma'il, a group of his descendants, who were well placed within the nascent Isma'iliyya, worked secretly for the creation of a unified Shi'i movement against the Abbasids. These leaders were, in fact, the Imams of that group that issued from the Mubarakiyya partisans of Muhammad b. Isma'il on his death, and who maintained the continuity of the Imamate in his progeny. These leaders, whose Fatimid 'Alid genealogy was in due course acknowledged by the Ismailis, made every effort to conceal their identity and places of residence. They also used different names and code names. Among other *taqiyya* tactics to protect themselves against Abbasid persecution, the central leaders of the movement did not openly claim the Imamate for three generations during the 'period of concealment' (*dawr al-satr*) in early Ismaili history.

In fact, the true identity and status of these leaders remained known only to a handful of trusted associates. Instead of openly claiming the Imamate, they organised the movement in the name of Muhammad b. Isma'il as the Mahdi, which was the doctrine of the bulk of the early Ismailis for a while. Organising a revolutionary movement in the name of a hidden Imam-Mahdi who could not be pursued by the Abbasid agents had obvious advantages. And this ingenious strategy served the central leaders of the early Ismailis until the year 899, when the then leader 'Abd Allah al-Mahdi felt secure enough to abandon the established disguising measures and claim the Imamate openly for himself and his predecessors, the same 'Alid leaders in the progeny of Muhammad b. Isma'il who had actually organised and led the early Ismailis. By the middle of the ninth century, there was a single Ismaili movement, instead of the earlier splinter groups. The Ismailis now referred to their religio-political campaign simply as *al-daʿwa* (the mission) or *al-daʿwa al-hadiya* (the rightly guiding mission), in addition to using expressions such as *daʿwat al-haqq* (summons to the truth).

Khuzistan in southwestern Persia

8

'Abd Allah b. Muhammad, also known as Wafi Ahmad

'Abd Allah was the eldest son of Muhammad b. Isma'il, and he had been designated by his father to succeed him. He became the leader of the early Ismaili *da'wa* not long after 795. As such, he would be the first of the second heptad of the Ismaili Imams. Biographical details are rather scarce about 'Abd Allah, who was one of the 'concealed Imams' (*al-a'imma al-masturin*) of the early Ismailis during the *dawr al-satr*, or the 'period of concealment', in their pre-Fatimid history. He received the epithet of 'al-Radi' and, in later Ismaili sources, is designated as 'al-Akbar' (the Elder), probably to distinguish him from his descendant 'Abd Allah al-Mahdi, the future founder of the Fatimid caliphate. In the Nizari Ismaili tradition, he is also known as Wafi Ahmad.

'Abd Allah was probably the first leader who was successful in organising in a systematic manner a dynamic, revolutionary Ismaili movement. Under these circumstances, and in order to escape Abbasid persecution, he sought refuge in different parts of Persia and Iraq before settling down in Salamiyya. However, at all times he did not reveal his true identity and place of residence except to a few trusted associates.

Initially, 'Abd Allah b. Muhammad seems to have spent a good portion of his life in 'Askar Mukram, near the city of Ahwaz in the southwestern Persian province of Khuzistan, where his father had spent the later years of his life. 'Askar Mukram was then a prosperous town about forty kilometres north of Ahwaz. Today the ruins of

'Askar Mukram, situated to the south of the town of Shushtar, are known as Band-i Qir. 'Abd Allah lived as a wealthy merchant in 'Askar Mukram, where he owned two houses. It was from there that he sent *da'i*s to different districts of Khuzistan and southern Iraq. Subsequently, one of these *da'i*s, Husayn Ahwazi, converted Hamdan Qarmat in the rural areas (Sawad) of Kufa. Hamdan and his chief assistant and brother-in-law 'Abdan, originally also from Ahwaz, organised the *da'wa* in various districts of southern Iraq and southern Persia.

Meanwhile, 'Abd Allah had encountered hostile reactions to his activities, obliging him to flee Khuzistan. He proceeded secretly to the nearby town of Basra, where he stayed for some time with his distant Aqilid Hashimid cousins, descendants of 'Aqil b. Abi Talib, 'Ali's brother. However, in Basra, too, he was soon harassed by opponents. It was at some unknown date in the first half of the ninth century that 'Abd Allah was once again forced to flee. This time he went into hiding in Syria, the region known in medieval Islamic sources as Sham.

8.1 Photograph of the dome of the Maqam al-Imam in Salamiyya, Syria. Erected around 1009 by the Fatimid commander, 'Ali b. Ja'far, who captured Salamiyya for the Fatimids, it holds the tomb of their forebear, Imam 'Abd Allah b. Muhammad, also known as Wafi Ahmad.

8.2 Page from a manuscript of *Istitar al-imam* by the Ismaili *da'i* Ahmad b. Muhammad al-Nisaburi (fl. 10th century). This copy was made in 1900. The work talks about the settlement in Salamiyya of Imam 'Abd Allah b. Muhammad in the 9th century.

Initially, 'Abd Allah found refuge in a Christian monastery in the hills of the Jabal al-Summaq, near Ma'arrat al-Nu'man. It was there that a group of his *da'i*s, who had been searching for him in different locations, finally established contact with their leader and prepared the ground for him to settle down in Salamiyya, in central Syria. At the time, the ancient town of Salamiyya, situated at the edge of the Syrian desert some thirty-five kilometres southeast of Hama, was being resettled by an Abbasid official in charge of the locality.

The Ismaili *da'i*s had acquired a plot of land in Salamiyya for 'Abd Allah, who now settled there permanently posing as a prosperous Hashimid merchant. 'Abd Allah constructed a mansion for himself in Salamiyya, which also served as the secret headquarters of the Ismaili *da'wa* for several decades until 902. In Salamiyya, too, 'Abd Allah continued to hide his true identity and role as the central leader of the Ismaili *da'wa*. 'Abd Allah al-Akbar died in Salamiyya, at an unknown date (perhaps not long after the middle of the ninth century). He had two sons in Salamiyya, Ahmad (who succeeded him) and Ibrahim. Around 1009, the Fatimids constructed a domed mausoleum over his grave in Salamiyya, which can still be seen and is locally known as the Maqam al-Imam.

It is worth mentioning here that in the anti-Ismaili Sunni polemical tradition, the 'Alid 'Abd Allah b. Muhammad, the Ismaili Imam, is deliberately conflated with a non-'Alid figure who lived a century earlier, namely 'Abd Allah b. Maymun al-Qaddah. The malicious intent in this substitution was to deny the 'Alid genealogy of the early Ismaili Imams and their successors as the Fatimid caliphs.

9

Ahmad b. 'Abd Allah, also known as Taqi Muhammad

10

Husayn b. Ahmad, also known as Radi al-Din 'Abd Allah

Ahmad succeeded his father, 'Abd Allah b. Muhammad b. Isma'il, to the central leadership of the Ismaili *da'wa* in Salamiyya at an unknown date after the middle of the ninth century. He continued to live in Salamiyya as a merchant affiliated to the Hashimid family, like his predecessors there. Similarly to other Imams of the *dawr al-satr*, or 'period of concealment', Ahmad too used different names and code names as dissimulating measures to hide his identity. In Nizari Ismaili tradition this Imam is also known as Taqi Muhammad. In Tayyibi Ismaili tradition, summarised in the comprehensive Ismaili history entitled *'Uyun al-akhbar*, written by Idris 'Imad al-Din (d. 1468), the authorship of the famous encyclopaedic work known as the *Rasa'il*

Ikhwan al-Safa is attributed to Ahmad b. 'Abd Allah, the second of the concealed Ismaili Imams (*al-a'imma al-masturin*). However, this claim is not endorsed by modern scholarship in the field.

Ahmad b. 'Abd Allah died in Salamiyya at an unknown date, after the middle of the ninth century, and was buried there in the family mausoleum. Ahmad had two sons: Husayn, who succeeded him in the leadership of the *da'wa*, and Abu 'Ali Muhammad, also known as Sa'id al-khayr and Abu'l-Shalaghlagh. It is rather impossible to distinguish the events that occurred under Ahmad's leadership from those under his son and successor Husayn, since we do not have reliable dates for either of these two Imams. However, it is known with certainty that Husayn, known in the Nizari Ismaili sources also as Radi al-Din 'Abd Allah, died in or around 881 in 'Askar Mukram and was buried there, when his son and future successor 'Abd Allah al-Mahdi (born in 873 or 874) was only eight years old. In fact, it was in view of his son's youthfulness that Husayn appointed his own brother Abu 'Ali Muhammad b. Ahmad (d. *c.* 899) as 'Abd Allah's guardian. It is related that Abu 'Ali Muhammad attempted several times unsuccessfully to usurp the leadership for his own sons ('Abd Allah's cousins), all of whom died prematurely.

Building on the work of his father, Ahmad b. 'Abd Allah led the Ismaili *da'wa* successfully, dispatching *da'is* to different regions. It was shortly after the middle of the ninth century, when the fragmentation of the Abbasid state was well under way, that the central Ismaili leadership (then probably still under Ahmad) intensified its activities. The *da'i* Husayn Ahwazi was now sent to southern Iraq where Hamdan Qarmat (d. 933) was converted at the latest in 874. Hamdan, and his chief assistant 'Abdan (d. 899), a learned theologian, organised the *da'wa* in the rural districts around Kufa and in other parts of southern Iraq as well as in southern Persia and eastern Arabia (then known as Bahrayn).

Ahmad b. 'Abd Allah himself reportedly visited Kufa and 'Askar Mukram, his ancestral home where the family had retained some properties. Ahmad's son and successor, Husayn, also maintained his ties with 'Askar Mukram where his own son and future successor 'Abd Allah was born in 873 or 874. It was in Kufa that Ahmad (or perhaps his son and successor Husayn) met Ibn Hawshab, later known as Mansur al-Yaman (the Conqueror of Yemen), who hailed from a prominent Imami Shi'i family. Ibn Hawshab (d. 914) was converted to Ismailism, like many of the early Ismaili *da'is* who originally belonged to the Imami (Twelver) community but had become confused and disillusioned with their own community, on the death of their eleventh Imam in 874.

Later, still in Ahmad's or Husayn's time, Ibn Hawshab was sent to Yemen in 879 to start the *da'wa* there. He was accompanied by 'Ali b. al-Fadl (d. 915), a Shi'i from Yemen

9–10.1 Title page of a manuscript of the *Rasaʾil Ikhwan al-Safaʾ*, an encyclopaedic compendium compiled in the early 10th century by a group of anonymous scholars in southern Iraq. This copy of the *Rasaʾil*, now held in Istanbul, was made around 1287.

who had been converted while on pilgrimage to the shrine of Imam Husayn in Karbala. The *da'wa* in Yemen won strong tribal support and met with astonishing success. It is worth noting that *Kitab al-kashf*, a collection of six short treatises, is one of a handful of early Ismaili texts extant from this period. This collection was redacted later by Ibn Hawshab's son Ja'far b. Mansur al-Yaman (d. *c.* 957). Another early text attributed to Ja'far is *Kitab al-'alim wa'l-ghulam*, an important source on pre-Fatimid Ismaili teachings and practices.

Meanwhile, the Ismaili *da'wa* had spread to many regions of the Iranian world, including the Jibal, Khurasan and later Transoxania. The ground for the extension of the *da'wa* to North Africa was also probably laid when Husayn b. Ahmad was the central leader. Abu 'Abd Allah al-Shi'i (d. 911), a native of Yemen, had been converted to Ismailism in Iraq before he was selected to work with Ibn Hawshab. In 892, he attached himself to some Kutama Berbers who had come to Mecca for the *hajj* pilgrimage, and accompanied them back to their native land in North Africa. He successfully led the *da'wa* in Ifriqiya, comprising today's eastern Algeria and Tunisia, preparing the ground for the establishment of the Fatimid caliphate. With the accession of 'Abd Allah b. Husayn al-Mahdi, the future founder of the Fatimid caliphate, the period of the concealed Imams ended and the Ismailis entered a new phase in their history when their Imams began to rule as Fatimid caliphs.

Part Four

The Early Fatimid Imam-Caliphs

al-Mahdi (d. 934)

al-Qaʾim (d. 946)

al-Mansur (d. 953)

al-Muʿizz (d. 975)

al-ʿAziz (d. 996)

al-Hakim (d. 1021)

al-Zahir (d. 1036)

al-Mustansir (d. 1094)

al-Mustaʿli
(d. 1101)

Nizar
(d. 1095)

Mustaʿlian Imams

Nizari Imams

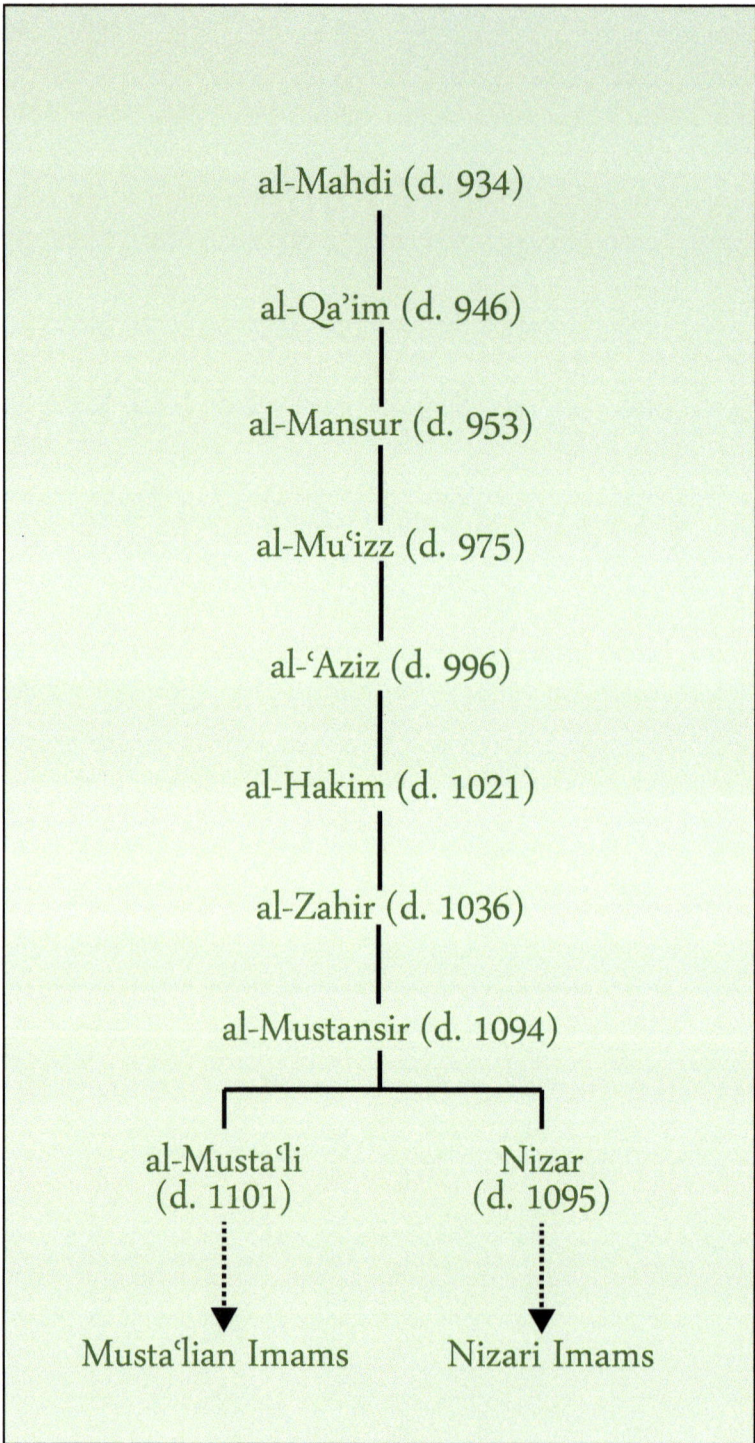

The early Fatimid Imam-caliphs

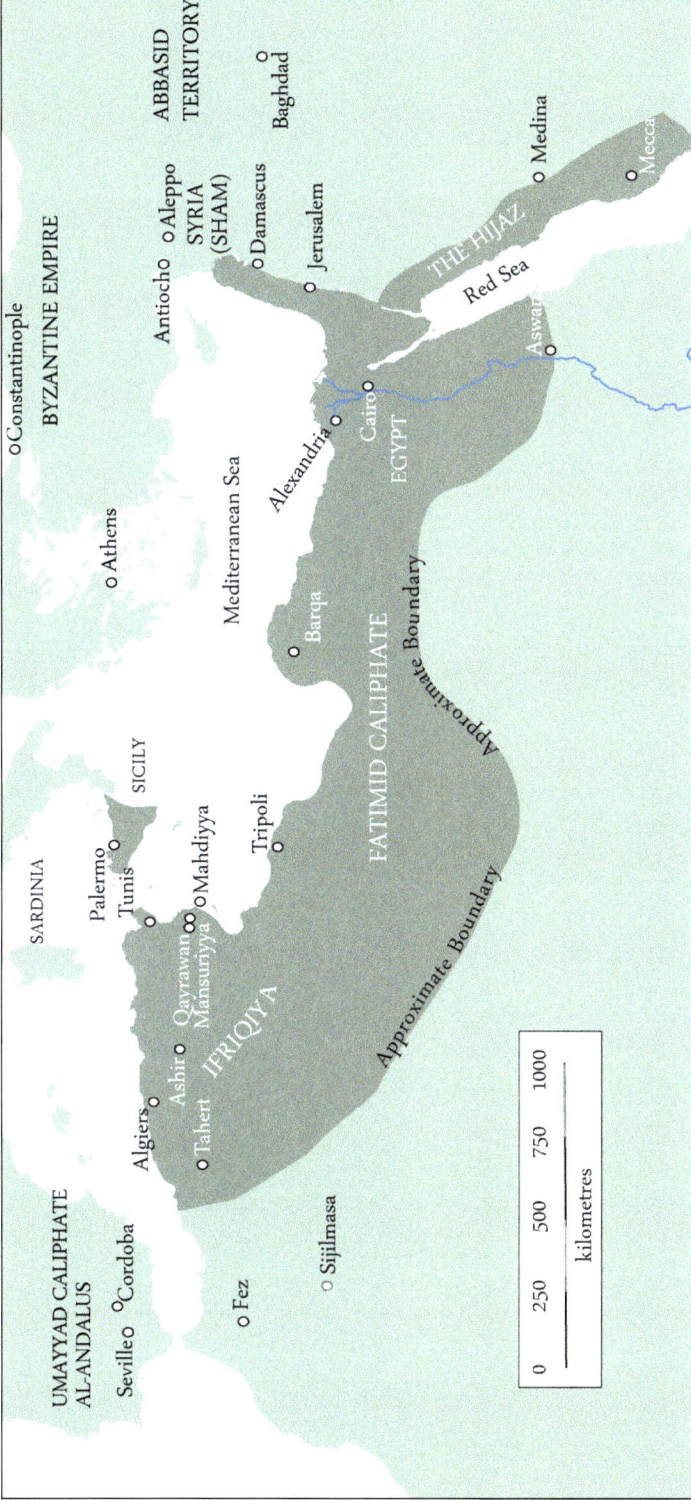

The Fatimid empire at its furthest extent

UMAYYAD CALIPHATE
AL-ANDALUS

Seville o ○Cordoba

o Fez

SARDINIA

o Constantinople

BYZANTINE EMPIRE

o Athens

ABBASID
TERRITORY

Baghdad o

Antioch o o Aleppo
SYRIA
(SHAM)
o Damascus

o Jerusalem

o Medina

o Mecca

Mediterranean Sea

Alexandria

Cairo
o
EGYPT

THE HIJAZ

Red Sea

Aswan
o

Barqa
o

FATIMID CALIPHATE

SICILY

Palermo
Tunis o
o
Qayrawan o o Mahdiyya
Mansuriyya
IFRIQIYA

Tripoli
o

Approximate Boundary

Algiers
o
Ashir o
o Tahert

Sijilmasa o

Approximate Boundary

0	250	500	750	1000

kilometres

11

al-Mahdi, Abu Muhammad 'Abd Allah (d. 934)

'Abd Allah b. Husayn al-Mahdi, the eleventh Ismaili Imam and the founder of the Fatimid caliphate, was born in 873 (or 874) in 'Askar Mukram in the southwestern Persian province of Khuzistan, where the family had continued to own properties since the time of Imam Muhammad b. Isma'il. This Husaynid branch of the 'Alid family had retained its roots in 'Askar Mukram even after relocating to Salamiyya in central Syria. Abd Allah was only eight years old when his father, Husayn b. Ahmad, died in 881 (or 882) in 'Askar Mukram and was buried there. 'Abd Allah had been designated by his father through the rule of the *nass* to succeed him as Imam and central leader of the Ismaili *da'wa*. However, due to 'Abd Allah's youthfulness his paternal uncle Abu 'Ali Muhammad b. Ahmad, also known as Sa'id al-khayr, had been appointed as his guardian. It has been reported that Abu 'Ali Muhammad attempted unsuccessfully several times to usurp the leadership for his sons, and perhaps also for himself.

Be that as it may, by the early 890s the central leaders of the *da'wa* had been quite successful in their activities while hiding their true identity. There was now a unified Ismaili movement instead of the earlier Kufan-based splinter groups. Under such guarded circumstances, the *da'is* of various regions maintained regular correspondence with the central headquarters of the *da'wa* in Salamiyya, receiving their main instructions from there. And the *da'wa* was generally propagated in the name of Imam Muhammad b. Isma'il as the expected Mahdi (or *qa'im*).

By 899, 'Abd Allah al-Mahdi, who was then firmly in charge of the *da'wa*, felt secure enough to dispense with the previously established *taqiyya* practices. In the event, instead of propagating the Mahdiship of Muhammad b. Isma'il, he now claimed the Imamate openly for himself and his ancestors, the same central leaders who had actually organised and directed the Ismaili *da'wa* after Muhammad b. Isma'il during the 'period of concealment'.

In a letter sent subsequently to the Ismaili community in Yemen, 'Abd Allah sought to reconcile his declaration with the actual course of events in early Ismaili history, divulging for the first time some of the dissimulating tactics of his predecessors. As explained in this letter, and corroborated by the few extant pre-Fatimid Ismaili sources, the central leaders of the *da'wa* before 'Abd Allah al-Mahdi had actually assumed the rank of *hujja*, proof or full representative, of the absent Imam-Mahdi Muhammad b. Isma'il. It was through the *hujja* that the Ismailis could establish contact with the hidden Imam. By his declaration, 'Abd Allah al-Mahdi, thus, elevated the ranks of himself and his predecessors from *hujjas* of the expected Mahdi to Imams, also emphasising that the leaders in question had all along regarded themselves as the legitimate 'Alid Imams from the progeny of Imam al-Sadiq, but they had not divulged this for security reasons. In other words, 'Abd Allah explained that hitherto the actual Ismaili Imams, in addition to assuming different code names, had also disguised themselves as the *hujjas* of the absent Imam. 'Abd Allah further explained that the earlier belief in the Mahdiship of Muhammad b. Isma'il had in fact been a misunderstanding, as it represented another *taqiyya* tactic. According to him, the name Muhammad b. Isma'il was itself a code name, a collective name, referring to every true Imam in the progeny of Ja'far al-Sadiq during the 'period of concealment', rather than having reference to the particular grandson of Imam al-Sadiq who actually bore that name.

At any rate, 'Abd Allah al-Mahdi's declaration split the Ismaili community into two rival factions. One faction remained loyal to the central leadership and accepted 'Abd Allah's explanation that the Ismaili Imamate had been handed down among his ancestors. These loyal Ismailis thus maintained continuity in the Imamate, which later became the official doctrine under the Fatimids. They recognised three 'concealed Imams' between Muhammad b. Isma'il and 'Abd Allah al-Mahdi. The loyalist camp included the bulk of the Yemeni Ismailis and those communities founded in Egypt, North Africa and Sind by *da'is* dispatched by Ibn Hawshab Mansur al-Yaman, who remained loyal to the central leadership.

On the other hand, 'Abd Allah's declaration was rejected by the communities in Iraq, Bahrayn and in parts of Persia. These dissident Ismailis, initially led by Hamdan Qarmat in Iraq, and Abu Sa'id al-Jannabi in Bahrayn, retained their original belief in the Mahdiship

11.1 A gold dinar of the first Fatimid Imam-caliph al-Mahdi (r. 909–934), minted in Qayrawan, in 911, obverse (left) and reverse (right).

of Muhammad b. Ismaʿil, and expected his return. Henceforth, the term Qarmati, derived from Hamdan Qarmaṭ's name, came to be applied specifically to the dissident Ismailis, who did not acknowledge as Imams ʿAbd Allah al-Mahdi or his predecessors and his successors in the Fatimid dynasty. In the same eventful year of 899, Abu Saʿid al-Jannabi (d. 913) founded the Qarmati state of Bahrayn that was to play a key role in preventing the Fatimid Imam-caliphs from extending their rule to the central lands of Islam.

Meanwhile, Zikrawayh b. Mihrawayh, a loyal *daʿi*, together with his sons, had embarked on an adventurous campaign for installing ʿAbd Allah al-Mahdi to a Fatimid state in Syria, without the Imam's authorisation. This premature campaign in fact compromised ʿAbd Allah al-Mahdi's position, as the Imam's true identity and place of residence in Salamiyya, were revealed to the Bedouin followers of Zikrawayh's campaign. Indeed, it was to escape capture by the Abbasid agents that ʿAbd Allah al-Mahdi secretly and hurriedly left Salamiyya in 902. Accompanied by his son and future successor, al-Qaʾim, his chamberlain Jaʿfar b. ʿAli, the chief *daʿi* Firuz, and a few attendants, ʿAbd Allah first went to Ramla, in Palestine, before arriving in Egypt in 904. The chamberlain Jaʿfar has left a valuable eyewitness account of this historic journey, which ended several years later in Ifriqiya and in al-Mahdi's installation to the Fatimid caliphate.

ʿAbd Allah al-Mahdi spent a year in Fustat, the capital of Tulunid Egypt, retaining his earlier disguise as a Hashimid merchant. In 905, al-Mahdi's stay in Egypt became untenable as an army was sent there to re-establish Abbasid rule. Instead of heading for Yemen, as expected all along by his companions, al-Mahdi now decided to set out for the Kutama Berber country in the Maghrib, where the loyal *daʿi* Abu ʿAbd Allah al-Shiʿi had already achieved much success. In the event, al-Mahdi joined a caravan of merchants travelling to the Maghrib. In Tripoli, he dispatched the *da'i* Abu'l-'Abbas Muhammad to the Kutama country to inform his younger brother, Abu 'Abd Allah al-Shi'i, of al-Mahdi's imminent arrival. However, the identity of Abu'l-'Abbas was discovered in Qayrawan (Kairouan), where he was arrested and imprisoned by the Aghlabids, who governed in the name of the Abbasids over Ifriqiya, covering the eastern part of the Maghrib, from 800 to 909. The Aghlabids had then been instructed by their Abbasid overlords to search for the Ismaili Imam and his companions.

Under the circumstances, al-Mahdi was once again obliged to change his plans. Accompanied by his son, al-Qa'im, and his faithful chamberlain Ja'far, al-Mahdi joined another caravan and finally arrived in the remote town of Sijilmasa (today's Rissani in southeastern Morocco), which lay on the fringes of the Sahara on an important trading route across the desert. 'Abd Allah al-Mahdi lived quietly there for four years (905–909) as one of this prosperous town's many merchant residents, also maintaining

11.2 Plan of the city of Mahdiyya, showing the Fatimid palaces, taken from the *Kitab ghara'ib al-funun*, produced in the mid-11th century.

11.3 Photograph of the Great Mosque of Mahdiyya showing the monumental entrance aligned with the dome of the *mihrab*, a feature of Fatimid mosque architecture.

his contacts with the *da'i* Abu 'Abd Allah al-Shi'i who was then preparing to launch the final, military phase of his operations in the Maghrib.

Abu 'Abd Allah Husayn, known as al-Shi'i due to his religious persuasion, had been active as a *da'i* among the Kutama Berbers of the Lesser Kabylia, in present-day eastern Algeria, since 893. Shi'i Islam had never taken deep root in the Maghrib, where the indigenous Berber clans generally adhered to diverse schools of Kharijism while the capital city of Qayrawan itself, founded by Arab soldier-tribesmen, was the stronghold of Maliki Sunnism. Subsequently, these realities continued to present major difficulties for the Fatimids in establishing their Shi'i rule over those parts of North Africa. At any rate, the *da'i* Abu 'Abd Allah personally taught the Kutama initiates Ismaili doctrines in regularly held lectures known as the 'sessions of wisdom' (*majalis al-hikma*). Separate sessions were held for women by the *da'i* himself or his subordinate *da'i*s. The *da'i* al-Shi'i organised the converted Kutama Berbers into a formidable army.

By 903, Abu 'Abd Allah had commenced his conquest of Ifriqiya, covering today's eastern Algeria and Tunisia. By 908, Abu 'Abd Allah's Kutama army had achieved much success, effectively signalling the fall of Qayrawan, the Aghlabid capital. Under the circumstances, the last Aghlabid ruler abandoned the palace city of Raqqada, in the suburbs of Qayrawan, and fled to Egypt. In March March 909, Abu 'Abd Allah entered Raqqada and received a delegation of the notables of Qayrawan, who had come to congratulate the Ismaili *da'i* on his victory. The *da'i* governed Ifriqiya for almost a year,

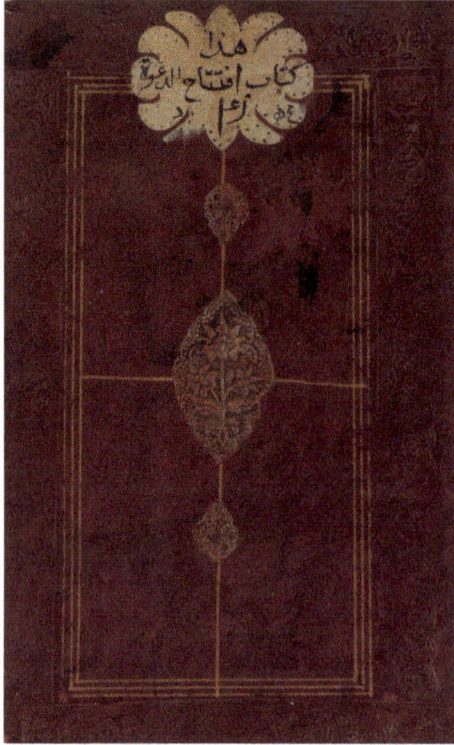

11.4 The cover of a manuscript of *Iftitah al-da'wa*.
Written by al-Qadi al-Nu'man around 957, it
recounts the events leading to the establishment of
the Fatimid state in North Africa in 909.

issuing a general guarantee of amnesty for the people and adding blessings on the *ahl al-bayt* in the *khutba* or sermon, at the Friday prayers.

In June 909, Abu 'Abd Allah al-Shi'i set off for Sijilmasa, at the head of his Kutama soldiers, to hand over the reins of power to Imam al-Mahdi. In August in Sijilmasa, al-Mahdi was acclaimed as caliph in ceremonies that lasted several days. 'Abd Allah al-Mahdi made his triumphant entry into Raqqada on 4 January 910. On the same day, he was publically acclaimed as ruler by the notables of Qayrawan and the Kutama Berbers. On the following day, the *khutba* was pronounced for the first time in the mosques of Qayrawan in the name of Abu Muhammad 'Abd Allah, with the caliphal title of al-Mahdi bi'llah, as the *amir al-mu'minin* (commander of the faithful). At the same time, a manifesto was read out from the pulpits announcing that the caliphate had finally come to be vested in the *ahl al-bayt*. The Shi'i caliphate of the Fatimids had now officially commenced in distant Ifriqiya. The new caliphate was named as Fatimid (Arabic, *Fatimiyya*), derived from the name of the Prophet's daughter Fatima, to whom al-Mahdi and his successors traced back their 'Alid ancestry.

'Abd Allah al-Mahdi, and his next three successors in the Fatimid dynasty, encountered numerous difficulties while consolidating their power in Ifriqiya. In addition to the continued enmity of the Abbasids, the Umayyads of Spain and the Byzantines, they confronted the hostility of the various Sunni and Khariji dynasties and Berber tribes in their immediate surroundings. Soon after his accession, al-Mahdi proclaimed his son Abu'l-Qasim Muhammad, who had accompanied him on the long journey from Salamiyya, as his heir-designate. In line with their universal aspirations, the Fatimids retained their *da'wa* organisation after assuming power. At any rate, as an expression of Fatimid universalism, al-Mahdi from early on concerned himself with extending his dominions eastwards. The conquest of Egypt, then ruled by the Ikshidids, who recognised Abbasid suzerainty, represented the first phase in the Fatimids' strategy of conquest towards the East. The Fatimids attacked Egypt twice unsuccessfully during al-Mahdi's reign; this objective was finally achieved in 969.

In 921, the Imam-caliph al-Mahdi settled in his new capital city of Mahdiyya, named after the founder of the Fatimid dynasty. He had personally selected the site of this royal city, which lay on the coast of Ifriqiya. The earliest Fatimid architectural structures are still preserved in Mahdiyya, Tunisia, including the mosque built there by al-Mahdi. Mahdiyya was equipped with an impressive shipyard, which soon enabled the Fatimids to possess a powerful fleet and operate extensively throughout the Mediterranean. As successors to the Aghlabids, the Fatimids had also inherited the island of Sicily (Siqilliyya) in southern Italy. They appointed governors to Sicily who played an important role in transmitting Islamic culture to Europe. Having laid the foundations of Fatimid rule in North Africa, from Morocco to the borders of Egypt, 'Abd Allah al-Mahdi died in Mahdiyya in March 934, after a caliphate of twenty-five years and an Imamate of at least thirty-five years.

12

al-Qaʾim, Abuʾl-Qasim Muhammad (d. 946)

In 934, the second Fatimid caliph and twelfth Ismaili Imam succeeded his father, ʿAbd Allah al-Mahdi, taking the caliphal title al-Qaʾim bi-Amr Allah. Born in Salamiyya, central Syria, in 890, he had accompanied his father on his fateful journey from Salamiyya to Sijilmasa and then to Qayrawan in Ifriqiya, where the Fatimid caliphate was established in 909. Before founding the Fatimid caliphate, al-Mahdi had operated as the leader of the Ismaili *daʿwa* as well as the Ismaili Imam. Accompanied by his son and future successor, on 4 January 910 al-Mahdi had triumphantly entered Qayrawan, the capital of Ifriqiya, where he formally initiated Fatimid rule.

From early on, al-Qaʾim had received training as a statesman; and he had been involved in the affairs of the Fatimid state before his accession. Already in al-Mahdi's reign, he had led several military expeditions in Ifriqiya in addition to leading two unsuccessful attempts to conquer Egypt during 913–915 and 919–921. Soon after his own accession, in 935 al-Qaʾim launched a third military expedition against Egypt, once again without success. In the course of his reign, al-Qaʾim also had several maritime confrontations with the Byzantines in Sicily and elsewhere in the Mediterranean.

The second Fatimid Imam-caliph maintained his father's policies of expansion and consolidation, and for the greater part of his reign Ifriqiya enjoyed relative peace despite the hostile stances of the indigenous Khariji Berber tribes, especially among the Zanata, and the Sunni Arab inhabitants of the urban areas led by their influential Maliki jurists.

12.1 A gold dinar of the Fatimid Imam-caliph al-Qaʾim (r. 934–946), minted in Mahdiyya in 935, obverse and reverse.

12.2 A folio from the famous Blue Qurʾan showing verses 55 to 60 of *Surat al-Furqan*. Scholars have long held that this Qurʾan was produced in Ifriqiya at the time of the Fatimids.

12.3 A green glass plaque moulded in Ifriqiya in the 10th century. In the middle of the image of a griffin, the inscription reads ʿal-Imam al-Qaʾim bi-Amr Allahʾ.

To at least partially offset the threat posed by the Maghrawa Berbers, an important branch of the Zanata, al-Qaʾim forged an enduring alliance with the Sanjaha Berbers led by Ziri b. Manad, who founded the city of Ashir in the central Maghrib in 936. Ziri served the Fatimids loyally until he lost his life in battle in 971 defending the cause of the Fatimids as an Ismaili. Ziriʾs son, Buluggin, later founded the Zirid dynasty that governed Ifriqiya on behalf of the Fatimids.

It was towards the end of al-Qaʾimʾs reign that the protracted anti-Fatimid rebellion of the Khariji Berbers led by Abu Yazid commenced. This revolt broadly capitalised on the socio-economic grievances of the Berbers as well as on the Sunni-Shiʿi, Khariji-Shiʿi and Zanata-Sanhaja rivalries in the Fatimid dominions of Ifriqiya; and it almost succeeded in uprooting the new Ismaili Shiʿi dynasty of the Fatimids.

Abu Yazid Makhlad b. Kaydad hailed from the Banu Ifran, the most important branch of the Zanata Berbers who adhered to Kharijism. Abu Yazid had eventually managed to become the *shaykh* or leader of the Nukkari Khariji Berbers in the Maghrib, representing one of the main subgroups of the Ibadi branch of Kharijism. With an ever-increasing number of Berbers swarming to his side, Abu Yazid launched a major revolt against the Fatimids in 943, and swiftly conquered almost all of southern Ifriqiya with its numerous towns. Abu Yazid readily defeated the Fatimid army, which had been divided into several sections for defensive purposes. By 945, the rebels had commenced their siege of Mahdiyya, the Fatimid capital, where al-Qa'im was residing. However, the Fatimid Imam-caliph succeeded in repeatedly repelling the Khariji Berber attempts to storm his capital. It was in the midst of this revolt that al-Qa'im died in Mahdiyya in May 946, after a reign of twelve years. By then, the tide of events had already begun to turn against Abu Yazid. At any rate, al-Qa'im's death was kept a secret for some time while his son and successor, al-Mansur, was mobilising an effective offensive against Abu Yazid and his rebellious movement.

13

al-Mansur, Abu Tahir Isma'il (d. 953)

Abu Tahir Isma'il, the third Fatimid caliph and thirteenth Ismaili Imam, succeeded his father al-Qaʾim in 946, with the caliphal title of al-Mansur bi'llah. He was born in 914 in Raqqada, and as such he was the first Fatimid Imam-caliph to have been born in Ifriqiya. He came to power in the midst of the widespread rebellion of Abu Yazid and his Khariji Berber supporters. Under the circumstances, the death of al-Qaʾim was not made public for just over a year while al-Mansur was engaged in a major offensive against the rebels.

Sunni and Ismaili sources are in unanimous agreement in praising al-Mansur for his bravery and wisdom in connection with his campaign against Abu Yazid. Soon after his accession, al-Mansur dispatched Fatimid reinforcements to Susa on the coast west of Mahdiyya, which was besieged, and defeated the rebels there. Subsequently, Abu Yazid was obliged to retreat towards Qayrawan, whose inhabitants had now turned against him. As a result, Abu Yazid's repeated attempts to seize Qayrawan proved futile and, in 946, he withdrew westwards in the direction of the Zab mountains, the original stronghold of his revolt. The Fatimid Imam-caliph now decided to hunt Abu Yazid personally at the head of his troops. In the event, Abu Yazid was defeated near Tubna and then around Masila. In August 947, al-Mansur, assisted by his faithful Ismaili Berber commander Ziri b. Manad, inflicted a decisive defeat on Abu Yazid in the mountains of Kiyana. Abu Yazid himself was captured and died of his wounds a few days later. Abu Yazid's son Fadl continued the revolt in the Awras and elsewhere for a few more months until he, too, was defeated and killed.

13.1 A gold dinar of the Fatimid Imam-caliph al-Mansur (r. 946–953), minted in Mahdiyya in 948, obverse and reverse.

It was in the immediate aftermath of Abu Yazid's demise that al-Mansur made public his father's death and his own accession to the Fatimid throne. The third Fatimid Imam-caliph built a new capital city, Mansuriyya, named after himself. This royal city, situated near the village of Sabra to the south of Qayrawan, served as the Fatimid capital from 948, when al-Mansur settled there, until the seat of the Fatimid state was transferred to Cairo in 973. Mansuriyya, with its Fatimid palaces, al-Azhar Mosque and its gates, served as a prototype for Cairo.

Having saved the Fatimid dynasty from a major threat, al-Mansur devoted the remainder of his brief reign to dealing with a number of internal and external challenges, including those posed by the Umayyads of Spain, who had supported Abu Yazid's rebellion, and by the Byzantines in Sicily. In 948 Fatimid rule in Sicily was entrusted to the faithful Kalbid family. The Kalbids ruled over Sicily for almost a century on behalf of the Fatimids. Meanwhile, al-Mansur was perhaps the first member of the Fatimid dynasty to devote some attention to the activities of the Ismaili *da'wa* in the East, though details are lacking. Having reasserted authority over various Fatimid dominions in North Africa and Sicily, al-Mansur died in March 953, after a short but eventful caliphate and Imamate of only seven years. He was succeeded as caliph and Imam by his eldest son, Abu Tamim Ma'add.

14

al-Muʿizz, Abu Tamim Maʿadd (d. 975)

Born in Mahdiyya in 931, Abu Tamim Maʿadd succeeded his father al-Mansur in 953 with the caliphal title al-Muʿizz li-Din Allah. The fourth Fatimid caliph and fourteenth Ismaili Imam was the last member of his dynasty to rule from Ifriqiya.

Fatimid rule was firmly established in North Africa only during the reign of al-Muʿizz. Taking advantage of the peace and internal security of the state that had been achieved largely through the loyalty of the Kutama and Sanhaja Berbers, al-Muʿizz was able to pursue successful policies of war and diplomacy, resulting in territorial expansion and friendly relations with the local dynasties of North Africa. Indeed, he succeeded in extending the authority and hegemony of his dynasty at the expense of their major rivals: the Umayyads of Spain, the Byzantines and especially the Abbasids.

The sources abound in praises of al-Muʿizz as a statesman with diplomatic skills as well as an efficient organiser who contributed significantly to the development of the Fatimid state's political, administrative and financial institutions. It was due to these skills and the outstanding military competence of his general Jawhar that al-Muʿizz soon succeeded in subduing the entire Maghrib as a prelude to implementing his policy of expansion eastwards. All in all, al-Muʿizz played a key role in transforming the Fatimid state from a regional power in Ifriqiya to a great empire, promoting intellectual, commercial and artistic activities which reached their full extent in Egypt.

Initially, al-Muʿizz concentrated on re-establishing Fatimid authority in the central and far western reaches of the Maghrib. These pacification campaigns were entrusted

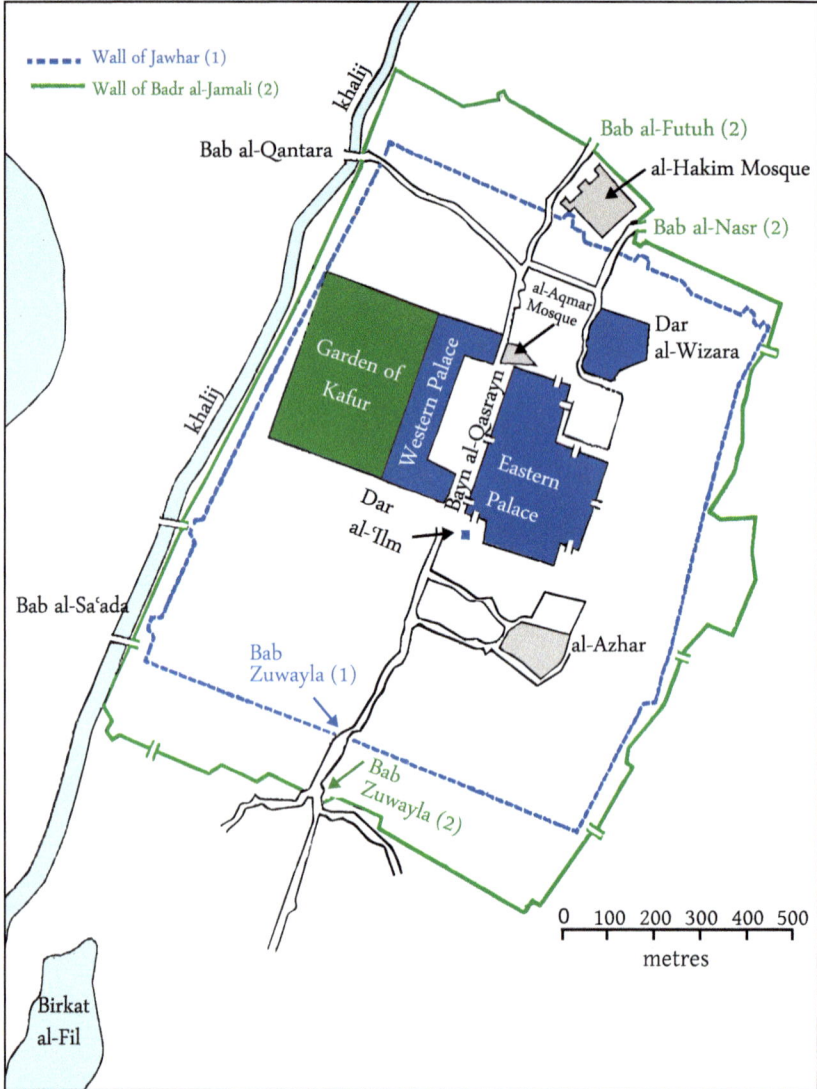

Plan of Fatimid Cairo

mainly to Jawhar, who was of Slav origins and had risen in rank under al-Mansur and al-Muʿizz to become the Fatimid chief general. After pacifying the Maghrib, al-Muʿizz started making meticulous plans for the conquest of Egypt, a vital Fatimid goal which the first two Imam-caliphs had not achieved. The preparations took some ten years. Meanwhile, the Ismaili *daʿwa* was intensified in Egypt then ruled by the enfeebled Ikhshidids on behalf of the Abbasids. After his remarkable successes in the Maghrib, al-Muʿizz had no hesitation in selecting Jawhar to lead the Egyptian expedition. In February 969, Jawhar led the Fatimid army out of Qayrawan after an elaborate ceremony presided over by al-Muʿizz. Jawhar entered Fustat, the old capital of Egypt, four months later in July 969. He camped his army outside the city, on a site about two kilometres north of the Mosque of Ibn Tulun and immediately held peace negotiations with the local notables. Jawhar behaved diplomatically and leniently towards the Egyptians, declaring a general amnesty (*aman*) and assuring the people of the safety of their lives and property through public proclamations. He introduced the Shiʿi modes of prayer only gradually.

Meanwhile, Jawhar proceeded to build a new city on his campsite. Initially called Mansuriyya, like its counterpart in Ifriqiya, the future Fatimid capital was later renamed 'al-Qahira al-Muʿizziyya' (the Victorious One of al-Muʿizz), al-Qahira (Cairo) for short. The new city, like its North African predecessor, was given northern and southern gates called Bab al-Futuh and Bab Zuwayla, respectively, as well as a mosque named al-Azhar. Jawhar also built two royal palaces there, for the Fatimid Imam-caliph and his heir-designate, separated by a wide area. Special buildings were erected for the various government departments and the Fatimid army. The plans of the new city had all been drawn up by al-Muʿizz himself. The Fatimid conquest of Egypt was celebrated by the Ismaili court poet Ibn Hani al-Andalusi (d. 973), the first great poet of the Maghrib.

Jawhar governed Egypt as the Fatimid viceroy for four years until 973. As the Fatimids had done after their takeover of power in Ifriqiya, Jawhar essentially retained the administrative and judiciary officials of the previous regime, easing the transition to Fatimid rule. In line with the erstwhile strategy of the Fatimids, in November 969 Jawhar dispatched the main body of the Fatimid army for the conquest of Palestine and Syria, where Fatimid success proved transitory. The Qarmatis of Bahrayn, then at the peak of their military power, in alliance with the Buyids and others, delayed the establishment of Fatimid hegemony over Syria for several more decades. However, soon after Jawhar's arrival in Egypt, Mecca and Medina submitted to al-Muʿizz. By and large, Fatimid suzerainty over the two holy cities in the Hijaz lasted until the fall of the dynasty.

14.1 A gold dinar of the Fatimid Imam-caliph al-Mu'izz (r. 953–975), minted in Cairo (Misr) in 969, obverse and reverse.

Meanwhile, al-Mu'izz had completed preparations for transferring the seat of the Fatimid state from Ifriqiya to Egypt. Accompanied by the entire Fatimid family, most of the Ismaili notables and *da'i*s, including al-Qadi al-Nu'man, and many Kutama chieftains, al-Mu'izz crossed the Nile and entered Cairo in June 973. He had also brought with him the Fatimid treasuries and the coffins of his predecessors, al-Mahdi, al-Qa'im and al-Mansur. This migration marked the termination of the North African phase (909–973) of the Fatimid caliphate.

The early Fatimids were primarily preoccupied with establishing and consolidating their rule in the hostile, anti-Shi'i milieu of North Africa, where the inhabitants were mostly Sunni and Khariji. Under the circumstances, al-Mu'izz's predecessors could not pay any meaningful attention to Ismaili *da'wa* activities beyond their dominions. Al-Mu'izz was, in fact, the first member of the dynasty to adopt a specific *da'wa* strategy. In particular, he seriously endeavoured to intensify the Ismaili *da'wa* outside the Fatimid dominions, partly seeking to win the support of the dissident Qarmatis as well as to prepare the ideological ground for Fatimid rule in those regions. It is worth noting that al-Mu'izz himself was well versed in literary and scholarly matters and is credited with composing a number of epistles, in addition to scrutinising the works of al-Qadi al-Nu'man (d. 974), the foremost Ismaili jurist of the Fatimid period.

The *da'wa* strategy of al-Mu'izz proved rather successful outside the confines of the Fatimid state. He also succeeded in establishing a Fatimid foothold in Sind, in South Asia. In 958, a Fatimid vassal state was founded there, with its seat at Multan,

14.2 The Mosque of al-Azhar built by the Fatimid Imam-caliph al-Mu'izz.

through the efforts of a *da'i* who converted the local ruler. In Multan, the *khutba* (sermon) now came to be read in the name of the Fatimid Imam-caliph instead of their Abbasid rivals. Ismaili rule persisted in Sind until 1005, when Sultan Mahmud of Ghazna invaded the region and persecuted the Ismailis. Subsequently, Ismailism survived there in a subdued form. On the other hand, the efforts of al-Mu'izz to gain the allegiance of the eastern Qarmatis were only partially successful. However, he won the allegiance of the *da'i* Abu Ya'qub al-Sijistani (d. after 971), who endorsed the Imamate of the Fatimids in the works he wrote after the accession of al-Mu'izz. Consequently, large numbers of al-Sijistani's Ismaili followers in Khurasan, Sistan, Makran and Central Asia, also switched their allegiance to the Fatimid Imam-caliphs. But Qarmatism persisted in many parts of Persia as well as in southern Iraq and Bahrayn.

It was also in al-Mu'izz's reign (953–975) and under his close supervision that Ismaili law was finally codified, mainly through the efforts of al-Qadi Abu Hanifa al-Nu'man b. Muhammad al-Tamimi al-Maghribi. He was officially commissioned by al-Mu'izz to prepare legal compendia. The learned al-Qadi al-Nu'man had served as

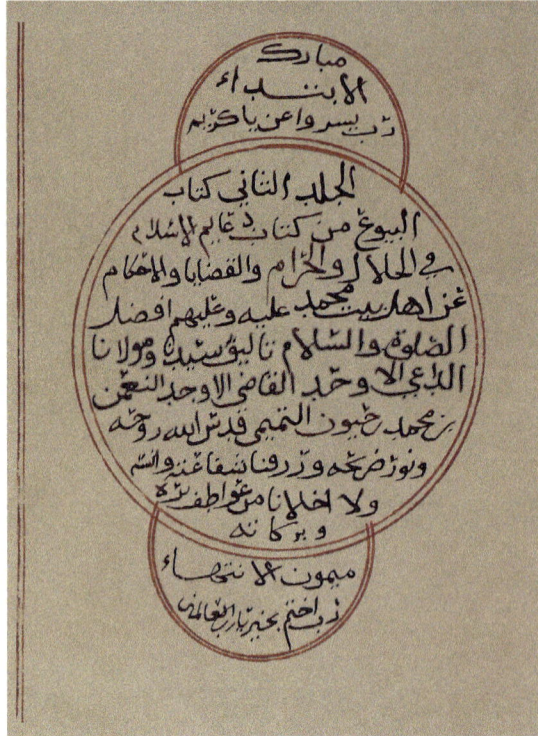

14.3 A page from a 17th-century copy of *Daʿaʾim al-Islam*, the Fatimid code of law, which was commissioned by the Imam-caliph al-Muʿizz and composed by al-Qadi al-Nuʿman (d. 974) in around 960.

the chief jurist (*qadi al-qudat*) of the Fatimid state from 948, before becoming also the chief *daʿi* (*daʿi al-duʿat*). Al-Qadi al-Nuʿman's legal work culminated in the compilation of *Daʿaʾim al-Islam* (The Pillars of Islam), which was read carefully by al-Muʿizz and endorsed as the official code of the Fatimid state. Like the Sunni Muslims and other Shiʿi Muslim communities, the Ismailis, too, now possessed a code of law and system of jurisprudence, which also delineated an Ismaili paradigm of governance. Ismaili law accorded special importance to the central Shiʿi doctrine of the Imamate. As a result, the authority of the infallible ʿAlid Imam and his teachings became another principal source of Ismaili law, in addition to the Qurʾan and the *sunna* which are accepted as the first two sources by all Muslim communities.

The rule of al-Muʿizz in Egypt lasted just over two years, devoted mainly to repelling a number of Qarmati incursions. At the same time, the Imam-caliph concerned himself with elaborating his governance in Egypt. In reorganising the financial system of the state, al-Mu'izz drew on the expertise of Ibn Killis (d. 991). A convert from Judaism, Ibn Killis was destined to become the first vizier of the Fatimid dynasty in 977. As well as being a patron of scholars, jurists and poets, Ibn Killis became an expert in Ismaili jurisprudence.

Al-Mu'izz considerably enhanced the power and fortune of his dynasty, and the territorial extent of the Fatimid state (*dawla*). Having transformed the Fatimid *dawla* into a flourishing empire with a proper administrative apparatus and a reinvigorated *da'wa* organisation, al-Mu'izz li-Din Allah died in December 975, at the young age of forty-four and after a caliphate and Imamate of twenty-two years. He was buried in the same mausoleum near the Fatimid palaces in which his predecessors and successors, as well as other members of the Fatimid family, were also buried.

15

al-ʿAziz, Abu Mansur Nizar
(d. 996)

Abu Mansur Nizar, the fifth Fatimid caliph and fifteenth Ismaili Imam, was born in 955 in Mahdiyya, Ifriqiya. He succeeded to the Fatimid throne with the caliphal title al-ʿAziz bi'llah on the death of his father al-Muʿizz in 975. The third son of al-Muʿizz, al-ʿAziz was the first member of the dynasty to commence his reign in Egypt. He had been designated as the heir-apparent (*wali al-ʿahd*) only about a year earlier, after the death of his elder brother ʿAbd Allah. The Imam-caliph al-Muʿizz had originally designated his second son ʿAbd Allah as his successor, in preference to Amir Tamim, his eldest son. Tamim devoted himself to literary activities and acquired a certain reputation as a poet. Many of Tamim's poems are in praise of the Imams, especially al-Muʿizz and al-ʿAziz. Tamim's panegyrics also contain references to Ismaili teachings under the Fatimids. Amir Tamim b. al-Muʿizz died at an early age in 985 in Cairo.

The consolidation and extension of Fatimid hegemony in Syria, at the expense of the Abbasids and the Byzantines, remained the primary objective of al-ʿAziz in his foreign policy. In the immediate aftermath of his accession, in 976 al-ʿAziz dispatched an army to Syria under the veteran commander Jawhar, to retake Damascus from Alftakin, a Turkish commander who had allied himself with the Qarmatis of Bahrayn. In the event, the Qarmatis forced Jawhar to retreat to Egypt, where he led a quiet life until his death in 992. Meanwhile, al-ʿAziz had led his army himself and defeated Alftakin and the Qarmatis near Ramla in 978. Nevertheless, Damascus remained only nominally in Fatimid hands for some time.

15.1 A gold dinar of the Fatimid Imam-caliph al-ʿAziz (r. 975–996), minted in Cairo in 975, obverse and reverse.

Al-ʿAziz also aimed to extend Fatimid hegemony to northern Syria. He made numerous attempts to conquer the Hamdanid principality of Aleppo without any success, mainly due to the intervention of Byzantium from the north. Al-ʿAziz avoided any direct confrontations with the Sunni Abbasids in Iraq and their Shiʿi overlords, the Buyids. In North Africa, he confirmed the Zirid Buluggin in his position of governor. However, under Buluggin's son and successor, al-Mansur (r. 984–996), the Zirids began to detach themselves from the Fatimids. Nonetheless, by the end of al-ʿAziz's reign the Fatimid empire had attained its greatest geographical extent, with Fatimid sovereignty recognised from the Atlantic and western Mediterranean to the Red Sea, the Hijaz, Syria and Palestine. The *khutba* was read in the name of al-ʿAziz, for a short while in 992 even in Mawsil, Iraq, then ruled by the Shiʿi ʿUqaylids. At the same time, Ismaili *daʿi*s continued to propagate the *daʿwa* in the name of the Fatimids in many eastern regions of the Muslim world, especially in various parts of Persia.

Al-ʿAziz was an excellent administrator, and he knew how to use the services of capable men, without much regard to their religious persuasion or ethnic background. In running the complex affairs of the Fatimid state al-ʿAziz was crucially helped by Ibn Killis, a convert from Judaism who had served the Fatimids in various administrative and financial capacities. In 977, al-ʿAziz made Ibn Killis his vizier, the first person to hold this office under the Fatimids. Ibn Killis retained the vizierate, with two brief interruptions, for over twelve years until his death in 991. The credit for utilising al-Azhar as a university also belongs to Ibn Killis.

15.2 Carved crystal ewer bearing the name of the Imam-caliph al-ʿAziz, now in the treasury of San Marco in Venice.

Subsequently, al-ʿAziz appointed several other individuals to the vizierate, including a Coptic Christian, ʿIsa b. Nasturus, who would be the first of several Christians to occupy that office under the Fatimids. Al-ʿAziz also appointed a number of Jews to high positions in the Fatimid state, though not the vizierate. The unusual policy of assigning high administrative posts to Christians and Jews, as well as to Sunni Muslims, in a Shiʿi state, was in line with the religious tolerance practised by the Fatimids. However, al-ʿAziz went further than his predecessors and set remarkable precedents in this domain. The tolerant religious policy of al-ʿAziz towards the non-Muslim subjects of the Fatimid state, or the *ahl al-dhimma*, led to growing discontent amongst Egypt's predominantly Sunni population, who later reacted by plundering several churches.

Like his father, al-ʿAziz encouraged the observance of the mourning ceremonies of ʿAshura commemorating the martyrdom of Imam Husayn at Karbala, and the Shiʿi feast of Ghadir, celebrating the investiture of Imam ʿAli b. Abi Talib by the Prophet at Ghadir Khumm. These distinctly Shiʿi ceremonies were actually inaugurated at Baghdad, the capital of the Sunni Abbasids, in 963, in the time of their Shiʿi Buyid overlord Muʿizz al-Dawla (r. 945–967). The Shiʿi Buyids, who hailed from northern Persia and originally adhered to Zaydi Shiʿism before inclining towards Twelver Shiʿism, also embellished the ʿAlid shrines of Iraq.

The Fatimid Imam-caliph al-ʿAziz had personally set out at the head of the Fatimid army on yet another expedition against Syria when he suddenly fell ill and died in October 996 at Bilbays, the first stop on the route to Syria. His caliphate and Imamate had lasted almost twenty-one years. Al-ʿAziz was succeeded by his sole surviving son, al-Hakim.

15.3 Fragment of a panel of carved Cypress wood. The panel dates from the 11th century and comes from the site of the Western Palace of the Fatimids in Cairo.

16

al-Hakim, Abu 'Ali al-Mansur (d. 1021)

In 996, Abu 'Ali al-Mansur succeeded his father al-'Aziz, as the sixth Fatimid caliph and sixteenth Ismaili Imam, with the caliphal title of al-Hakim bi-Amr Allah. Born in 985 in the Fatimid palace in Cairo, al-Hakim was only eleven years old at the time of his accession. The first Fatimid Imam-caliph to have been born in Egypt, al-Hakim had been proclaimed as heir-apparent (*wali al-'ahd*) in 993, on the death of his older and sole brother, Muhammad.

Al-Hakim confronted numerous difficulties and riots during his relatively long reign (996–1021). He did not lose any territories in North Africa, but the Ismaili communities of those regions were now severely victimised by Sunni mobs. Relations between the Fatimids and the Qarmatis of Bahrayn also continued to remain hostile. On the other hand, al-Hakim was successful in Syria and extended Fatimid hegemony to the northern principality of Aleppo.

Above all, the persistent rivalries between the various factions of the Fatimid army overshadowed the other difficulties in al-Hakim's caliphate. Al-Hakim's father al-'Aziz had encouraged the employment of non-Berber groups, especially the Turks, in the Fatimid forces. This policy had been adopted to facilitate the Fatimid conquest of the eastern lands, since the Turks were known as skilful fighters in addition to having had the valuable experience of serving in the Abbasid armies. To the discontent of the Berbers, who were mainly Kutama tribesmen, Turkish officers had rapidly risen through the ranks of the Fatimid army. The serious rivalry between these two factions of the army reached the point of open warfare during al-Hakim's reign.

16.1 A gold dinar of the Fatimid Imam-caliph al-Hakim (r. 996–1021), minted in Cairo in 996, obverse and reverse.

Furthermore, by the time of al-Hakim, the Fatimids had generally realised the difficulty of achieving a speedy conquest of the Muslim East. Nonetheless, they still aimed at extending their rule to the eastern lands. Under al-Hakim, the *da'wa* organisation was systematically expanded outside the Fatimid dominions, especially in Iraq and Persia, and he also concerned himself with the training of the *da'is*. A large number of *da'is* were assigned to these territories, where they targeted various social strata. In Iraq, the seat of the Abbasid caliphate, the *da'is* particularly concentrated their efforts on local rulers and influential Arab tribal chiefs.

Foremost amongst the Ismaili *da'is* operating in the eastern regions in al-Hakim's time, was Hamid al-Din al-Kirmani (d. after 1020). He was an eminent philosopher and perhaps the most learned Ismaili theologian of the entire Fatimid period. Being of Persian origin, al-Kirmani spent the greater part of his career as a Fatimid *da'i* in Iraq. The activities of al-Kirmani and other *da'is* soon bore fruit, and several *amirs* and tribal chiefs in Iraq acknowledged the suzerainty of al-Hakim. Alarmed by these developments, the Abbasid caliph al-Qadir (r. 991–1031) decided to take retaliatory measures. In addition to commissioning several refutations of Ismaili doctrine, in 1011 he assembled a number of Sunni and Shi'i scholars at his court in Baghdad and commanded them to declare in a written document that al-Hakim and his predecessors lacked genuine Fatimid 'Alid ancestry. This so-called 'Baghdad manifesto' was read in mosques throughout the Abbasid domains to the deep annoyance of al-Hakim.

One of al-Hakim's most important acts was the foundation of the Dar al-'Ilm (House of Knowledge), sometimes also called the Dar al-Hikma (House of Wisdom), which

16.2 Door panels donated by the Imam-caliph al-Hakim (r. 996–1021) to the Mosque of al-Azhar. The inscription at the top reads, 'Our Lord, the commander of the faithful, the Imam al-Hakim bi-Amr Allah, may the blessings of God be upon him and upon his ancestors, the Pure Ones, and his descendants'.

was set up in 1005 in a section of the Fatimid palace in Cairo. A wide range of religious and other subjects were taught at this institution of learning, which was also equipped with a vast library. Scholars of different religious persuasions used this academy, where the Ismaili *da'i*s also received at least part of their training. Al-Hakim himself often attended the lectures given there. He also completed the construction of a mosque started by his father and which still survives under his own name in Cairo.

Al-Hakim's reign witnessed the genesis of what was to evolve into the Druze religion. From around 1017 (the opening year of the Druze era), a number of *da'i*s who had come to Cairo from Persia and Central Asia, started a movement proclaiming the divinity of al-Hakim. The extremist teachings of these *da'i*s, including especially al-Akhram, Hamza and Muhammad al-Darazi (after whom the movement was later designated as al-Daraziyya or al-Durziyya), caused much unrest during the final years of al-Hakim's reign. Contrary to the claims of some later Sunni authors, however, there is no evidence suggesting that al-Hakim himself had encouraged the ideas held by the founders of the Druze movement. In fact, the leadership of the *da'wa* organisation in Cairo was categorically opposed to this movement, launching a campaign against it. As part of this campaign, al-Kirmani, being the most eminent *da'i* of the time, was invited to Cairo to refute the new doctrine on theological grounds.

Al-Hakim also concerned himself with the moral standards of his subjects and issued many edicts (*sijillat*) of an ethico-social nature. The Christian chronicler Yahya al-Antaki (d. 1066), and several later Sunni historians, have painted a highly distorted and fanciful image of this Fatimid Imam-caliph, depicting him as a person of strange and erratic behaviour. However, modern scholarship in Ismaili and Fatimid studies is beginning to reveal a different account on the basis of al-Hakim's own edicts and the complex religio-political circumstances of his reign. As a result, al-Hakim is now emerging as a ruler who was rather popular with his subjects.

In the closing years of his reign, al-Hakim displayed a growing inclination towards asceticism. He dressed simply and, unaccompanied by guards, rode on a donkey through the streets of Cairo. He also took to nocturnal and solitary excursions in the

16.3 Entrance portal to the Mosque of al-Hakim in Cairo. The construction of this mosque was begun by al-Hakim's father and predecessor, the Imam-caliph al-'Aziz, and was completed by al-Hakim.

16.4 View of the Mosque of al-Hakim in Cairo.

16.5 A copy of the *Kitab al-masabih fi ithbat al-imama* by the Fatimid *da'i* Hamid al-Din al-Kirmani (d. after 1020). This is a treatise on the concept and nature of the Imamate, in particular defending the legitimacy of al-Hakim's Imamate.

countryside. On 13 February 1021, al-Hakim left for one of his usual outings to the Muqattam hills outside Cairo and never returned. A futile search was conducted for the thirty-six-year-old Imam-caliph, whose caliphate and Imamate had lasted twenty-five years; only his donkey and bloodstained garments slashed by daggers, were found. The mystery of al-Hakim's disappearance was never resolved.

17

al-Zahir, Abu'l-Hasan 'Ali (d. 1036)

Born in 1005 in the Fatimid palace in Cairo, Abu'l-Hasan 'Ali succeeded to the Fatimid throne in 1021, with the caliphal title al-Zahir li-I'zaz Din Allah, on the disappearance of his father al-Hakim. He was the seventh Fatimid caliph and seventeenth Ismaili Imam.

In the immediate aftermath of al-Hakim's enigmatic demise, his half-sister Sitt al-Mulk played a unique role in ensuring the smooth succession of al-Hakim's sole son, al-Zahir. Sitt al-Mulk, also known as Sayyidat al-Mulk and al-Sayyida al-'Amma (Princess-Aunt), was born in 970 in Mansuriyya, the last Fatimid capital in Ifriqiya. Similarly to many other Fatimid princesses, she never married for dynastic reasons. The favourite daughter of the Imam-caliph al-'Aziz, Sitt al-Mulk was an influential Fatimid princess with a large retinue and substantial wealth. For many years before his accession, the future al-Zahir had enjoyed the protection of his aunt Sitt al-Mulk at her palace, where he was also brought up and educated, as he had apparently fallen into disfavour with his father.

Be that as it may, about forty days after al-Hakim's disappearance, Sitt al-Mulk had her sixteen-year-old nephew proclaimed as caliph while retaining the reins of government in her own hands as regent. Until her death two years later in 1023, Sitt al-Mulk ruled efficiently and restored order to the state, also addressing certain religious and social grievances, all traceable to al-Hakim's final years. It may be noted that starting with al-Zahir, henceforth the Fatimid throne usually fell to minors while regents, viziers and military commanders effectively held power for extended periods.

After Sitt al-Mulk, real political authority in the Fatimid state remained vested in al-Zahir's capable vizier ʿAli b. Ahmad al-Jarjaraʾi. He retained the vizierate and his influence, also under al-Zahir's successor, until his death in 1045. Meanwhile, in 1024 Egypt suffered a famine which lasted several years and led to serious economic crises and riots in Cairo. Similar natural catastrophes befell Fatimid Egypt in subsequent times as well.

In al-Zahir's time, the Ismaili *daʿwa* continued to be active in many regions beyond the Fatimid dominions, especially in Iraq where many *daʿis* won converts. On the other hand, Fatimid control of Syria was now seriously undermined due to the hostility of a number of local rulers and tribal chiefs, including the Jarrahids of Palestine and the Kalbis and Kilabis of Syria. However, Fatimid domination was re-established in Syria in 1038, mainly due to the efforts of Anushtigin al-Duzbari, a capable Turkish commander in the service of the Fatimids. The Fatimid Imam-caliph al-Zahir died in 1036 in his thirty-first year, after a caliphate and Imamate of fifteen years. He was succeeded by his son Abu Tamim Maʿadd who was a minor.

17.1 A gold dinar of the Fatimid Imam-caliph al-Zahir (r. 1021–1036), minted in Cairo in 1029, obverse and reverse.

17.2 A gold case with filigree and granulation patterns, about 4.7 × 3.9 cm in size, designed to hold a miniature Qur'an. This unique object was made in Fatimid Egypt in the 11th century.

17.3 A piece of *tiraz* textile, produced during the reign of the Fatimid Imam-caliph al-Zahir. The inscription woven into the bands of decoration of this *tiraz* piece includes the Shiʿi *shahada* and the name of the Imam-caliph al-Zahir.

17.4 A glass weight from the Fatimid period bearing the name
of the Imam-caliph al-Zahir. These official weights ensured that
goods were sold in a regulated and orderly fashion.

18

al-Mustansir, Abu Tamim Ma'add (d. 1094)

Abu Tamim Ma'add, the eighth Fatimid caliph and eighteenth Ismaili Imam, was born in 1029 in Cairo. He succeeded his father, the Imam-caliph al-Zahir, in 1036 at the age of eight with the title al-Mustansir bi'llah. He had been designated as heir-apparent (*wali al-'ahd*) in 1030, when he was only eight months old. Al-Mustansir's caliphate and Imamate, lasting almost sixty lunar years (1036–1094), was the longest of his dynasty.

In the first decade of al-Mustansir's reign, real political authority remained in the hands of al-Jarjara'i, who had retained the vizierate since 1021, while the Imam-caliph's mother Rasad, a Sudani, acted as the regent. On al-Jarjara'i's death in 1045, all power was seized and maintained for a long time by the queen-mother. Meanwhile, ethnic rivalries in the Fatimid army had begun to provide a major source of unrest in the state, often erupting into factional fighting. The persistent intrigues at the Fatimid court added their own share of troubles to the chaotic situation unfolding in Egypt.

In 1050, as an exception, the vizierate was entrusted to the capable judge Abu Muhammad b. 'Ali al-Yazuri, who held that office until his death in 1058 and succeeded in restoring some order to the disrupted affairs of the state. However, after al-Yazuri, factional fights in the army and internal disorders erupted even more intensively than before. Numerous ineffective viziers followed one another while the Fatimid state now witnessed a period of decline, accompanied by chaos in the army and the depletion of the public treasury.

Matters came to a head in 1062, when open warfare broke out in Cairo between the Turks, aided by Berbers, and the black Sudani troops of the Fatimid army. On the defeat of the Sudanis in 1067, the victorious Turkish commander, Nasir al-Dawla, established himself as the effective authority in Egypt. By 1070, he even had the *khutba* pronounced in Alexandria and elsewhere in lower Egypt in the name of the Abbasid caliph al-Qa'im (r. 1031–1075). In the meantime, Egypt was also experiencing a serious economic crisis and suffering from a famine lasting seven years (1065–1072), in addition to the persistent ravaging of the land by the rebellious Turkish troops. The Fatimid palace, too, was eventually looted by the Turkish guards. The deteriorating situation culminated in the complete breakdown of law and order in Egypt.

It was under such circumstances that al-Mustansir appealed for help to Badr al-Jamali (d. 1094), an Armenian general in Syria. In 1074, Badr arrived in Cairo with his Armenian troops, and immediately proceeded to quash the rebellious Turkish soldiery. Badr al-Jamali restored order and soon acquired the highest positions in the state and the *da'wa*. He became commander of the armies (*amir al-juyush*), the main source of his power as well as the title by which he was best known, in addition to the posts of chief judge and chief *da'i*. Thus, Egypt enjoyed peace and relative prosperity during the last two decades of al-Mustansir's reign.

Meanwhile, al-Basasiri, a Turkish general in Iraq, drawing on effective Fatimid support had seized several towns there, and had the *khutba* read in the name of al-Mustansir. Al-Basasiri finally entered Baghdad itself in 1058 and had the *khutba* pronounced in the name of the Fatimids for one full year even in the Abbasid capital. But he kept the Abbasid caliph al-Qa'im under house arrest instead of sending him to Cairo, as expected by al-Mustansir. This great Fatimid victory was, however, short-lived, as al-Basasiri was soon abandoned by the Fatimid regime. Subsequently, he was pursued and defeated by Tughril, founder of the Saljuq empire, who was then establishing his rule over Iraq as the Abbasids' new overlord.

All in all, by the end of al-Mustansir's reign, only a few coastal towns of Syria, like Acre and Tyre, still remained in Fatimid hands, while in North Africa the Fatimid dominions had been reduced practically to Egypt itself. On the other hand, the Ismaili *da'wa* activities reached their peak in al-Mustansir's time. An extensive network of *da'is* now operated not only inside Egypt and other Fatimid dominions but also outside the Fatimid state. The *da'wa* was particularly active in Iraq, various regions of Persia, and in Central Asia, in addition to Yemen.

Amongst the most prominent *da'is* of this period operating in the Iranian lands was al-Mu'ayyad fi'l-Din al-Shirazi. After his initial successes in Fars, and at the Buyid

18.1 A gold dinar of the Fatimid Imam-caliph al-Mustansir (r. 1036–1094), minted in Cairo in 1036, obverse and reverse.

court there, this learned *da'i* migrated to Egypt. In 1058, he was appointed as chief *da'i* (*da'i al-du'at*), and, with the exception of two brief periods, he held that post until shortly before his death in 1078. The distinctive Ismaili tradition of organising 'sessions of wisdom' (*majalis al-hikma*) for the benefit of different Ismaili audiences, reached its peak under al-Mu'ayyad. These lectures on esoteric Ismaili doctrines, known as *hikma*, composed and delivered by this chief *da'i* have survived in eight volumes entitled *al-Majalis al-Mu'ayyadiyya*, each volume containing one hundred lectures.

Another important Ismaili personality of al-Mustansir's time was Nasir-i Khusraw. Born in 1004, near Balkh, in greater Khurasan, Nasir was a *da'i*, a theologian, a philosopher and a renowned traveller, as well as one of the greatest Persian poets. After a three-year stay in Cairo, where he furthered his Ismaili education, Nasir served as the chief *da'i*, or *hujja*, of Khurasan and spread the *da'wa* throughout Badakhshan, now divided between Afghanistan and Tajikistan. Indeed, the contemporary Ismailis of Badakhshan and their offshoot communities in Hunza and other northern regions of Pakistan regard Shah Sayyid Nasir, as they call him, as the founder of their communities.

Nasir-i Khusraw was also the last great exponent of a unique tradition of learning initiated by the Ismaili *da'i*s of the Iranian lands, starting with Muhammad b. Ahmad al-Nasafi (d. 943), Abu Hatim al-Razi (d. 934) and Abu Ya'qub al-Sijistani (d. after 971); and, subsequently, further developed by Hamid al-Din al-Kirmani (d. after 1020). These *da'i*s harmonised their Ismaili theology with a variety of philosophical traditions,

18.2 A gold ring decorated with filigree and granulation, signature metalwork techniques of the Fatimid period. The inscription in Arabic may have served a talismanic function, protecting the wearer from an ill fate.

18.3 Bab al-Nasr was one of the main gates of Cairo rebuilt in stone by the *amir al-juyush* Badr al-Jamali. Bab al-Nasr and Bab al-Futuh were built at the northern end of the city in 1087.

18.4 Title page of a 19th-century manuscript of the *Diwan* of Nasir-i Khusraw, the Ismaili *da'i* of Khurasan (d. after 1070). Nasir-i Khusraw was also a philosopher and poet who produced an important body of writings in Persian on Ismaili beliefs.

18.5 Title page of the *Safar-nama* of Nasir-i Khusraw, edited and published for the first time by Charles Schefer (1820–1898) in Paris in 1881. The work recounts Nasir-i Khusraw's travels during the years 1035 to 1042 from Khurasan to Cairo where he studied to become an Ismaili *daʿi*.

notably Neoplatonic philosophy. This led to the elaboration of an intellectual tradition within Ismailism, now designated as 'philosophical theology' and also as 'philosophical Ismailism'. These Iranian da'is wrote for the ruling elite and the educated classes, aiming to attract them intellectually and win their support for the Ismaili da'wa. This explains why they expressed their *kalam* theology, revolving around the central Shi'i doctrine of the Imamate, in terms of the then most modern and fashionable philosophical themes, without compromising the essence of their religious message.

Yemen was another region outside the Fatimid state where the Ismaili da'wa achieved exceptional success. Since the time of the da'i Ibn Hawshab Mansur al-Yaman (d. 914), the da'wa had survived in Yemen in a highly subdued manner. However, in 1047 the da'i 'Ali b. Muhammad al-Sulayhi (d. 1067), an important chieftain of the Banu Hamdan, established himself in the mountain region of Haraz, marking the foundation of the Sulayhid dynasty which ruled over Yemen as vassals of the Fatimids for almost a century until 1138. From the latter part of the reign of 'Ali's son and successor, al-Mukarram Ahmad (d. 1084), effective authority in the Sulayhid state was exercised by his consort, al-Sayyida Arwa (d. 1138), also known as al-Malika al-Hurra. In due course, this remarkable queen was appointed by the Fatimid Imam-caliph al-Mustansir, as the *hujja*, or chief da'i, in Yemen. This was the highest rank in the da'wa hierarchy ever attained by a woman. It may be also added here that the Sulayhids played a key role in the renewed efforts of the Fatimids to spread the da'wa on the Indian subcontinent, starting with Gujarat.

The Fatimid Imam-caliph al-Mustansir died in December 1094, after an eventful reign lasting almost sixty years. The dispute over his succession led to a permanent schism in the hitherto unified Ismaili da'wa and community resulting in two rival branches, later designated as Nizari and Musta'lian, named after two of the deceased Imam-caliph's sons who laid claim to his heritage. Subsequently, the two communities acknowledged different lines of Imams in the progenies of these two sons, Nizar and al-Musta'li.

19

Nizar (d. 1095)

Abu Mansur Nizar was the eldest son of the Fatimid Imam-caliph al-Mustansir. Born in September 1045 in Cairo, Nizar had been designated by his father through the rule of the *nass* as his successor to the Fatimid caliphate and the Ismaili Imamate. Nizar, who was thus expected to succeed al-Mustansir, was about fifty years old at the time of his father's death in 1094. However, al-Afdal, who a few months earlier had succeeded his own father Badr al-Jamali as the all-powerful 'commander of the armies' (*amir al-juyush*), had other plans.

Nizar and his brothers, 'Abd Allah and Isma'il, were the eldest sons of al-Mustansir. But, aiming to retain the reins of power in his own hands, al-Afdal favoured al-Mustansir's youngest son Abu'l-Qasim Ahmad, who was born in 1074. At the time of al-Mustansir's death in December 1094, Ahmad was about twenty years old and already married to al-Afdal's sister. Under the circumstances, al-Afdal moved swiftly and, on the day after al-Mustansir's death, placed Ahmad on the Fatimid throne with the title al-Musta'li bi'llah. Supported by the army, al-Afdal quickly obtained the *ba'ya*, or oath of allegiance, for al-Musta'li from the notables of the Fatimid court and the Ismaili *da'wa* in Cairo.

The dispossessed Nizar, refusing to endorse the investiture of his much younger half-brother, hurriedly fled to Alexandria accompanied by his brother 'Abd Allah and a few supporters, where he rose up in revolt early in 1095. In Alexandria, which was the centre of military factions suppressed earlier by Badr al-Jamali, Nizar received a great deal of local support. Amongst other notables, the city's governor, Nasir al-Dawla Aftakin, who aspired to replace al-Afdal, and its Ismaili *qadi*, Ibn 'Ammar, along with the Arab inhabitants of the area, joined forces with Nizar. It was under such circumstances that Nizar received the general oath of allegiance of the population of

Alexandria as caliph with the title al-Mustafa li-Din Allah. The proclamation of Nizar b. al-Mustansir as caliph and Imam in Alexandria is attested on a gold dinar minted in 488 AH/1095 AD. The sole known example of this unique dinar, discovered in 1994, is now preserved in the coin collection of the Ismaili Special Collections Unit at The Institute of Ismaili Studies in London.

Drawing on a wide base of support in Alexandria, Nizar was initially very successful in his revolt. He repelled the Fatimid forces sent against him and even advanced to the vicinity of Cairo. However, towards the end of 1095, al-Afdal personally took the field against him. He besieged Alexandria and obliged Nizar, whose coalition of forces had meanwhile broken up, to surrender. Nizar was taken to Cairo, where he was imprisoned and then executed on the order of al-Mustaʿli at the end of 1095.

There are conflicting, sectarian, accounts of this important episode in Ismaili history. Subsequently, the leaders of the Mustaʿlian Ismailis circulated an account alleging that on his deathbed al-Mustansir had named al-Mustaʿli as his heir. However, it is a historical fact that Nizar's rights to the succession were never revoked by al-Mustansir, and that al-Afdal secured the succession of al-Mustaʿli in what amounted to a palace coup. This explains why Nizar himself refused to endorse al-Afdal's designs and the Ismaili leadership in Persia upheld al-Mustansir's *nass* for Nizar. By this decision, Hasan-i Sabbah (d. 1124), the then leader of the Persian Ismailis, had in fact founded the independent Nizari Ismaili *daʿwa*. He now severed his relations with the Fatimid regime and the *daʿwa* headquarters in Cairo, which had recognised al-Mustaʿli as the new Imam-caliph in succession to al-Mustansir.

Be that as it may, the dispute over al-Mustansir's succession left a decisive mark on the Ismaili community and its subsequent history. By supporting al-Mustaʿli, al-Afdal had permanently split the Ismailis into two rival factions, later designated as Nizari and Mustaʿlian. The Imamate of al-Mustaʿli, who was installed to the Fatimid caliphate, was acknowledged by the *daʿwa* establishment in Cairo, as well as most Ismailis in Egypt, many in Syria, and the entire Ismaili community in Yemen and that in western India dependent on it. These so-called Mustaʿlian Ismailis, who later traced their Imamate in al-Mustaʿli's progeny, maintained their relations with the Fatimid regime and the *daʿwa* establishment in Cairo, hereafter serving as the headquarters of the Mustaʿlian Ismaili *daʿwa*.

On the other hand, Hasan-i Sabbah, the leader of the Persian Ismailis, upheld Nizar's right to the Ismaili Imamate based on al-Mustansir's original *nass*. In this decision, Hasan-i Sabbah was supported by all the Ismaili communities of the Saljuq domains, notably in Persia and Iraq. Nizar also had partisans within the Fatimid territories,

19.1 A gold dinar of Imam Nizar, minted in Alexandria in 488/1095, obverse and reverse. This unique coin was recovered in 1994.

particularly in Syria and Egypt. For these Ismailis, later designated as Nizari, Nizar was the rightful successor after al-Mustansir to the Ismaili Imamate; and as such he would be counted as the nineteenth in their line of Imams.

Nizar became the progenitor of the Nizari Ismaili Imams; his immediate descendants, as we shall see, later emerged at the fortress of Alamut in northern Persia, and took charge of the affairs of their state, *daʿwa* and community. Meanwhile, Nizar's name and caliphal title (al-Mustafa li-Din Allah) appeared on the coins minted at Alamut, with his progeny being blessed anonymously. Nizar's own Imamate had lasted just about one year.

Part Five

The Imams at Alamut

da'is and hujjas

Hasan-i Sabbah (1090–1124)

Kiya Buzurg-Umid (1124–1138)

Muhammad b. Buzurg-Umid (1138–1162)

Imams

Hasan 'ala dhikrihi'l-salam (1162–1166)

Nur al-Din Muhammad (1166–1210)

Jalal al-Din Hasan (1210–1221)

'Ala al-Din Muhammad (1221–1255)

Rukn al-Din Khurshah (1255–1256)

Ismaili rulers at Alamut (1090–1256)

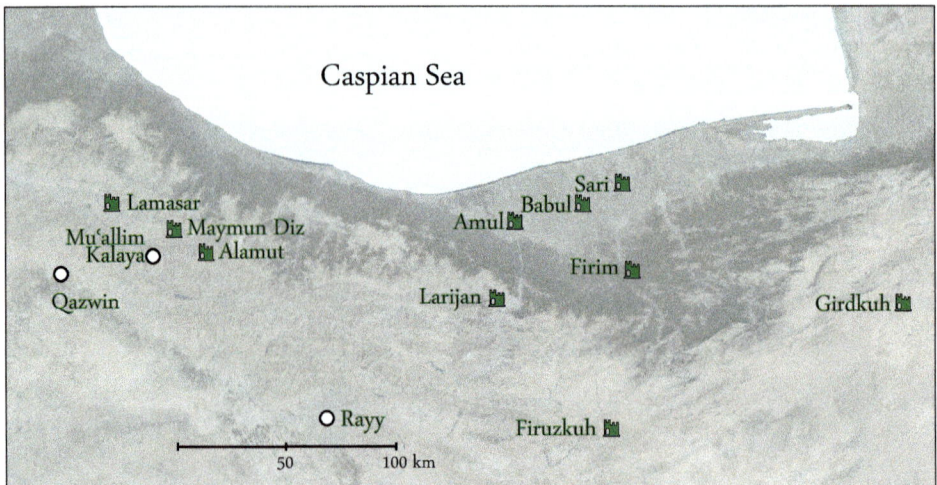

Ismaili castles in northern Persia

20–22

Concealed Imams: al-Hadi, al-Muhtadi, al-Qahir

By the time of Nizar b. al-Mustansir's tragic end in Cairo in 1095, Hasan-i Sabbah had already emerged as the undisputed leader of the Ismailis of Persia and other Saljuq domains, notably Iraq. Operating as an Ismaili *daʿi* on behalf of the Fatimids, Hasan had visited Cairo earlier during 1078–1080, when Badr al-Jamali was the chief *daʿi* and the effective political authority in Egypt. The shrewd Hasan-i Sabbah had then become fully cognisant of the declining power of the Fatimid regime and its inability to help the Persian Ismailis in their struggle against the ardently hostile Sunni Saljuqs. It was under such circumstances that Hasan-i Sabbah had begun to design his own revolutionary strategy against the Saljuq Turks, whose alien rule was detested by Persians of all classes.

Hasan-i Sabbah's seizure of the fortress of Alamut in northern Persia in 1090 represented a first step in his strategy of uprooting the Saljuqs, also marking the foundation of what was to become known as the Nizari Ismaili state of Persia. Alamut continued to serve as the central headquarters of that state, which would be composed of a network of inaccessible fortresses and several territories with their towns in different parts of Persia, as well as a subsidiary in Syria. The Ismaili state of Persia was finally destroyed by the all-conquering Mongols in 1256.

As the Ismaili revolt against the Saljuqs was successfully unfolding in Persia, the dispute over the Fatimid Imam-caliph al-Mustansir's succession in 1094 split the

Ismailis into two rival factions. Opposing the decision of the Fatimid vizier al-Afdal to deprive Nizar of his succession rights, Hasan in fact upheld al-Mustansir's original *nass* for his eldest son Nizar and broke off relations with the Fatimid regime that had recognised Nizar's much younger half-brother al-Musta'li as the next caliph and Imam. By this decision, Hasan-i Sabbah had now also founded the Nizari Ismaili *da'wa* independently of the Fatimid regime.

The Nizari Ismailis of Persia and elsewhere soon confronted another major difficulty when, after his abortive revolt, Nizar himself was executed in Cairo in 1095. Nizar's demise, in fact, initiated another period of concealment (*dawr al-satr*), similar to that witnessed by the pre-Fatimid Ismailis, in the early history of the Nizari Ismailis. As a result, very little is known of the lives and careers of the three concealed Imams who are traditionally held to have lived secretly during this period.

It is a historical fact that Nizar did have male progeny. The sources give the names of at least two of Nizar's sons: Abu 'Ali al-Hasan and Abu 'Abd Allah al-Husayn. It is also known that a line of the descendants of Nizar's sons continued to live in Egypt and in the Maghrib until the demise of the Fatimid dynasty. Some of these Nizarid Fatimids

20–22.1 Recent excavations at the castle of Alamut, centre of the Ismaili state in Persia founded in the name of Imam Nizar by the *da'i* Hasan-i Sabbah in the late 11th century.

were also pretenders to the Fatimid throne and they may also have claimed the Ismaili Imamate; as such they were involved in anti-Fatimid revolts. Abu ʿAbd Allah al-Husayn himself launched an abortive revolt against the Fatimid caliph al-Hafiz (d. 1149) from his base in the Maghrib, but he was captured and executed in 1131. Another descendant of Nizar, whose name is not given in the sources, was involved in another abortive revolt staged in 1148, again in the Maghrib, with considerable support from the Kutama and other local Berbers. The last known attempt by a Nizarid Fatimid based in the Maghrib to uproot the Fatimids of Egypt occurred in the reign of al-ʿAdid (r. 1160–1171), the last Fatimid caliph. In 1161, Muhammad b. al-Husayn b. Nizar, a grandson of Nizar, came to Barqa from his base in the Maghrib. Aiming to seize Cairo, he rose in revolt with much popular support and adopted the caliphal title of his ancestor, al-Mustansir biʾllah. However, he was betrayed by one of his chief allies who arranged for his arrest and dispatch to Cairo where he was executed.

At any rate, after Nizar, the Nizari Ismailis were left without an accessible Imam. It is also possible that the Persian Ismailis may have remained uninformed for quite some time about Nizar's own tragic fate. Indeed, numismatic evidence from the early Alamut period in Nizari Ismaili history reveals that Nizar's name and caliphal title (al-Mustafa li-Din Allah) continued to appear on coins minted at Alamut for about seventy years

20–22.2 View from the south of the rock of Alamut showing the remains of the castle on its peak.

20–22.3 Ruins of the castle of Maymun Diz in Daylaman, near Alamut.

after his death in 1095, during the reigns of Hasan-i Sabbah's (d. 1124) next two successors at Alamut, namely Kiya Buzurg-Umid (r. 1124–1138) and his son Muhammad (r. 1138–1162). In the inscriptions on these rare coins, Nizar's progeny are generally blessed anonymously. The latest known specimens of such coins, gold dinars minted at Kursi al-Daylam, that is Alamut, in 1158 and 1161, bear the legend *'Ali wali Allah/ al-Mustafa li-Din Allah Nizar*, with blessings on Nizar's anonymous progeny.

Be that as it may, Hasan-i Sabbah and his next two successors, as 'lords of Alamut', did not divulge the name of any Imam after Nizar himself. In the absence of a manifest Imam, it seems that Hasan-i Sabbah, as head of the *da'wa*, was eventually acknowledged by the community as the *hujja* of the inaccessible Imam. It had been already held by the pre-Fatimid Ismailis that when the Imam was concealed and inaccessible, his *hujja* would be his chief representative for his community. Drawing on this tradition and as the Nizari Ismailis were now experiencing another period of concealment (*dawr al-satr*), Hasan-i Sabbah, and then his next two successors, each came to be regarded as the Imam's full representative and living proof, or *hujja*, in the community, acting as the custodian of the Nizari Ismaili *da'wa* until the time of the Imam's manifestation.

20–22.4 A gold fractional dinar from the time of Muhammad b. Buzurg-Umid (r. 1138–1162), the third lord of Alamut and the *da'i* and *hujja* of the Imam. The mint name is Kursi al-Daylam and the date 1141. The inscriptions on the reverse (right) mention Imam Nizar and bless his descendants anonymously.

There were alternative versions of the Nizarid Fatimid ancestry of the Imams who later openly emerged at Alamut, starting with Hasan *'ala dhikrihi'l-salam* (d. 1166). These versions, at least some of which must have circulated within the contemporary Nizari Ismaili community, are related in the Ismaili histories of 'Ata-Malik Juwayni (d. 1283), Rashid al-Din Fadl Allah (d. 1318) and Abu'l-Qasim Kashani (d. 1337), who had access to the Ismaili chronicles of the Alamut period which have not survived directly. According to these sources, already in Hasan-i Sabbah's time many Nizari Ismailis held the belief that a son or grandson of Nizar b. al-Mustansir had been brought from Egypt to Alamut, and he became the progenitor of the line of the Nizari Ismaili Imams who would emerge at Alamut, starting with the fourth lord of Alamut, Hasan *'ala dhikrihi'l-salam*.

Indeed, several non-Ismaili sources allude to the existence of an unnamed Imam at Alamut. In this context, the same sources relate that a number of Nizaris maintained that in 1095 a certain *qadi* called Abu'l-Hasan Sa'idi had gone from Egypt to Alamut secretly taking with him either Nizar's son al-Hadi or his grandson known as al-Muhtadi. This Nizari tradition must have had wide currency by the final years of Hasan-i Sabbah's life as it is corroborated by an anti-Nizari polemical epistle issued by the Fatimid chancery in Cairo in 1122. In this epistle, entitled *al-Hidaya al-Amiriyya*, the Fatimid caliph al-Amir (r. 1101–1130) ridicules the idea that a descendant of his uncle Nizar was then living in Persia.

20–22.5 Map of the Caspian Sea with the mountains of Daylaman at the top. Daylaman, or Rudbar, in northern Persia was the heartland of the Ismaili state founded by Hasan-i Sabbah. The map comes from the *Kitab ghara'ib al-funun*, produced in Egypt, some time between 1020 and 1050.

On the basis of the genealogy subsequently circulating amongst the Nizari Ismailis there were three concealed Imams between Nizar and Hasan ʿala dhikrihi'l-salam, namely, al-Hadi, al-Muhtadi and al-Qahir. It is possible that al-Hadi may be identified with one of Nizar's sons living in North Africa, such as Abu ʿAli al-Hasan, and that it was the second concealed Imam (al-Muhtadi) who arrived in Alamut. Be that as it may, the descent of these concealed Imams from Nizar is attested to in a recently recovered manuscript of the *Haft bab* from Badakhshan. This work was written, a few decades after the declaration of the *qiyama* at Alamut, by Hasan-i Mahmud-i Katib, an Ismaili historian and poet. More cannot be said on these concealed Imams given our present state of knowledge. In this connection, it should also be added here that in the list of the Imams recognised by the Muʾmin-Shahi Nizari Ismailis – who are now represented by a small community only in Syria – Nizar's successor to the Imamate is named as his son al-Hasan b. Nizar, whose existence is attested in the historical sources.

23

Hasan ʿala dhikrihi'l-salam (d. 1166)

Hasan, whom the Ismailis called *ʿala dhikrihi'l-salam* (on his mention be peace), was the fourth lord of Alamut, and also counted as the twenty-third Ismaili Imam. Born in 1126, he succeeded to the leadership of the Ismaili state, *daʿwa* and community in 1162 on the death of Muhammad b. Buzurg-Umid (r. 1138–1162), the third lord of Alamut.

From his youth Hasan had shown an interest in Ismaili teachings as well as studying philosophical and Sufi writings. He had also mastered the art of *taʾwil*, or esoteric exegesis, which had been applied by the earlier Ismailis to Qurʾanic passages as well as the commandments and prohibitions of the *shariʿa*. Already in the reign of Muhammad b. Buzurg-Umid, Hasan had acquired followers who considered him as the Imam promised by Hasan-i Sabbah (d. 1124). The latter, and his next two successors as lords of Alamut, had operated as *daʿi*s and *hujja*s, or chief representatives of the concealed Imam, during the period of concealment (*dawr al-satr*).

The most significant event of Hasan's brief reign (1162–1166) was the declaration of *qiyama*, or Resurrection, which initiated a new phase in the history of the Nizari Ismaili community. On 8 August 1164, in the presence of representatives of different Ismaili territories invited to Alamut, Hasan delivered a *khutba* or sermon and conveyed new instructions from the concealed Imam. According to these instructions, the Ismailis had now been brought to the *qiyama*, or the Last Day when humankind would be judged and committed to either Paradise or Hell.

Expounding Ismaili *taʾwil*, and drawing on earlier Ismaili teachings, however, the *qiyama* or the end of the world was interpreted symbolically and spiritually. The *qiyama*

23.1 A gold fractional dinar of Imam Hasan ʿala dhikrihiʾl-salam (r. 1162–1166), obverse and reverse; the mint is Kursi al-Daylam and the date 1163.

was interpreted to mean the manifestation of the unveiled truth (*haqiqa*), which had hitherto been hidden in the *batin* or the esoteric dimension of the Islamic message, in the person of the Ismaili 'Imam of the time'. As a result, the Ismailis, who acknowledged the rightful Imam, were now capable of comprehending the truth or spiritual reality, and indeed the esoteric essence of the religious laws. The Ismailis were thus collectively admitted into a spiritual Paradise on earth. On the other hand, the 'outsiders', or all those who did not acknowledge the Ismaili Imam, were henceforth rendered spiritually non-existent. In line with earlier Ismaili teachings, the Imam initiating the *qiyama* would be the *qaʾim al-qiyama*, or Lord of the Resurrection.

Soon afterwards, on 18 October 1164, a similar ceremony was held at the fortress of Muʾminabad, where the same *khutba* and message were delivered by *muhtasham* Muzaffar, the head of the Ismaili community in Quhistan, southeastern Khurasan. At Alamut, Hasan had been named not only as the Imam's *daʿi* and *hujja*, like the previous lords of Alamut, but also as the Imam's *khalifa*, or deputy with plenary authority, a higher rank which was not defined at the time. But at Muʾminabad the status of Hasan was further clarified. The lord of Alamut now also declared that just as previously the Fatimid al-Mustansir had been God's *khalifa* or representative on earth, so now Hasan himself was the *khalifa* of God. Hasan had thus, in two stages, claimed the Imamate for himself.

Subsequently, in his epistles (*fusul*) and addresses, Hasan implied more explicitly that he was the Imam and the *qaʾim al-qiyama*, the son of a concealed Imam from the

23.2 View of the rock of Alamut from the north, photographed by the renowned pioneer of Ismaili studies, W. Ivanow (1886–1970).

progeny of Nizar b. al-Mustansir, though in appearance he had been considered to be the son of Muhammad b. Buzurg-Umid. The contemporary Ismailis did unanimously accept this claim, which was reiterated more elaborately by Hasan's son and successor.

A year and a half after the declaration of the *qiyama*, on 9 January 1166, Hasan *'ala dhikrihi'l-salam* was stabbed to death in the fortress of Lamasar, situated to the west of Alamut, by a brother-in-law who was opposed to his new policies. Hasan was succeeded by his nineteen-year-old son Muhammad. Thus, after a period of some seventy years following Nizar b. al-Mustansir's death in 1095, the line of the Nizari Ismaili Imams had emerged openly at Alamut, and the Nizari Ismailis henceforth acknowledged the lords of Alamut, beginning with Hasan *'ala dhikrihi'l-salam*, as their Imams.

23.3 The castle of Furk in Quhistan, part of the Ismaili state in southeastern Khurasan which was governed by a *muhtasham* on behalf of Alamut.

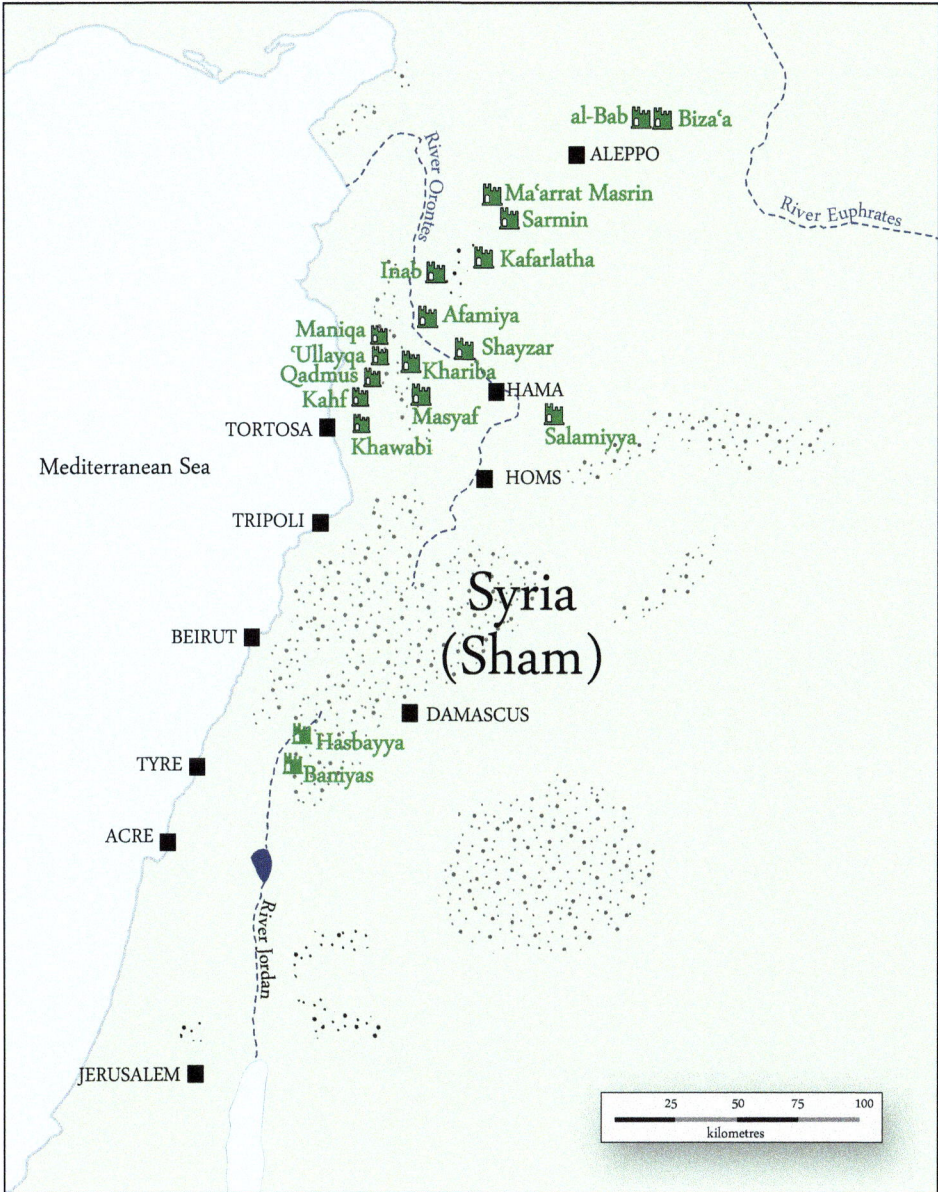

Ismaili castles in Syria

24

Nur al-Din Muhammad, also known as Aʻla Muhammad (d. 1210)

On 9 January 1166, Muhammad succeeded his father, Hasan *ʻala dhikrihi'l-salam*, as the fifth lord of Alamut. He is also counted as the twenty-fourth Ismaili Imam. Born in March 1148, he was nineteen years old at the time of his accession. Also known as Aʻla Muhammad in the Nizari Ismaili tradition, he reigned for forty-four years, longer than any other lord of Alamut.

Muhammad was a scholar and a prolific writer, and he contributed actively to the Ismaili thought of his time. In particular, he devoted his life to the systematic elaboration and refinement of the teachings associated with the declaration of the *qiyama*, or Resurrection, made by his father in 1164, in terms of a coherent doctrine. In this context, he placed the present (*hadir*) and living Ismaili Imam at the very centre of the doctrine of the *qiyama*. The exaltation of the teaching authority of the present Imam over those of all previous authorities, which had already been highlighted in the doctrine of *taʻlim* propagated by Hasan-i Sabbah (d. 1124), in fact became the outstanding feature of the Nizari Ismaili thought of Nur al-Din Muhammad's time. Furthermore, he claimed the Imamate for his father and, therefore, for himself in the fullest possible physical sense, explaining that his father was the son of a descendant of Nizar b. al-Mustansir who had secretly found refuge near the fortress of Alamut. As noted, this genealogical claim is also confirmed in a contemporary Ismaili source entitled *Haft bab*, written by Hasan-i Mahmud-i Katib.

24.1 The citadel of Masyaf, centre of the Ismailis in Syria.

24.2 Khawabi, one of the castles of the Ismailis in Syria.

24.3 The castle of Maniqa, one of a network of Ismaili castles in the Syrian mountains bordering the coastal strip.

Nur al-Din Muhammad also devoted his long reign to managing the affairs of the Nizari Ismaili *da'wa* and state from his central headquarters at the fortress of Alamut, in northern Persia. However, politically his reign was rather uneventful. Outside Syria, the Ismailis of the *qiyama* times, who had rendered the outside world spiritually irrelevant, generally ignored the Sunni Muslims and did not launch any campaigns against their enemies. Meanwhile, by the final decade of Muhammad's reign, the Sunni Khwarazmians, who were then carving out their own empire, had replaced the Saljuqs as the main adversary of the Nizari Ismailis of Persia.

Nur al-Din Muhammad's reign coincided with the rise to prominence of Rashid al-Din Sinan as the chief *da'i* of the Syrian Nizari Ismailis. Sinan led the Syrian Ismailis to the peak of their fame and glory for three decades until his death in 1193. Sinan entered into an intricate network of shifting alliances with the major neighbouring powers and rulers, especially the Crusaders, the Zangids and Salah al-Din (Saladin of the medieval European sources), founder of the Ayyubid dynasty. As a result, he managed to secure the independence of his fragile community under highly adverse circumstances.

It was also in Sinan's time that the Crusaders came into contact with the Nizari Ismailis of Syria and made them famous in Europe as the Assassins. This was because the Crusaders and their European chroniclers were responsible for fabricating and putting into circulation a number of legends regarding the supposed secret practices of the Nizari Ismailis, fictitious tales rooted in 'imaginative ignorance' that found their culmination in an account popularised by Marco Polo.

Nur al-Din Muhammad died in September 1210, after an Imamate of forty-four years. He was succeeded by his son Jalal al-Din Hasan.

25

Jalal al-Din Hasan (d. 1221)

Jalal al-Din Hasan succeeded to the leadership of the Ismaili state, *da'wa* and community as the sixth lord of Alamut and twenty-fifth Ismaili Imam in September 1210 on the death of his father Nur al-Din (or A'la) Muhammad. Born in 1166, he was the oldest son of Nur al-Din Muhammad, and had been designated by the rule of the *nass* from his childhood to succeed to the Ismaili Imamate.

Weary of the isolation of the Ismailis from the outside world in the *qiyama* times, initiated by his grandfather and retained by his father, Jalal al-Din Hasan devoted his relatively brief reign to establishing better relations with Sunni Muslims and their rulers. Immediately upon his accession, he publicly repudiated the doctrine of the *qiyama*, and ordered his followers to observe the *shari'a* in its Sunni form. He sent messengers to the Abbasid caliph al-Nasir (r. 1180–1225), Muhammad Khwarazmshah (r. 1200–1220), and other Sunni rulers telling them of his reform. Indeed, he did his utmost to convince the Sunni world of his changed policy. Finally, in August 1211, the caliph al-Nasir issued a decree formally confirming Jalal al-Din Hasan' new dispensation.

The lord of Alamut was now accepted as an *amir* among other Muslim *amir*s, and his rights to the territories of the Ismaili state were officially acknowledged for the first time by the Abbasid caliph, who showed the Ismaili Imam all manner of favours. The Ismailis of Persia and Syria accepted Jalal al-Din's reform without any dissent, continuing to regard him as the infallible Imam who guided his community and contextualised the interpretation of the *shari'a* as he saw fit. As was explained later, the Nizari Ismailis evidently viewed their Imam's declaration as a reimposition of *taqiyya*, or precautionary dissimulation, which had been lifted in the *qiyama* times. And the reimposition of *taqiyya* could be taken to imply any sort of accommodation with the outside world as deemed necessary by the 'Imam of the time'.

For the Ismailis who had hitherto survived rather precariously, Jalal al-Din Hasan's rapprochement with the Sunni world had obvious advantages in terms of peace and security. In particular, the Ghurid attacks on the Ismailis of Quhistan, in southeastern Khurasan, now ceased. And in Syria, where the Nizari Ismailis confronted renewed Crusader campaigns, they received timely assistance from the Ayyubids.

The Ismailis had not succeeded in their initial revolt, and had subsequently been marginalised in their fortress communities as 'heretics'. Under the circumstances, it seems that many Ismailis had gradually become disenchanted with their isolation. Jalal al-Din Hasan had, in fact, boldly accommodated his community to the outside world, situating the Ismailis at the very centre of contemporary Muslim affairs. The resulting improved relations were also beneficial to the Sunnis, as the Ismaili Imam now played an active role in the caliphal alliances of al-Nasir.

Furthermore, towards the final years of Jalal al-Din's reign many Sunni Muslims, including their Sunni scholars, who were fleeing from the Mongols now invading Khurasan and other eastern regions, found refuge in the Ismaili towns and fortress communities of Quhistan, where they were treated most lavishly by the local Ismaili *muhtasham* or leader. Jalal al-Din was evidently the first Muslim ruler to engage successfully in negotiations with the Mongols after they had crossed the Oxus in Central Asia. Jalal al-Din Hasan died in November 1221, after a reign of eleven years, and was succeeded at Alamut by his sole son, Muhammad.

26

'Ala al-Din Muhammad
(d. 1255)

'Ala al-Din Muhammad, the seventh lord of Alamut and twenty-sixth Ismaili Imam, was the only son of Imam Jalal al-Din Hasan; his mother was a sister of Kayka'us b. Shahanshah, the ruler of Kutum, in Gilan, in northern Persia. Born around 1212, he succeeded his father in November 1221 at the age of nine.

The vizier appointed earlier by Jalal al-Din Hasan continued to run the affairs of the Ismaili state in Persia for some time, also retaining the policy of rapprochement with the Abbasids and the Sunni Muslims generally. However, the observance of the Sunni *shari'a*, imposed earlier, was gradually relaxed and the ideas associated with the *qiyama*, declared in 1164, were once again revived.

Politically, 'Ala al-Din's reign was an extremely turbulent period not only for the Ismaili state, but for Persia and the entire Muslim East, which had now begun to experience a foretaste of the Mongol menace. However, initially the Ismaili leadership at Alamut seems to have reached an understanding with the Mongols, who did not target any of the Ismaili towns and fortresses of Persia for some time. Indeed, it has been reported how in the 1220s the Ismaili *muhtasham*s or leaders in Quhistan, Khurasan, shared the stability and prosperity of their community with an increasing number of refugees, who had fled before the invading Mongols and found asylum in the Ismaili fortress communities of Persia.

Meanwhile, in the wake of the Mongol invasions, relations between Alamut and the Khwarazmians, who had replaced the Saljuqs as the foremost enemy of the Ismailis,

26.1 A detail of a miniature from a copy of the *Akhlaq-i Nasiri* produced in Lahore, *c.* 1590–1595. This work was written by the Persian scholar and polymath Nasir al-Din al-Tusi (d. 1274).

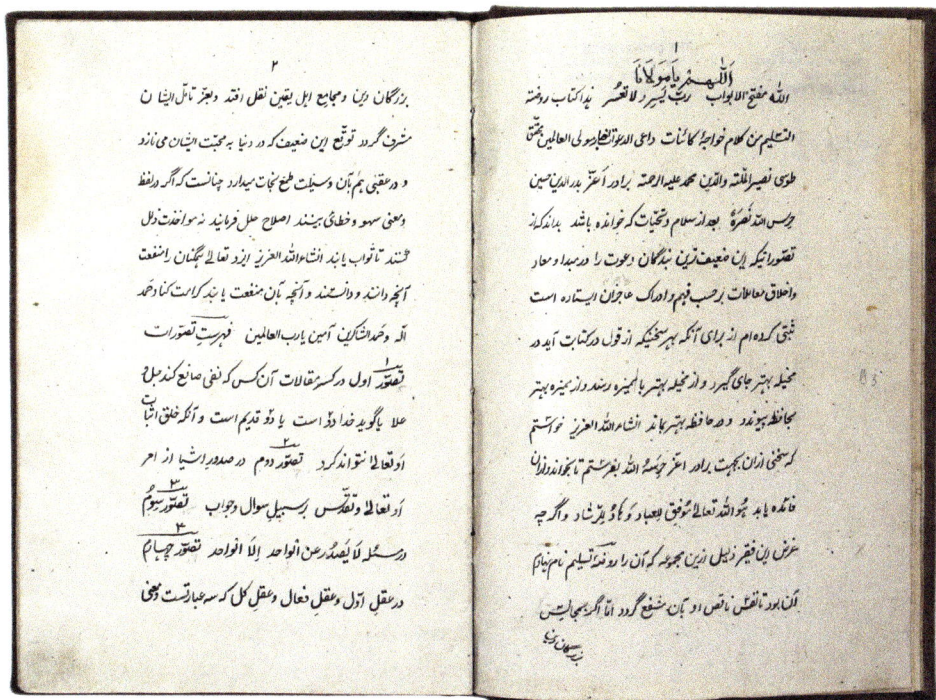

26.2 The opening pages of a copy of the *Rawdat al-taslim* of Nasir al-Din al-Tusi. It contains a comprehensive exposition of the Ismaili teachings of the Alamut period.

were characterised by warfare and diplomacy until the Mongols finally defeated the Khwarazmians in 1231. Ismaili fortunes were rapidly reversed after the collapse of the Khwarazmian empire. The Ismailis now directly confronted the Mongols, who were then making renewed efforts to conquer all of Persia. After some unsuccessful initial Ismaili peace overtures to the Mongol Great Khan Güyük (r. 1246–1248), Ismaili–Mongol relations deteriorated beyond repair. By 1253, under Güyük's successor Möngke (r. 1251–1259), the Mongols had destroyed numerous Ismaili towns and fortresses in Quhistan and elsewhere in Persia.

'Ala al-Din Muhammad's reign was also a period of intense intellectual activity in the Ismaili community of Persia. In particular, the Ismaili leadership now made a systematic effort to explain the various religious policies of the lords of Alamut, since Hasan-i Sabbah's time, within a coherent theological framework. At the same time, the intellectual life of the community was invigorated by the influx of outside scholars, who availed themselves of the Ismaili libraries at Alamut and other fortresses and their patronage of learning.

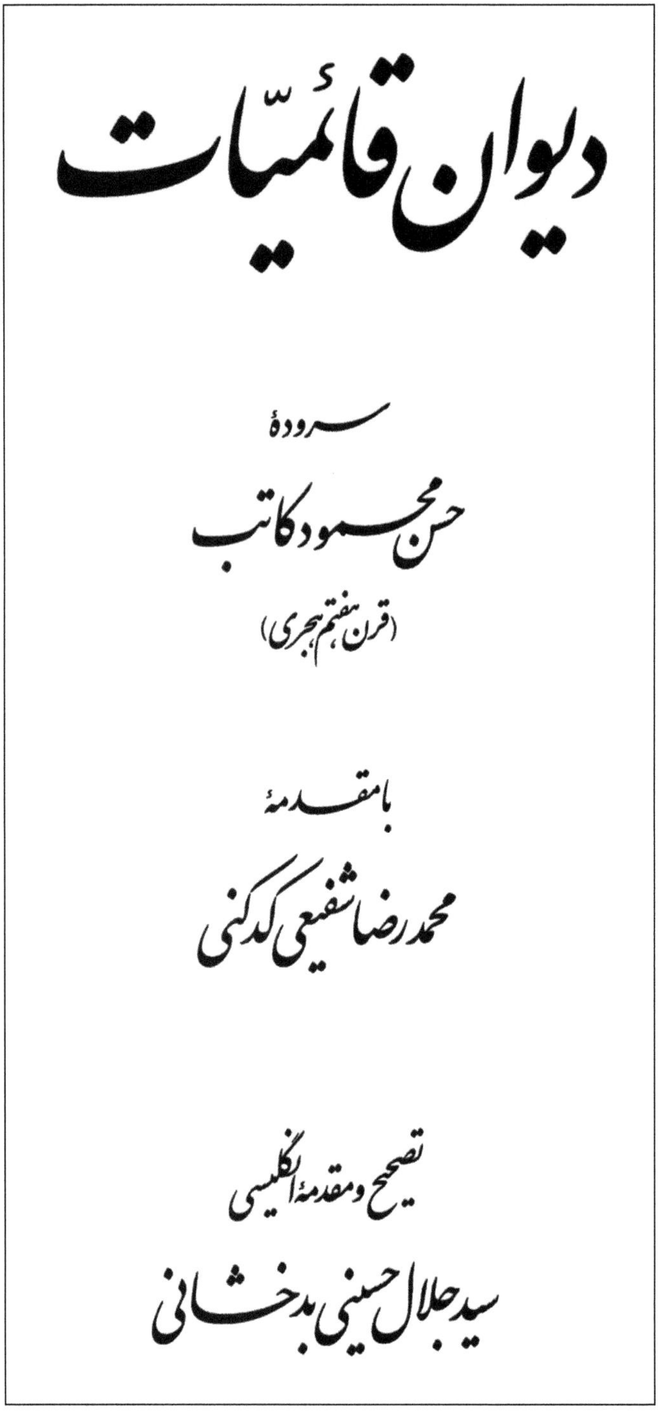

دیوان قائمیّات

سرودهٔ

حسن محمود کاتب

(قرن هفتم هجری)

بامقدمهٔ

محمد رضا شفیعی کدکنی

تصحیح و مقدمهٔ انگلیسی

سید جلال حسینی بدخشانی

26.3 The title page of the first edition of the *Diwan-i qa'imiyyat*, published in 2011. The core of this work was composed at Alamut by Hasan-i Mahmud-i Katib, and further poems by other poets were added over subsequent centuries.

26.4 A silver dirham of Imam 'Ala al-Din Muhammad (r. 1221–1255), minted at Baldat al-Iqbal, or the 'city of good fortune', viz. Alamut, in 1222, obverse and reverse.

Foremost among such scholars of this period was Khwaja Nasir al-Din Muhammad al-Tusi (1201–1274), who, in 1227, entered the service of Nasir al-Din b. Abi Mansur (d. 1257), the Ismaili *muhtasham* in Quhistan and himself a learned man. It was to this *muhtasham* that al-Tusi dedicated both his great works on ethics, *Akhlaq-i Nasiri* and *Akhlaq-i muhtashami*. All in all, al-Tusi spent some three decades in the Ismaili castles of Persia until 1256, converted willingly to Ismailism, and made important contributions to the Ismaili thought of his time. In fact, it is mainly through al-Tusi's Ismaili writings that modern scholars have come to have a better understanding of the Ismaili teachings of the Alamut period.

It may be added here that it was probably in 'Ala al-Din Muhammad's reign (1221–1255) that the Nizari Ismaili *da'wa* was introduced to the Indian subcontinent by Persian *da'is* dispatched originally to Sind. At the same time, the Persian-speaking Ismailis of Badakhshan and other regions of Central Asia, who seem to have remained outside the Nizari-Musta'lian division in Ismailism, explicitly acknowledged the Nizari Ismaili Imamate and *da'wa* in 'Ala al-Din's time.

While the Mongols were incessantly conducting intensive military campaigns against the territories of the Ismaili state in Persia, on 1 December 1255 'Ala al-Din Muhammad was found murdered in the castle of Shirkuh, near Alamut, under obscure circumstances. Imam 'Ala al-Din, the penultimate lord of Alamut who reigned for thirty-five years, was succeeded in the Ismaili leadership by his oldest son, Rukn al-Din Khurshah.

27

Rukn al-Din Khurshah (d. 1257)

Rukn al-Din Khurshah succeeded to the leadership of the Ismaili state, *daʿwa* and community as the eighth lord of Alamut and twenty-seventh Ismaili Imam upon the death of his father, ʿAla al-Din Muhammad, on 1 December 1255. Hasan, born around 1230 in Rudbar, northern Persia, was better known as Khurshah (also Khayrshah) with the honorific title of Rukn al-Din. He was the oldest son of ʿAla al-Din who had designated him in his childhood to be his successor.

Rukn al-Din's brief, eventful reign as the last lord of Alamut coincided with the completion of the Mongol conquests of Persia and the final year in the history of the Ismaili state of the Alamut period. By the time of Rukn al-Din's accession, the Persian Ismailis had already experienced a foretaste of the destructive power of the Mongol hordes. However, it remained for the Mongol conqueror Hülegü, leading a major expedition from Mongolia to Persia in 1253, to destroy the Ismaili state.

Vacillating between surrender and resistance, and receiving conflicting advice from his courtiers, Rukn al-Din was drawn into a complex and ultimately futile web of negotiations with Hülegü, who arrived in Persia in April 1256. Rukn al-Din dispatched several embassies, headed variously by his vizier Shams al-Din Gilaki and a number of his own brothers, to Hülegü who continuously demanded Rukn al-Din's total submission and the surrender of the Ismaili strongholds.

Having grown weary of the delaying tactics of the Ismailis, in September 1256 Hülegü decided to launch his own assault on Rudbar, the main territory of the Ismaili state in the central Alburz mountains of northern Persia. In the event, he ordered all the

27.1 A depiction of the Mongol assault on the fortress of Alamut from a copy of the *Chingiz-nama*, dated 1596, produced in India during the Mughal era.

main Mongol forces operating in Persia to converge on the stronghold of Maymun Diz, in the vicinity of Alamut, where Rukn al-Din was then residing. After the failure of one last round of negotiations, followed by a few days of intense fighting, Rukn al-Din was finally obliged to surrender to the Mongols. On 19 November 1256, accompanied by his vizier Mu'ayyad al-Din, Nasir al-Din al-Tusi, and other Ismaili dignitaries, Rukn al-Din descended from MaymunDiz and presented himself to Hülegü. This marked the end of the Ismaili state of Persia, which had been founded some 166 years earlier by Hasan-i Sabbah. Rukn al-Din Khurshah had ruled over that state for exactly one year.

Subsequently, Rukn al-Din was treated respectfully by the Mongols while they still needed his cooperation to persuade the Ismaili strongholds to surrender. Soon about forty fortresses in Rudbar had fallen into Mongol hands in this manner; they were duly demolished after their garrisons were taken into custody by the Mongols. Alamut, the

27.2 A depiction of the Mongol siege of Alamut from a copy of the *Taʾrikh-i jahan-gusha* of ʿAta-Malik Juwayni (d. 1283).

27.3 The castle of Girdkuh in northern Persia.

traditional seat of the Ismaili state, surrendered in December 1256, but Lamasar held out for another year while the fortress of Girdkuh, in Qumis near Damghan, resisted an army of Mongol besiegers until 1270. The historian ʿAta-Malik Juwayni (d. 1283), who took part in the final truce negotiations between his master Hülegü and the Ismailis, has left a vivid account of the fortress of Alamut and its famous library, before the old castle was destroyed by the Mongols.

Later, Hülegü arranged for the visit of Rukn al-Din to Mongolia as the Ismaili Imam wished to meet the Great Khan Möngke. On 9 March 1257, Rukn al-Din set out on his fateful journey to Qaraqorum, accompanied by nine companions and some Mongol guards. But once the Ismaili Imam was in the Mongol capital or its vicinity, the Great Khan declined to meet with him, on the pretext that several major Ismaili strongholds had not yet surrendered to the Mongols. By then, the Great Khan had already sanctioned a general massacre of the Persian Ismailis in Mongol custody. Rukn al-Din Khurshah's own tragic end came in the late spring of 1257, when on his return journey to Persia, he was put to the sword by his Mongol guards somewhere along the edge of the Khangai mountains in northwestern Mongolia. His Imamate had lasted just over a year.

Part Six

The Early Imams after Alamut

The first five centuries after the demise of the Ismaili state in Persia, and the fall of Alamut and other Ismaili strongholds into Mongol hands, represent the longest obscure phase in the entire history of the Ismailis. Many aspects of Ismaili activity and thought in this period are still not adequately studied and understood, mainly due to the lack of primary sources.

A variety of factors, related to the very nature of the Ismaili communities living during these centuries, have served to create special research difficulties here. In the aftermath of the destruction of their state, many of the Persian Ismailis who had survived the Mongol catastrophe migrated to adjacent lands in Afghanistan, Central Asia and Sind, where Ismaili communities already existed. Other Ismaili groups, isolated in remote areas outside their traditional territories in Persia, soon either disintegrated or were assimilated into the religiously dominant communities of their milieu.

Meanwhile, the central *da'wa* organisation and the direct leadership of the Ismaili Imams, or their chief representatives, who had ruled as the lords of Alamut (1090–1256) had also disappeared. But the Ismaili Imamate continued in the progeny of Rukn al-Din Khurshah (d. 1257), the last lord of Alamut. However, the Imams remained in hiding and inaccessible to their followers for about two centuries. Under the circumstances, various Nizari Ismaili communities developed on a regional basis and in isolation from one another. In due course, the communities of Central Asia and South Asia expanded significantly compared to their co-religionists in Persia and Syria.

More complex research difficulties arise from the widespread observance of *taqiyya*, or precautionary dissimulation, in different forms and at different times, by the Nizari Ismailis of different regions. To that end, they not only concealed their true beliefs and religious literature, but also adopted a variety of Sufi, Sunni, Twelver (Ithna'ashari) Shi'i and Hindu disguises in the hostile surroundings of the Iranian world and the Indian subcontinent. It goes without saying that carrying out *taqiyya* practices for extended periods would inevitably lead to irrevocable influences exerted on the very religious identity of the dissimulating Ismaili community, with results ranging from total acculturation or full assimilation to various degrees of interfacing between 'Ismaili' and 'other' traditions.

All in all, three main phases may be distinguished in the post-Alamut history of the Nizari Ismailis. The earliest phase, covering the first two centuries after the fall of Alamut in 1256, remains rather obscure. It was also during this phase that a succession dispute in the family of the Imams split the Nizari Ismaili community and its Imamate into two rival branches: the Muhammad-Shahi (or Mu'mini) and the Qasim-Shahi. The Qasim-Shahi Nizari Imams, who were gradually acknowledged by the majority of the Nizari Ismailis, emerged in the village of Anjudan, in central Persia, around the middle of the fifteenth century, initiating the so-called Anjudan revival in their *da'wa* and literary activities. The Anjudan phase lasted for over two centuries until the end of the seventeenth century. In the third post-Alamut phase, coinciding essentially with the eighteenth century, the Imams also acquired some political prominence in Persia. By the 1840s, when the Qasim-Shahi Nizari Ismaili Imam had become known as the Aga Khan and the seat of the Ismaili Imamate had been transferred to India, the Ismailis entered the modern phase of their history under the progressive leadership of their hereditary Imams.

28

Shams al-Din Muhammad (d. c. 1310)

Shams al-Din Muhammad, the first post-Alamut Imam, succeeded to the Ismaili Imamate on the death of his father, Rukn al-Din Khurshah, in the late spring of 1257. Born in the late 1240s, Shams al-Din was evidently the sole surviving son of the last lord of Alamut. In some legendary accounts, and as related in the oral tradition of the Ismailis, Imam Shams al-Din has been identified with Shams-i Tabrizi, the spiritual guide of Mawlana Jalal al-Din Rumi (d. 1273).

A group of Ismaili dignitaries had evidently managed to conceal Shams al-Din, who had received the *nass* to the Imamate, a few months before the castle of Alamut fell into Mongol hands in December 1256. Subsequently, Shams al-Din was taken to Adharbayjan, in northwestern Persia, where he lived clandestinely as an embroiderer, whence his nickname of Zarduz.

Certain allusions in the versified *Safar-nama* (travelogue) of Nizari Quhistani, a contemporary Nizari Ismaili poet, indicate that he saw Imam Shams al-Din in Tabriz, the capital of Adharbayjan, in 1280. Hakim Saʿd al-Din b. Muhammad, better known as Nizari Quhistani, was born in 1247 in Birjand, Quhistan. As a child he had witnessed the Mongol invasion of his native land. Nizari Quhistani served in the administration of the Kart dynasty of Khurasan and Afghanistan. Subsequently, he spent some time in the service of the Mihrabanid Maliks of neighbouring Sistan. It was mainly in his official capacity that Nizari travelled widely and saw the Ismaili Imam. Nizari, who died destitute in 1320, praises the contemporary Ismaili Imams in many of his poems, occasionally also referring to himself as a *daʿi*.

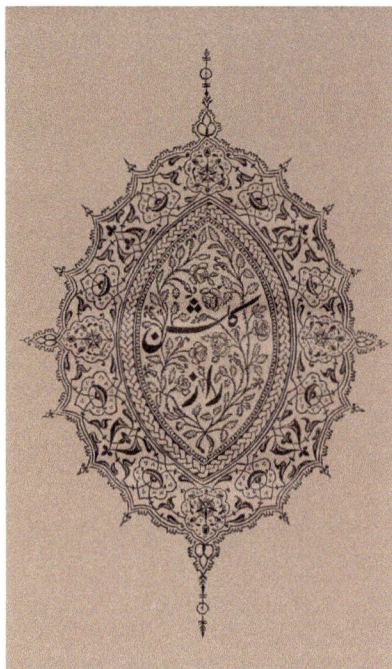

28.1 Title page of the *Gulshan-i raz* of Mahmud-i Shabistari (d. after 1339). This page is from the first edition of the work together with its German translation by the Austrian Orientalist, J. von Hammer-Purgstall (1774–1856), published in 1838.

Shams al-Din's long Imamate coincided with an obscure period in the early post-Alamut history of the Ismaili community. The Ismailis of Rudbar, the main territory of the former Ismaili state in northern Persia, evidently soon reorganised themselves under some form of local leadership. In less than two decades after the fall of Alamut in 1256, they were making periodic attempts to reoccupy that stronghold and other key fortresses in the region. The Mongols themselves had at least partially reconstructed Alamut, Lamasar and other major castles for their own use. By 1275, the Ismailis of Rudbar were strong enough to seize Alamut, which was later wrested from them by a Mongol force dispatched by Hülegü's son and successor in the Ilkhanid dynasty, Abaqa (r. 1265–1282). In the meantime, by 1273, the Ismailis of Syria had been completely subjugated by the Mamluks, but they were permitted to remain in their traditional abodes in the Jabal Bahra.

Shams al-Din Muhammad, the twenty-eighth Ismaili Imam, died in Adharbayjan around 1310, after an Imamate of almost half a century. His succession was disputed, leading to the Qasim-Shahi and Muhammad-Shahi (also known as Mu'mini) schism in the line of the Nizari Ismaili Imams and their following. According to this obscure

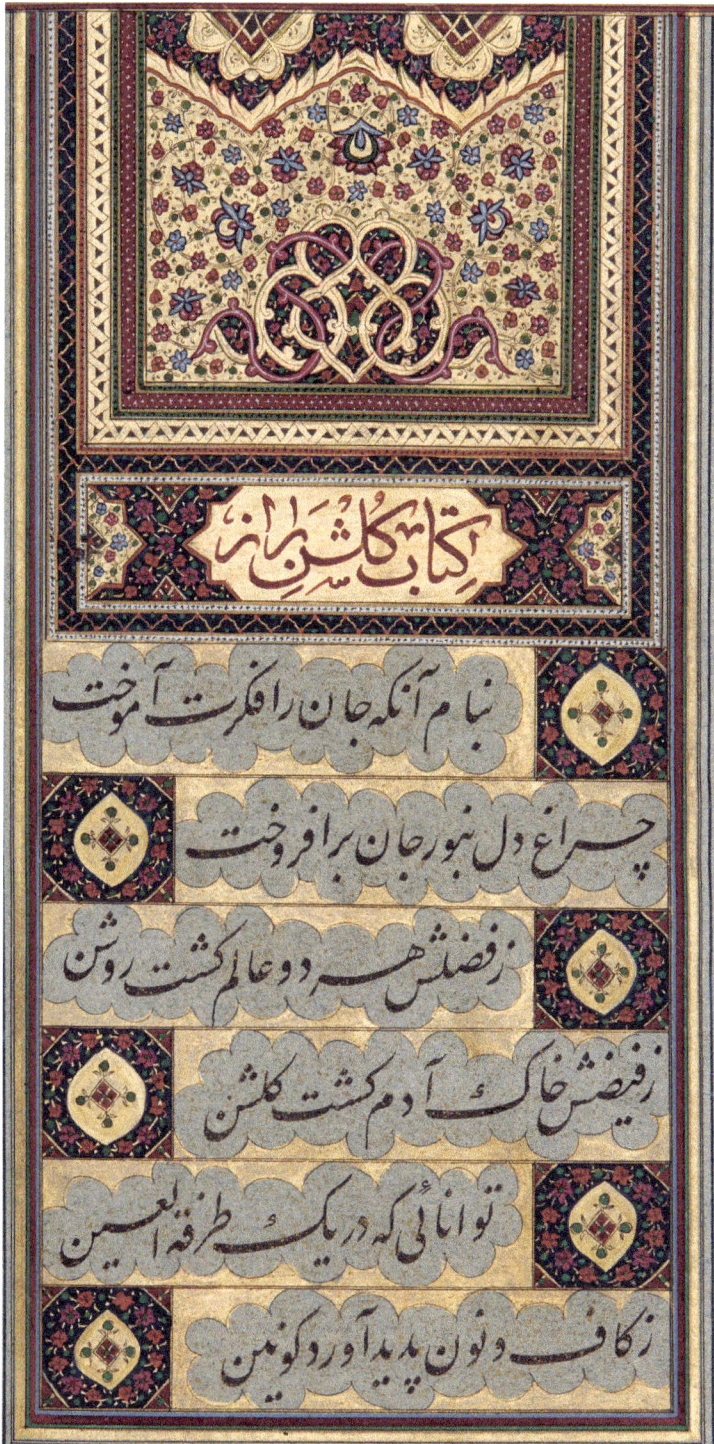

28.2 Title page of an illuminated manuscript of Mahmud-i Shabistari's *Gulshan-i raz* made for Nasir al-Din Shah Qajar (r. 1848–1896), dated 1893.

28.3 A miniature depicting a group of Sufis in contemplation and during a session of *sama'* from a copy of the *Mathnavi* of Jalal al-Din Rumi (d. 1273), dated *c*. 1530.

schism, Shams al-Din's succession was claimed by two of his sons, namely, Qasim Shah and Muhammad Shah. It is also possible that these two individuals were actually sons of Muʾmin Shah b. Shams al-Din, and as such the grandsons of the deceased Imam. Matters become even more complicated as Muʾmin Shah's name is omitted in the current list of the community.

Be that as it may, the Muhammad-Shahi line of Imams was discontinued by the end of the eighteenth century, while the Qasim-Shahi line has endured to the present day. The Qasim-Shahi Imams, who in modern times have been known internationally as the Aga Khans, are now the sole Nizari Ismaili Imams. According to the established tradition of this line, Imam Shams al-Din Muhammad was in due course succeeded by his son, Qasim Shah.

 **29**

Qasim Shah

 **30**

Islam Shah

 **31**

Muhammad b. Islam Shah (d. c. 1463)

Not much is known about Qasim Shah and his next two successors, Islam Shah and Muhammad b. Islam Shah, who followed one another in the Ismaili Imamate of the Qasim-Shahi Nizari Ismailis. Furthermore, certain developments are associated with all three Imams. For these reasons we shall treat these Imams as a group rather than individually and separately from each other.

Qasim Shah succeeded to the leadership of the Qasim-Shahis of the Ismailis around 1310, on the death of Shams al-Din Muhammad. Like his predecessor, Qasim Shah,

29–31.1 Title page of a manuscript of the *Mantiq al-tayr* by Farid al-Din ʿAttar (d. *c.* 1221). This copy was made by the calligrapher Sultan ʿAli Mashhadi (d. 1520).

too, lived clandestinely, probably in Adharbayjan, northwestern Persia. He was either the son or grandson of Shams al-Din Muhammad, and it was early in his leadership that the Nizari Ismailis split into rival Qasim-Shahi (named after him) and Muhammad-Shahi branches, as explained in the preceding entry on Imam Shams al-Din Muhammad. Be that as it may, Qasim Shah devoted his long Imamate of some sixty years mainly to defending the legitimacy of his succession. He died around 1370 and was succeeded by his son Ahmad, better known as Islam Shah, who was a contemporary of Timur (r. 1370–1405), founder of the Timurid dynasty of Persia and Transoxania. Islam Shah died around 1425 and was, in turn, succeeded in the Ismaili Imamate by his son, Muhammad.

It was evidently Islam Shah who transferred the seat of his line of the Ismaili Imams to localities around Qum and Mahallat, in central Persia, during the early decades of his fifty-five-year Imamate. It is noteworthy that Islam Shah's name as Imam is indeed mentioned in some *ginan*s, devotional literature of the Ismaili Khojas of South Asia. In fact, Islam Shah may have been the very first Imam of his line to establish a foothold in the village of Anjudan, near Mahallat, which was soon afterwards to become the permanent *da'wa* headquarters of the Qasim-Shahi Imams. The Persian chroniclers of Timur's reign, such as Sharaf al-Din 'Ali Yazdi (d. 1454), author of the *Zafar-nama*, in fact refer to Ismaili activities in his time in Anjudan and mention the curious episode of a military expedition led by Timur himself in May 1393 against the Ismailis living in Anjudan, who by then had obviously attracted quite a bit of attention. Timur was then conducting various campaigns in Persia, and it is related that his soldiers killed many Anjudani Ismailis, pillaging their properties. It was, however, under Muhammad b. Islam Shah's son and successor, Mustansir bi'llah (d. 1480) who assumed the Imamate around 1463, that the Imams of the Qasim-Shahi line became firmly established in Anjudan.

It was during the Imamates of these three Imams, if not somewhat earlier in post-Alamut times, that the Persian Ismailis, as part of their general *taqiyya* practices, concealed themselves under the mantle of Sufism, without establishing formal affiliations with any one of the Sufi *tariqa*s, or orders, then spreading throughout post-Mongol Persia and Central Asia. The origins and early development of this complex Ismaili–Sufi relationship remain rather obscure. It is a fact, however, that the ideas of the Persian Ismailis now became increasingly infused with Sufi teachings and terminology. At the same time, the Sufis themselves, who, like the Ismailis, adhered to *batini ta'wil*, or esoteric exegesis, began to use or adopt ideas that were more widely associated with the Ismailis. As part of this coalescence, the Persian-speaking Nizari

Ismailis began to adopt Sufi ways of life even externally. Thus, it has been reported that Imam Shams al-Din Muhammad's immediate successors in the Qasim-Shahi line of Imams lived clandestinely for the most part as Sufi *pir*s, or masters, while their followers adopted the typically Sufi title of *murid* or disciple. This association is reflected in the fact that henceforth the word 'shah' (often used by Sufi masters) also appears as part of the names of the Ismaili Imams, starting with Qasim Shah.

The adoption of a Sufi exterior by the Ismailis would not have been so readily possible if these two esoteric traditions in Islam had not had doctrinal grounds in common. As an early instance of this type of Ismaili–Sufi interaction, mention may be made of the celebrated versified Sufi treatise entitled *Gulshan-i raz* (The Rose-Garden of Mystery) composed by the Sufi *shaykh*, Mahmud-i Shabistari (d. after 1339) and a later partial commentary (*ta'wilat*) on it by a Persian Ismaili author. As a result of their close relationship with Sufism in early post-Alamut times, the Ismailis have considered some of the greatest mystic poets of Persia as their co-religionists and have preserved their works as part of their own heritage and literature. Among such poets, mention may be made of Sana'i (d. 1140), Farid al-Din 'Attar (d. *c.* 1221) and Mawlana Jalal al-Din Rumi (d. 1273), as well as other Sufi personalities like 'Aziz al-Din Nasafi (d. *c.* 1262) and Qasim-i Anwar (d. *c.* 1433).

Part Seven

The Imams of the Anjudan Period

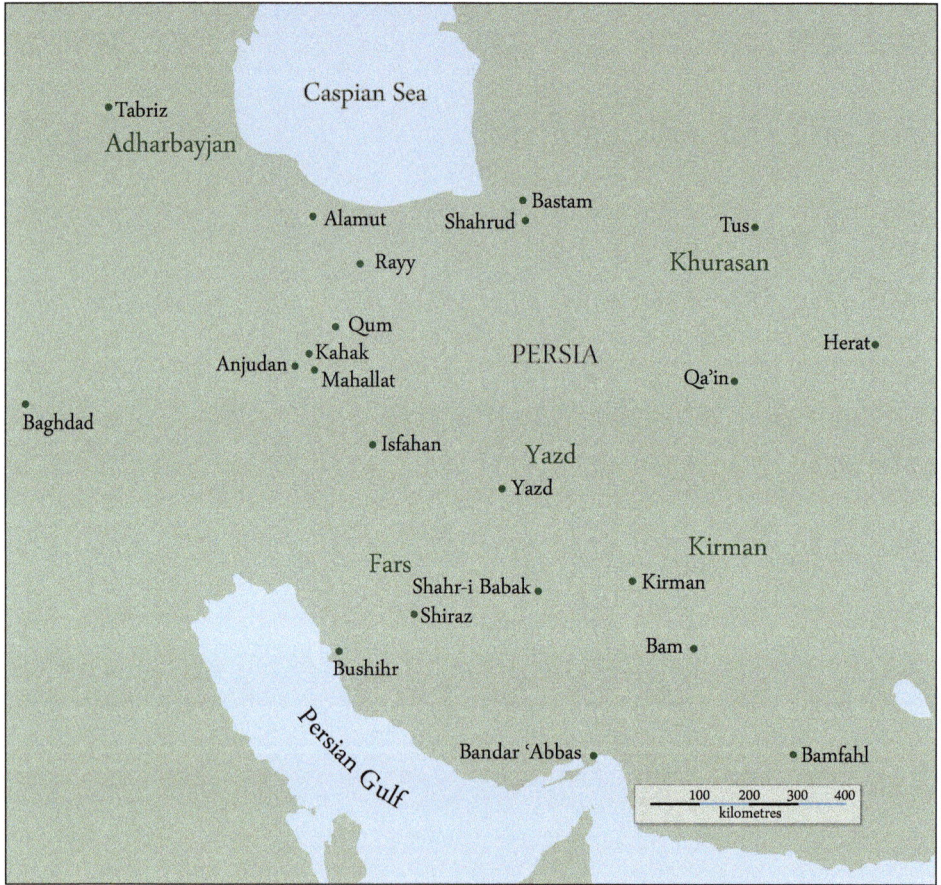

Persia in Safawid times

❋ 32 ❋

Mustansir bi'llah
(d. 1480)

❋ 33 ❋

'Abd al-Salam Shah

❋ 34 ❋

Gharib Mirza, also known as
Mustansir bi'llah (d. 1498)

Muhammad b. Islam Shah, the thirty-first Imam, was succeeded in the Ismaili Imamate by his son 'Ali Shah, better known as Mustansir bi'llah, who is the first post-Alamut Imam with definite connections to Anjudan. This village, in central Persia, situated at the foot of a rocky range some thirty-seven kilometres east of Arak (formerly known as Sultanabad) and about the same distance west of Mahallat, remained the seat of the

Imams of this Nizari Ismaili branch until the final decades of the seventeenth century, coinciding with almost the entire period of Safawid rule over Persia. The Ismaili antiquities of Anjudan include a wooden mosque and three mausoleums containing the tombs of several of the Imams and their relatives.

Imam Mustansir bi'llah succeeded to the leadership of the Ismailis, as their thirty-second Imam, around 1463 and died in Anjudan in 1480, the date mentioned in the inscription in his mausoleum. This mausoleum, the oldest surviving Ismaili monument in Anjudan, is locally referred to as Shah Qalandar, which was evidently Imam Mustansir bi'llah's Sufi name. It should be added here that Ismaili oral tradition erroneously holds that Mustansir bi'llah and his immediate successors resided in Shahr-i Babak in the Persian region of Kirman.

Mustansir bi'llah was succeeded in the Imamate by his son, 'Abd al-Salam Shah, in 1480. The grave of this Imam, the thirty-third of the line, who died in 1493 according to oral tradition, has not been discovered. However, the mausoleum of his son and successor, 'Abbas Shah, who also carried the honorific title of Mustansir bi'llah, is

32–34.1 Mausoleum of Imam Mustansir bi'llah (d. 1480), also known as Shah Qalandar, in Anjudan.

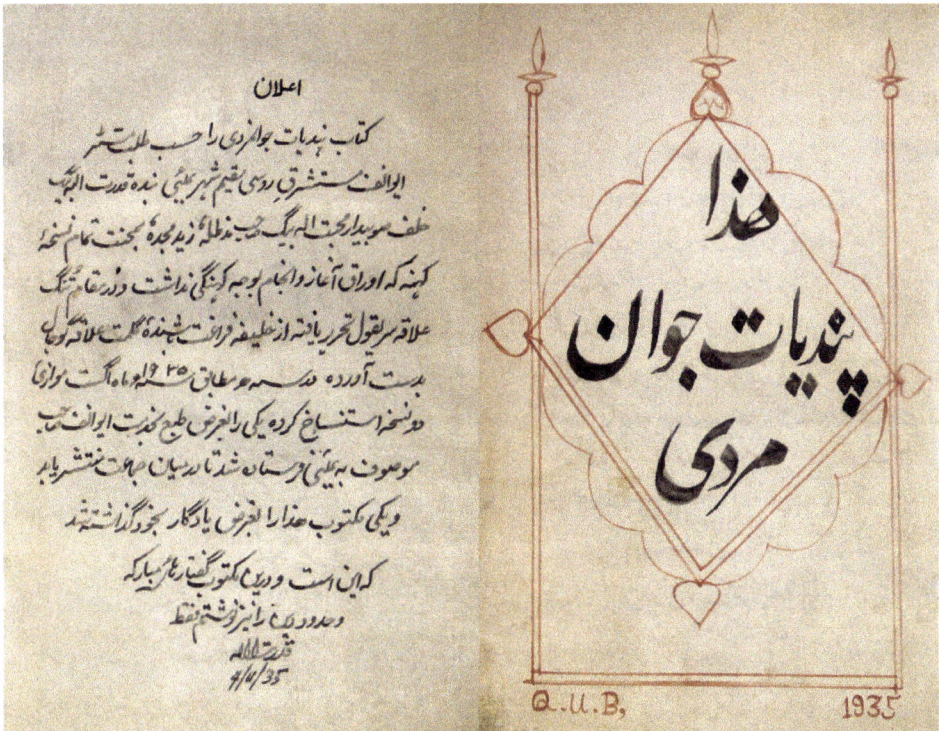

اعلان

كتاب پندیات جوانمردی را صاحب طلائشر
ایوالله مستشرق روسی مقیم شهر عینی بنده قدرت البهاء

[handwritten Persian text continues]

32–34.2 Title page and opening page of a manuscript of the *Pandiyat-i javanmardi*, a collection of the sermons of Imam Mustansir bi'llah. This copy was made in 1935 in Hunza for the pioneer of Ismaili studies, W. Ivanow (1886–1970), who at the time lived in Bombay.

preserved in Anjudan. This Imam, the thirty-fourth of the line, was also known as Gharib Mirza, and is still referred to as Shah Gharib by the local inhabitants of Anjudan, who have remained unaware of the Ismaili identity of these dignitaries buried in their village. Gharib Mirza died in August 1498, after a brief Imamate of about five years, according to the date (Muharram 904 AH) that was inscribed on the wooden box placed on his grave, and which identified him as Shah Mustansir b. Shah 'Abd al-Salam. This box, like several other Ismaili antiquities of Anjudan, has disappeared in recent decades.

The Anjudan revival in Ismaili *da'wa* and literary activities was effectively initiated with the settlement of Mustansir bi'llah, the thirty-second Imam, in Anjudan. However, the Ismailis were still obliged, in pre-Safawid Persia, to practise *taqiyya* and continue to dissimulate to the outside world, mainly in the guise of Sufism. So to the outside world, the Ismaili Imams appeared as Sufi *pir*s, *murshid*s or *shaykh*s and they were also regarded as pious 'Alid sayyids, descendants of the Prophet through Fatima and 'Ali.

32–34.3 Mausoleum of Imam Shah Gharib, also known as Mustansir bi'llah, in Anjudan.

Similarly, the followers of the Imams posed as their *murid*s, who were guided along the *tariqa* or path to *haqiqa* or truth by their revered spiritual master. This explains why, in the course of the Anjudan period, and indeed earlier starting with Qasim Shah, it became customary for the Ismaili Imams to adopt Sufi names, often also adding the words shah and ʿAli to their names, as Sufi masters did.

Meanwhile, the general religio-political circumstances of Persia had become somewhat more favourable for the activities of the Ismailis, and certain groups influenced by Shiʿi ideas. In this context, mention may be made of the political fragmentation of Persia, after the collapse of the Mongol Ilkhanid dynasty and the widespread circulation of Shiʿi tendencies and ʿAlid loyalism, especially through a number of Sufi *tariqa*s, or orders, notably the Niʿmat Allahiyya and the Safawiyya. The Sufi orders in question remained outwardly Sunni, while being particularly devoted to ʿAli and the *ahl al-bayt*, or the Prophet's household, acknowledging ʿAli's spiritual guidance. In time, at least some of the same Sufi orders came to profess formally their adherence to Shiʿi Islam. Be that as it may, Imam Mustansir bi'llah, the thirty-second Imam, whose Sufi name was Shah Qalandar, may have been the first Imam of his Qasim-Shahi line who developed an association with the Niʿmat Allahi Sufi order,

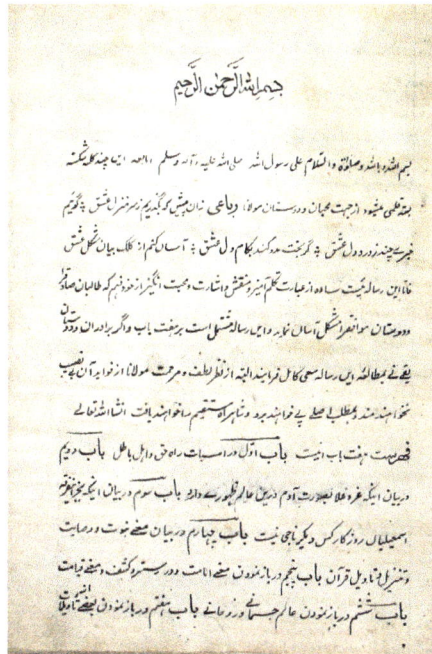

32–34.4 Title page of the *Haft bab* of Abu Ishaq Quhistani (d. after 1498). This was one of the first works on Ismaili doctrine produced after the fall of Alamut in 1256.

though substantiating evidence is lacking. Under these circumstances, the Imams now began to conduct their *da'wa* activities somewhat more openly. By adopting a title like Mustansir bi'llah, first used by a Fatimid Imam-caliph, it seems that the Imams were now striving to revive the old glories of the Ismailis.

The Ismaili *da'wa* was now reorganised and reinvigorated from its central headquarters at Anjudan, where the Imams resided. The objectives of these renewed *da'wa* efforts were to win new converts and to reassert the central authority of the Imams over the various regions where their followers lived, especially Central Asia and the Indian subcontinent, which had increasingly come under the control of their local and hereditary dynasties of *pir*s. In order to achieve these objectives, the Imams required the necessary financial resources and loyal *da'i*s who would faithfully carry out their guidance. These points are, indeed, reiterated throughout a Persian treatise entitled *Pandiyat-i javanmardi* (Admonitions on Spiritual Chivalry), containing the sermons of Mustansir bi'llah, the thirty-second Imam, to the true believers or *mu'min*s. These admonitions, or *pandiyat*, have been preserved also in Sindhi (Khojki) and Gujarati versions, which were sent to India for the religious guidance of the Nizari Ismailis there, known as Khojas. Copies of the original Persian version of this work are still preserved

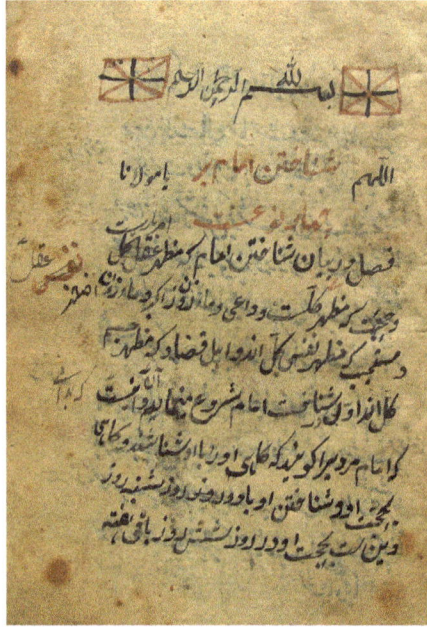

32–34.5 A manuscript of the *Fasl dar bayan-i shinakht-i imam*, a work by the 16th-century Ismaili *daʿi* and poet Khayrkhwah-i Harati (d. after 1553), composed around 1545. It consists of a summary of Khayrkhwah's ideas concerning the Imamate and other teachings of the Anjudan period.

in the manuscript collections of the Ismailis of Badakhshan and adjacent regions in Hunza, and other northern areas of Pakistan, as well as in the Sinkiang (Xinjiang) province of China.

The Anjudan revival in *daʿwa* activities was accompanied by a revival in literary activities amongst the Nizari Ismailis, especially in Persia. The earliest results of these efforts, representing the first doctrinal treatises produced after the fall of Alamut in 1256, appear in the works of Abu Ishaq Quhistani (d. after 1498), and Khayrkhwah-i Harati (d. after 1553). By the time of Khayrkhwah, who was also a poet with the pen name of Gharibi – derived from the name of Gharib Mirza, one of his contemporary Imams – the term *pir* had acquired wide currency among the Ismailis; it was used in reference to *daʿi*s of different ranks and the head of any Ismaili community, as well as to the person of the Imam himself.

32–34.6 A miniature from a manuscript of the *Haft awrang* of the Sufi poet Jami (d. *c.* 1492), commissioned by the Safawid prince Sultan Ibrahim Mirza in 1556.

35

Abu Dharr ʿAli

36

Murad Mirza (d. 1574)

According to the traditional sequence of the Qasim-Shahi Nizari Imams, Gharib Mirza was succeeded in 1498 by his son Abu Dharr ʿAli, also known as Nur al-Din Muhammad, who is counted as the thirty-fifth Imam in the line. Abu Dharr ʿAli's Imamate coincided with the advent of the Safawid dynasty in 1501 and their immediate proclamation of the Twelver (Ithnaʿashari) form of Shiʿi Islam as the state religion of Persia. These developments seemed to promise yet more favourable opportunities for the activities of the Ismailis and other Shiʿi communities in Safawid Persia. The Ismailis did in fact reduce the intensity of their *taqiyya* practices during the initial decades of Safawid rule. At the time, they were led by Imam Abu Dharr ʿAli who was contemporary with Shah Ismaʿil I (r. 1501–1524), founder of the dynasty, and partially contemporary with Ismaʿil's son and successor, Shah Tahmasp I (r. 1524–1576). In fact, the improved conditions evidently permitted the thirty-fifth Imam to marry a sister, or a daughter, of Shah Tahmasp.

The new optimism of the Ismailis proved short lived, however, as the Safawids soon adopted intolerant policies towards most Sufi orders and those Shiʿi communities that fell outside the boundaries of Twelver Shiʿism. Meanwhile, the increased and more overt activities of the Ismailis had begun to attract the attention of the Safawid monarchs and their Twelver 'ulama, or religious scholars, despite the continued use of Sufi guises. In the event, the Ismailis too were targeted for renewed persecution in the reign of Shah Tahmasp, after Abu Dharr 'Ali's son and successor Murad Mirza had succeeded to the Ismaili Imamate, as the thirty-sixth Imam, at an unknown date during 1524–1573.

Several Persian chroniclers, including Qadi Ahmad Qumi (d. 1606), refer to the persecution of the Ismailis of Anjudan in 1573, during the Imamate of Murad Mirza. The same sources also relate that this Imam had numerous followers in India, who regularly sent him their religious dues from Sind and elsewhere. Apparently, Murad Mirza, like his predecessor, did not reside in Anjudan. Furthermore, departing from his family's tradition, Murad Mirza was engaged in obscure political activity outside Anjudan, perhaps in league with the Nuqtawis, a Shi'i-related movement influenced by Sufism and Ismaili esoteric teachings. Also known as the Pasikhaniyya, the Nuqtawis had split from the Hurufiyya, whose doctrines were derived from Persian Sufism and

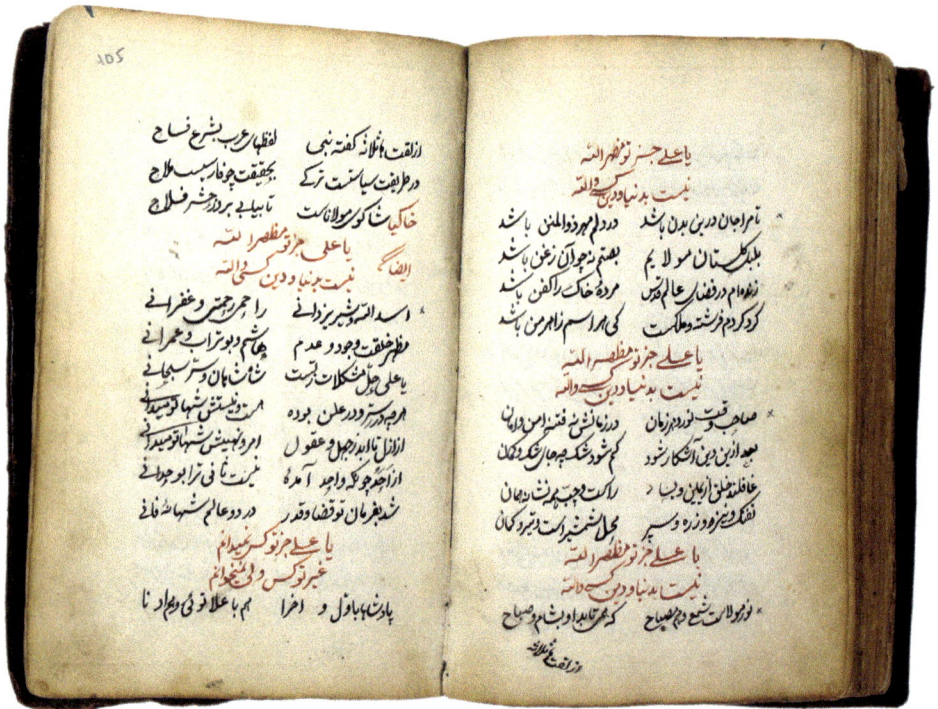

35–36.1 A manuscript of the *Diwan* of the Ismaili poet Khaki Khurasani (d. after 1646). This copy was made in the 1890s. The poems refer to the spreading influence of the Ismailis in Khurasan and western Persia as well as in the Indian subcontinent. They also eulogise the Imams Dhu'l-Faqar 'Ali and Nur al-Dahr.

35–36.2 A Safawid miniature from the mid-16th century depicting a young man seated on the branch of a tree reading.

35–36.3 Painting of a prince reading a poem about the Prophet Yusuf.

Ismailism. By the time of the early Safawids, the Nuqtawi movement had become very popular in many cities in Persia, including Kashan and the areas around Anjudan.

At any rate, Murad Mirza himself seems to have acquired substantial supporters in Kashan and other localities in central Persia. Alarmed by this Imam's popularity, in 1573 Shah Tahmasp ordered the governor of Hamadan to proceed to the Anjudan area and capture Murad Mirza, also dealing with his followers or *murid*s there. The governor killed many of the Anjudani Ismailis and took much booty from them, but failed to arrest Murad Mirza, who was then staying in a fortress in the district of Kamara near Anjudan. Murad Mirza was, however, captured and imprisoned shortly afterwards. Then in October 1573, the Imam escaped from prison assisted by a high Safawid official who was a secret convert to Ismailism. Subsequently, Murad Mirza fled to the vicinity of Qandahar, in Afghanistan, en route receiving help from his followers in Fars, Makran and Sind. But a few months later, in 1574, he was captured in Afghanistan by a contingent of Safawid soldiers sent after him. The Ismaili Imam was brought before Shah Tahmasp, who ordered his execution. The graves of Abu Dharr ʿAli and Murad Mirza, who were Imams from 1498 to 1574, have not been found in Anjudan.

It was perhaps after Murad Mirza's tragic fate that the Ismaili Imams and their followers, in addition to their Sufi cover, began to practise *taqiyya* in the guise of Twelver Shiʿism, which was the 'politically correct' form of Shiʿism under the Safawids. In this connection, it should be added that Shah Tahir al-Husayni (d. 1549), the thirty-first and most famous Imam of the Muhammad-Shahi Nizaris, had a few decades earlier already propagated his form of Ismailism in the guise of Twelver Shiʿism. Nevertheless, he did not escape persecution from the Safawids. Shah Tahir was eventually obliged to flee from Persia in 1520. Two years later he settled in Ahmadnagar, the capital of the Nizam-Shahi state in the Deccan, in India. There, he converted Burhan Nizam Shah (r. 1509–1554) from Sunni Islam to Twelver Shiʿism, before that form of Shiʿism was proclaimed in 1537 as the official religion of his state. Subsequently, by the time this line of Imams was discontinued in the final decades of the eighteenth century, the Muhammad-Shahi Nizaris had either switched their allegiance to the Qasim-Shahi line of Imams or were fully assimilated into the Twelver Shiʿi communities of India, Persia and elsewhere. At present, the only known members of this Nizari group are located in Syria. Locally known as the Jaʿfariyya, they are still awaiting the reappearance of their last known Imam (Amir Muhammad al-Baqir), counted as the fortieth in their line of Imams, and who is believed to have gone into concealment around 1796.

37

Dhu'l-Faqar ʿAli (d. 1634)

38

Nur al-Din (al-Dahr) ʿAli (d. 1671)

39

Khalil Allah ʿAli (d. 1680)

In 1574, Murad Mirza's son Khalil Allah succeeded to the Imamate of the Ismailis as their thirty-seventh Imam. He also carried the Sufi name of Dhu'l-Faqar ʿAli. He and the next two succeeding Imams re-established themselves again in Anjudan, which had been abandoned by Murad Mirza, the thirty-sixth Imam. Furthermore, the Imams now once again remained aloof from any political activity, in contrast to Murad Mirza who had lost his life due to his political activity. Aiming to safeguard the security of their community, Dhu'l-Faqar ʿAli, and his immediate successors, quietly concerned themselves primarily with conducting the affairs of their *daʿwa* and community while they continued to dissimulate under the double mantle of Twelver Shiʿism and Sufism.

As a result of their quiescent policies, and successful *taqiyya* practices, the Imams were able to develop friendly relations with the Safawid ruling establishment. These improved relations are reflected, for instance, in the fact that Imam Dhu'l-Faqar ʿAli married a Safawid princess, perhaps a sister of Shah ʿAbbas I (r. 1587–1629), the greatest member of the dynasty who transferred the Safawid capital from Qazwin to Isfahan in 1598. Shah ʿAbbas continued his predecessors' policies against the Sunni Muslims, and certain radical Shiʿi movements, such as the Nuqtawiyya, but he was quite tolerant towards the Ismailis, even when their true identity was revealed.

Be that as it may, friendly relations between Imam Dhu'l-Faqar ʿAli and Shah ʿAbbas are further attested by an epigraph, recovered in 1976 in Anjudan by the author. This epigraph contains the text of a royal decree issued by Shah ʿAbbas in March 1627 (Rajab 1036 AH) and addressed to Amir Khalil Allah Anjudani, the contemporary Ismaili Imam (Dhu'l-Faqar ʿAli). According to this decree, the Shiʿi inhabitants of

37–39.1 A stone inscription reproducing the edict of Shah ʿAbbas I (r. 1587–1629), made in 1627 and addressed to Imam Amir Khalil Allah Anjudani (Dhu'l-Faqar ʿAli), granting the Shiʿi inhabitants of Anjudan exemption from a number of taxes.

37–39.2 Among these tombstones in the mausoleum of Imam Shah Gharib in Anjudan is that of Imam Shah Khalil Allah (d. 1680), the last Imam of the Anjudan period.

Anjudan were exempted, like other Ithna'ashari Shi'is living around Qum, from paying certain taxes to the state treasury. It is interesting to note that in this decree the Anjudani Shi'is were regarded as Ithna'asharis, proving that by that time the Persian Ismailis had been very successful in dissimulating as Twelver Shi'is.

Imam Dhu'l-Faqar 'Ali, mentioned as Amir Khalil Allah in the above-mentioned Safawid decree, may indeed be identified with a certain Khalil Allah who, according to his tombstone at Anjudan, died at the age of sixty-eight in March 1634 (Ramadan 1043 AH), some seven years after the date of the above decree. His long Imamate had lasted sixty years. He was succeeded in the Imamate by his son Nur al-Dahr (also known as Nur al-Din) 'Ali, carrying another Sufi name. This Imam, the thirty-eighth in the line of the Qasim-Shahi Nizari Imams, may be identified with Nur al-Dahr b. Khalil Allah, who died in November 1671 (Rajab 1082 AH), according to his tombstone at Anjudan. His Imamate had, thus, lasted some thirty-seven years. The Persian Ismaili poet Imam-Quli Khaki Khurasani (d. after 1646), a contemporary of the thirty-seventh and thirty-eighth Imams, frequently eulogises them as Shah Dhu'l-Faqar (Khalil), possibly also called Haydar, and Shah Nur al-Dahr b. Dhu'l-Faqar, in his *Diwan* of poems. He also mentions Anjudan as their place of residence, which he apparently visited himself.

Imam Nur al-Dahr's son and successor, Shah Khalil Allah, was the last Imam of his line to reside at Anjudan. This Imam, the thirty-ninth in the line, died in January 1680 (Dhu'l-Hijja 1090 AH), after a brief Imamate of some nine years. His tombstone, along with several others, was preserved until recent times, set in one of the walls of the mausoleum of Gharib Mirza, the thirty-fourth Imam, in Anjudan. By the time of this Imam, the Ismaili *da'wa* of the Qasim-Shahi Nizaris had become very successful with many followers in Khurasan, Kirman and other regions of Persia, as well as Badakhshan, Afghanistan, Multan and elsewhere in India. Indeed, by the closing decades of the seventeenth century, when the residence of the Imams was transferred to the neighbouring village of Kahak, the Anjudan revival had achieved lasting success. As a result, the *da'wa* of the Qasim-Shah Nizari Ismailis gained the allegiance of the bulk of the Nizari Ismailis, at the expense of the Muhammad-Shahi Nizaris. At the same time, the Ismaili *da'wa* of the Qasim-Shahi line of the Imams had expanded significantly, especially in Central Asia and several regions of the Indian subcontinent, including especially Sind and Gujarat.

The *da'wa* organisation of the Ismailis was a relatively simple one during the Anjudan period. It was naturally headed by the Imam, who was followed in the hierarchy (*hudud*) by a single *hujjat*. The latter was the highest administrative officer of the *da'wa* and the Imam's chief assistant. The *hujjat*, who lived in close proximity to the Imam, was often selected from among the close relatives of the Imam who were not generally in the direct line of succession to the Imamate. Next as a rank in the *da'wa* hierarchy, there was a single category of *da'i*, a summoner at large who visited different Ismaili communities. Then came the rank of *mu'allim* or teacher, who was normally in charge of the *da'wa* activities in a particular community or region. The *mu'allims* were appointed by the *hujjat*, in consultation with the Imam. Every *mu'allim* was assisted by two categories of *ma'dhun* or assistant. The senior one, *ma'dhun-i akbar*, was permitted to teach Ismaili doctrines and to seek converts on his own initiative. The junior assistant, *ma'dhun-i asghar*, who held the lowest rank in the hierarchy, could perform these tasks only after receiving the *mu'allim's* permission.

The ordinary Ismaili initiates, as in earlier times, were referred to as *mustajibs*, now often also designated as *murids*. They did not occupy a rank in the *da'wa* hierarchy. By the middle of the sixteenth century in the Anjudan period, the Sufi term *pir* had come to be generally used in reference to the higher ranks in the *da'wa* organisation, notably the Imam himself as well as *hujjat*, *da'i* and *mu'allim*. However, the term *pir* fell into disuse in Persia after the Anjudan period, while it was retained by the Ismaili communities of Central Asia and South Asia.

Part Eight

The Imams in the Eighteenth Century

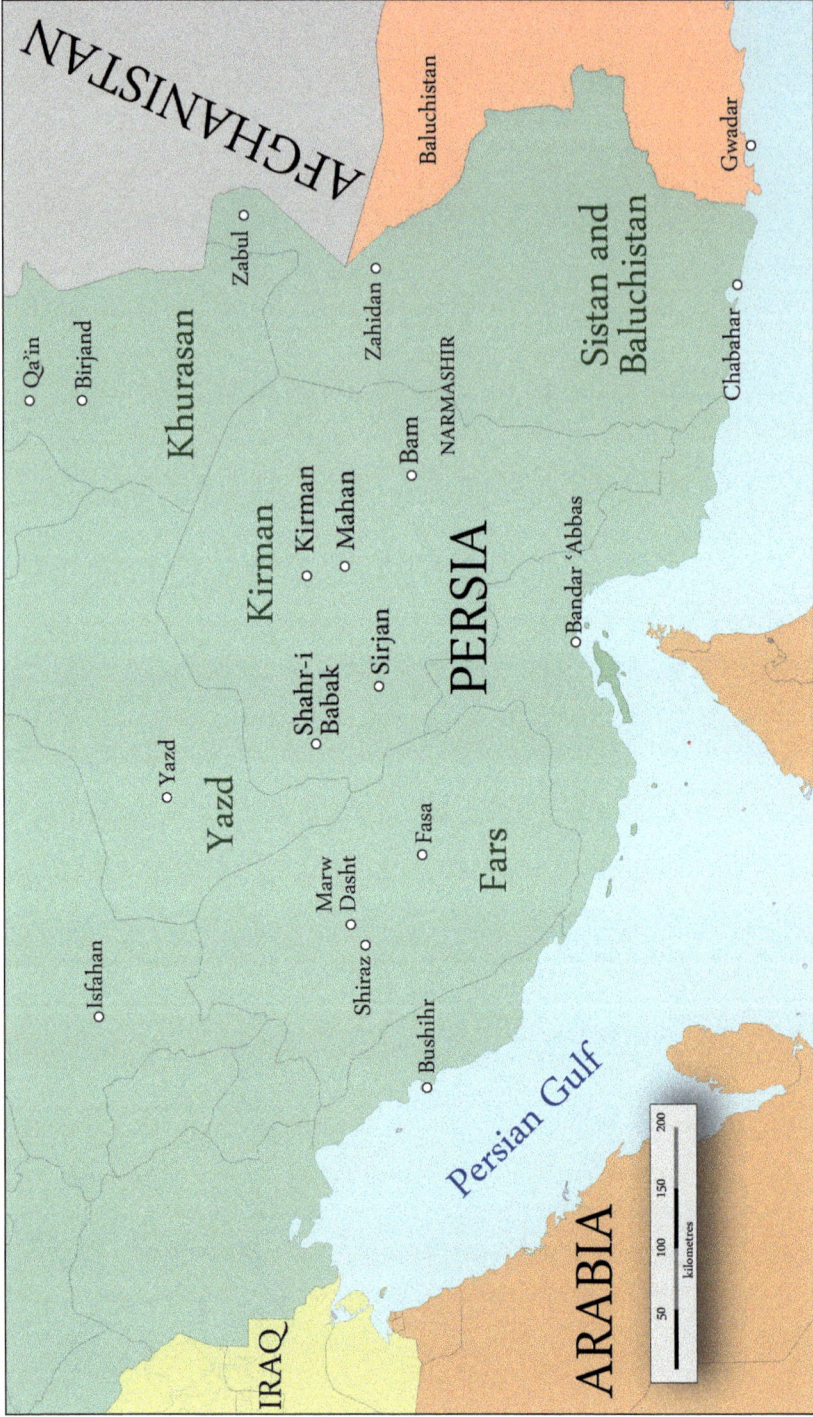

Southern Persia

40

Shah Nizar (d. 1722)

Imam Khalil Allah, the thirty-ninth Ismaili Imam, died in 1680 and was succeeded in the Imamate by his son, Shah Nizar. By that time, the Ismaili Imams had established deep roots in central Persia, in Mahallat, Anjudan and adjacent areas. Shah Nizar, the fortieth Imam, transferred his residence and the headquarters of the *da'wa* from

40.1 The restored mausoleum of Imam Shah Nizar in Kahak. Kahak was a stopping point on the road between Qum and Arak to which this Imam moved at the beginning of his Imamate.

40.2 The tombstone of Imam Shah Nizar, dated AH 1134 (1722).

Anjudan to the nearby village of Kahak. The reasons for this move, which took place during the early decades of his Imamate (1680–1722), remain unknown. At any rate, this event marked the end of the Anjudan period in Ismaili history, which had lasted just over two centuries from the 1450s. Anjudan was now abandoned permanently by the Ismaili Imams.

Kahak is located about thirty-five kilometres northeast of Anjudan and northwest of Mahallat in central Persia. Separated from Anjudan by a number of shallow ranges, Kahak evidently enjoyed importance in Safawid times as a resting place for caravans on the road between Qum and Arak (formerly known as Sultanabad). This is attested by the ruins of a fairly large caravanserai in the vicinity of the village. Today Kahak is a small village with an Ithna'ashari population of about 500 persons. Both Shah Nizar and his immediate successor lived in Kahak, although it was later abandoned as the residence of the Imams for other localities in the region of Kirman.

40.3 A Safawid caravanserai near Kahak.

However, the Imams retained a foothold there at least until the beginning of the nineteenth century.

The Ismaili Imams had evidently maintained some sort of relationship with the Niʿmat Allahi Sufi *tariqa*, or order, intermittently from early Anjudan times. However, the earliest definite evidence for this association may be traced to Imam Shah Nizar. He had close ties with this Sufi order, which had not yet been revived in Persia. This also explains Nizar's adoption of the *tariqa* name of ʿAta Allah, and why certain tribal groups of his followers came to be designated as ʿAta Allahis. With the encouragement of Shah Nizar, these Ismailis, who were originally nomadic tribesmen in Khurasan, had settled down in Sirjan and other districts of Kirman.

Imam Shah Nizar died, according to the inscription on his tombstone preserved in Kahak, in September 1722 (Dhu'l-Hijja 1134 AH), shortly before the Afghan invasion of Persia which extended to Kahak. This invasion contributed to the downfall of the Safawids in the dying decades of the dynasty. Ismaili tradition erroneously places Shah Nizar's death almost a century earlier, in 1628. He was buried in one of the chambers of the building that served as his residence, and which is still preserved at the western end of Kahak. This building has several chambers, each one containing a few graves. In the compound and its garden there are also several tombstones with inscriptions in Sindhi (Khojki) characters, attesting to the pilgrimage of the Ismaili Khojas, who regularly embarked on the long and perilous journey from India to Persia for the *didar*, or seeing, of their Imam in Kahak. In fact, Kahak is mentioned in some *ginan*s, devotional poems of the Khojas, as the place of residence of the Imams. By the time of Shah Nizar, indeed, close relations had developed between the Ismaili Imams and their Khoja followers in Sind, Panjab, Gujarat and other regions of the Indian subcontinent.

41
Sayyid ʿAli

42
Hasan ʿAli

43
Qasim ʿAli

On Shah Nizar's death in 1722 his son Sayyid ʿAli succeeded to the Ismaili Imamate as the forty-first Imam. He was, in turn, succeeded by his son Sayyid Hasan ʿAli, also known as Sayyid Hasan Beg, counted as the forty-second Imam of his line. At an unknown date, Imam Hasan ʿAli was succeeded by his son Qasim ʿAli, also known as Sayyid Jaʿfar, who is counted as the forty-third Imam of the line. No specific dates are available for these three Imams other than the fact that their cumulative Imamates lasted from 1722 until the 1750s.

These Imams lived during an extremely turbulent period in the history of Persia, covering the first half of the eighteenth century. By the time of Shah Nizar's death in

1722, the Safawid dynasty had effectively been uprooted, although minor Safawid princes continued to rule over Khurasan and a few other regions. The decline of the Safawids coincided with the Afghan invasion of Persia in 1722, which led to the utter disruption of law and order until Nadir Shah expelled the Afghans and founded his own short-lived Afsharid dynasty (1736–1796). After Nadir (d. 1747), other Afsharids, notably Shah Rukh, ruled over Kirman and other parts of Persia. Meanwhile, Karim Khan Zand (r. 1751–1779), founder of another short-lived dynasty, had come to control Fars, Kirman and other Persian territories. It was under such unsettled conditions that the three Imams covered in this section led the Ismailis of Persia, Central Asia, India and other regions for about three decades, during which their residence and *daʿwa* headquarters was established in the region of Kirman.

It seems that Sayyid ʿAli's Imamate did not last much beyond a decade. It was during the Imamate of his son, Hasan ʿAli, that Nadir Shah expelled the Afghans from Persia and proclaimed himself king in 1736. It is related that towards the final years of Nadir Shah Afshar's reign (1736–1747), Imam Hasan ʿAli, the forty-second Imam, moved his residence from Kahak to Shahr-i Babak in the region of Kirman, about 180 kilometres southeast of the city of Kirman itself, between the towns of Rafsanjan and Sirjan. This important decision seems to have been motivated by the Imam's concern for the safety of the Khoja pilgrims who were then coming in increasing numbers to see their Imam.

Earlier, in the unsettled conditions prevailing over Persia, the Khojas who travelled to the Kahak and Mahallat areas to see their Imam and remit to him their religious dues – known as *dassondh* in India – were often attacked and plundered between Naʾin and Yazd by various tribesmen, notably the Bakhtiyaris, in addition to suffering extortion at the hands of various government officials. In the event, Imam Hasan ʿAli transferred his residence to Shahr-i Babak in southeastern Persia, a location closer to the ports on the Persian Gulf and a safer route for the land journey of the Khojas after they had completed their sea voyage from the Indian subcontinent to the ports of Persia. A number of Ismailis had already lived for some time in Shahr-i Babak, which now became a significant Ismaili centre after the settlement there of the Imam himself.

Improvements in the financial situation of the *daʿwa* organisation enabled Imam Hasan ʿAli to acquire extensive properties in Shahr-i Babak as well as a comfortable winter residence in the city of Kirman itself. He also abandoned much of the traditional *taqiyya* practices of his predecessors and so emerged from the virtual state of concealment under which they had lived. Indeed, he became actively involved in the affairs of the province of Kirman, which was retained as the seat of the Ismaili

41–43.1 Portrait of Nadir Shah Afshar (r. 1736–1747), founder of the Afsharid dynasty, painted in oil on canvas, *c.* 1740, by Muhammad Rida Hindi.

Imamate by his successors until the last decade of the eighteenth century. Imam Hasan ʿAli established close relations with the Afsharid prince Shah Rukh, who ruled over Kirman for a while after Nadir Shah's murder in 1747. The close ties between the Ismaili Imam and the Afsharid ruler of Kirman culminated in the marriage of Imam Hasan ʿAli's daughter and Shah Rukh's son, Lutf ʿAli Khan. The Ismaili sources relate a number of apparently legendary accounts concerning Hasan ʿAli, including this Imam's severe persecution by Nadir Shah who is said to have eventually blinded him. Alternatively, the Imam is said to have accompanied Nadir Shah on his famous Indian campaign in 1738.

By the 1750s, Kirman had been annexed to the territories controlled by Karim Khan Zand, founder of the Zand dynasty (r. 1751–1794). Subsequently, the chaotic conditions of Persia deteriorated further when Agha Muhammad Khan, founder of the Qajar dynasty, appeared on the political scene in 1779. Meanwhile, Imam Hasan ʿAli was succeeded, at an unknown date not long before 1750, by his son Qasim ʿAli, counted as the forty-third Imam. Not much is known about this Imam, who retained his residential ties with both Shahr-i Babak and the city of Kirman during his relatively brief Imamate of only a few years.

44

Abu'l-Hasan 'Ali
(d. 1792)

Abu'l-Hasan 'Ali, also known as Sayyid Abu'l-Hasan Kahaki and Baqir Shah or Baqir 'Ali Shah, succeeded his father Qasim 'Ali as the forty-fourth Ismaili Imam at an unknown date, probably in the early 1750s. This Imam played a very prominent role in the political affairs of Kirman, which he governed for several decades, as well as in the contemporary dynastic rivalries in Persia. He was a warrior, a diplomat and an accomplished political strategist, who chose his alliances carefully at a time when a number of claimants to the throne of Persia were vying with one another for the control of Kirman and other regions. Early in his career, the Imam was favoured by Karim Khan Zand (r. 1751–1779), founder of a short-lived dynasty in Persia, but later he lent his support to Agha Muhammad Khan (r. 1779–1797), the future founder of the Qajar dynasty who was then successfully challenging Zand rule in different parts of Persia.

Imam Abu'l-Hasan 'Ali had friendly relations with Karim Khan Zand and his governor of Kirman, Mirza Husayn Khan. The latter placed several towns and districts of Kirman, such as Sirjan and Zarand, under the Ismaili Imam's rule and treated him most respectfully. Later, Sayyid Abu'l-Hasan was appointed as the *beglerbegi*, or governor, of the city of Kirman under the Zands. He continued to be popularly referred to by his title of *beglerbegi*, even after being appointed, around 1756 or a few years later, by Karim Khan Zand to the governorship of the entire province of Kirman.

Meanwhile, Imam Abu'l-Hasan had continued to receive substantial religious offerings from his followers, which enabled him to acquire further property in Kirman and also spend generously for the benefit of the people of Kirman. At any rate, the Imam was extremely popular amongst the Kirmanis, who held him in high regard. All in all, he contributed to the prosperity of Kirman. He laid out a large square next to the Friday mosque, which is still known as the Maydan-i Khwarbar. He also constructed a summer palace and a garden is Zarisuf, outside the city, which is known as Bagh-i Aqa (garden of the Aqa), and which became the place where the formal investiture of Kirman's governors was traditionally held.

The Imam's standing among the people of Kirman made it possible for him to continue to rule that region in an independent manner when the Zand dynasty disintegrated upon Karim Khan's death in 1779. Subsequently, he supported or opposed various Zand rulers, who competed with one another and soon were confronted by their greatest common enemy, Agha Muhammad Khan Qajar. In the rivalries for the succession that erupted amongst the members of the Zand family, Sayyid Abu'l-Hasan lent his valuable support to Karim Khan Zand's brother Sadiq Khan (r. 1779–1781), who was assisted by the Imam in mobilising an army in Kirman and asserting his authority in Shiraz, the Zand capital in Fars. As a token of his appreciation, Sadiq Khan formally reinstated Sayyid Abu'l-Hasan as the governor of Kirman, though the Imam did not in fact need this reinstatement.

Under the chaotic conditions of the time in many regions of Persia, which led to further Afghan invasions, Sayyid Abu'l-Hasan lost control of certain parts of Kirman, including Narmashir and the ancient citadel of Bam. The border territories between Kirman and Afghanistan, including Narmashir, were now frequently invaded by the Afghan and Baluchi forces of Aʿzam Khan, an *amir* from Qandahar. This Afghan warlord was eventually defeated in battle by an army of 7,000 men sent after him by the Ismaili Imam and led by his cousin, Mirza Sadiq, a capable military commander. However, sometime later, when Imam Abu'l-Hasan was on one of his regular visits to Shahr-i Babak, an important Ismaili centre in Kirman, Aʿzam Khan once again crossed the border and ravaged various districts of Kirman, leading his forces as far as the gates of the city. This time, the Imam personally led his forces from Shahr-i Babak and inflicted a decisive defeat on Aʿzam Khan outside the city of Kirman.

The governorship of Imam Abu'l-Hasan was more seriously challenged when Muhammad Hasan Khan Sistani, who controlled Bam, encouraged Lutf ʿAli Khan Zand (r. 1789–1794), the last effective member of the Zand dynasty, to invade Kirman. Lutf ʿAli Khan's father, Jaʿfar Khan (r. 1785–1789), was briefly ruling over a number of territories when Agha Muhammad Khan Qajar made himself master of northern Persia and established his capital in Tehran in 1786. Lutf ʿAli Khan and Agha Muhammad

44.1 The *Diwan* of Hafiz (d. *c.* 1390). This manuscript was produced in the second half of the 18th century for Imam Abu'l-Hasan ʿAli (d. 1792), the 44th Ismaili Imam.

44.2 Miniatures from the *Diwan* of Hafiz made for Imam Abu'l-Hasan ʿAli. It is likely that these are portraits of members of his family.

44.3 Portrait of Karim Khan Zand (r. 1751–1779), founder of the Zand dynasty by an unknown artist, in watercolour on paper.

Khan struggled intensely with each other for the throne of Persia, which eventually resulted in the victory of the Qajar dynasty.

It was under such unsettled circumstances that in October 1790 Lutf ʿAli Khan arrived in Kirman aiming to seize Shahr-i Babak, the Imam's main Ismaili stronghold in the province, where he had numerous followers amongst the Khurasani and ʿAta Allahi tribesmen. The Imam also had a fortress in Shahr-i Babak, which was guarded by a large number of Ismailis under the command of his cousin, Mirza Sadiq. Being informed of the difficulty of capturing Shahr-i Babak, Lutf ʿAli Khan changed his plans and instead headed for the city of Kirman. In view of the political circumstances, with Agha Muhammad Khan then rapidly extending his control over Persia, Imam Abu'l-Hasan prudently refused Lutf ʿAli Khan entry into the city. He reinforced the city's defences and made preparations to withstand a prolonged siege. However, in January 1791, due to adverse weather conditions, the Zand ruler was obliged to lift the siege and return to Shiraz.

It was in Imam Abu'l-Hasan ʿAli's time that the Niʿmat Allahi Sufi order was revived in Persia by that *tariqa*'s master, Rida ʿAli Shah (d. 1796) who, like his predecessors, resided in the Deccan, India. The Persian Niʿmat Allahi Sufis, who had been isolated for several centuries from their spiritual master (*qutb*), had persistently asked him to send them a trusted representative. Rida ʿAli Shah, who led the Niʿmat Allahis for more than half a century, eventually dispatched a disciple, Maʿsum ʿAli Shah (d. 1796), who arrived in Shiraz around 1770 and soon acquired numerous disciples including Nur ʿAli Shah (d. 1797). This disciple, and another one called Mushtaq ʿAli Shah, arrived in Mahan in 1785, to be near the shrine of the founder of their order, Shah Niʿmat Allah Wali (d. 1431). In due course, they acquired an increasing number of disciples in the city of Kirman and settled there. With these developments, relations between this Sufi order and the Ismaili Imams were also revived. Imam Abu'l-Hasan himself was among the notables of Kirman who lent their support to Nur ʿAli Shah and Mushtaq ʿAli Shah.

The widespread success of the Niʿmat Allahi Sufis in Kirman aroused the traditional animosity of the local Twelver Shiʿi *ulama* against them. However, Imam Abu'l-Hasan's support for the Sufis protected them against any intended harm. At any rate, a certain Mulla ʿAbd Allah, an influential cleric of Kirman, persisted in his anti-Sufi campaign; and he found a suitable opportunity to act when Imam Abu'l-Hasan left Kirman to restore order to Shahr-i Babak and Sirjan where tribesmen were menacing the local population. In May 1792, when Imam Abu'l-Hasan and Nur ʿAli Shah were both out of town, Mulla ʿAbd Allah, while preaching in the Friday mosque of Kirman, noticed the presence of Mushtaq ʿAli Shah who had come there to pray. In the event, Mulla ʿAbd Allah succeeded in inciting those present to stone the Niʿmat Allahi Sufi to death as an infidel. Mushtaq ʿAli Shah was buried near the same mosque and his mausoleum, known as the Mushtaqiyya, is still preserved and visited by the Persian dervishes. Imam Abu'l-Hasan ʿAli died a few months later in the same year, 1792, and was evidently buried in Mushtaq ʿAli Shah's mausoleum. His Imamate had lasted about four decades.

Imam Abu'l-Hasan ʿAli was succeeded briefly as governor of Kirman by his cousin Mirza Sadiq, who had been initiated into the Niʿmat Allahi Sufi *tariqa*. Soon after, Agha Muhammad Khan Qajar seized Shiraz and sent his nephew and future successor Fath ʿAli Khan to conquer Kirman. Fath ʿAli Khan replaced Mirza Sadiq with his own appointee. Subsequently, Lutf ʿAli Khan Zand briefly held Kirman before losing it permanently in 1794 to the Qajars. Thereupon, Agha Muhammad Khan Qajar massacred a large number of people in Kirman, but spared the Ismailis in appreciation of the fact that earlier Imam Abu'l-Hasan had denied the Zand ruler entry into Kirman. The Ismaili sayyids and their families, relatives of the Imam, who lived in Shahr-i Babak, were permitted to relocate to Kahak, where the Qajar conqueror gave them new landed properties in compensation for what they had left behind in Kirman. At the same time, a few hundred Ismaili ʿAta Allahi families of Shahr-i Babak were settled outside the city of Kirman. Indeed, Kirman remains one of the few provinces in Iran where Ismaili communities are still found to this day.

45

Shah Khalil Allah (d. 1817)

On his death in 1792, Imam Abu'l-Hasan ʿAli was succeeded in the Ismaili Imamate by his eldest son Khalil Allah ʿAli, designated also as Shah Khalil Allah, who is counted as the forty-fifth Imam in his line.

In 1794, Agha Muhammad Khan Qajar, the founder of the Qajar dynasty of Persia, seized Kirman from his rivals in the Zand dynasty. Thereupon, he proceeded to massacre a large number of the people of Kirman, which had been governed by Imam Abu'l-Hasan ʿAli for almost four decades until 1792. But he spared the region's Ismailis, and permitted the new Imam and his relatives to move to Kahak. At the same time, he gave Shah Khalil Allah new landed properties in Kahak in compensation for what had been left behind in Kirman. Shah Khalil Allah remained in Kahak until 1815.

Shah Khalil Allah maintained his father's friendly relations with the Niʿmat Allahi Sufis. He married Bibi Sarkara, the daughter of Muhammad Sadiq Mahallati (d. 1815), who bore the next Imam, Aga Khan I, in 1804 in Kahak. Muhammad Sadiq Mahallati, a brother of the previous Imam, Abu'l-Hasan, was himself a Niʿmat Allahi and carried the Sufi name of Sidq ʿAli Shah. Muhammad Sadiq Mahallati's son, ʿIzzat ʿAli Shah, was another prominent Niʿmat Allahi dervish. This maternal uncle of Aga Khan I developed close relations with Zayn al-ʿAbidin Shirvani (d. 1837), who carried the Sufi name of Mast ʿAli Shah and would become the master (*qutb*) of one of the main branches of the Niʿmat Allahi *tariqa*. ʿIzzat ʿAli Shah spent the greater part of his life in Mahallat, which was then enjoying the patronage of the Ismaili Imams, and died there

45.1 A view of the city of Yazd, showing the monumental portal and dome of the Friday Mosque.

around 1829. Imam Shah Khalil Allah himself carried a Niʿmat Allahi Sufi name, but he did not apparently have any active interest in Sufism (*tasawwuf*). Jean Baptiste Rousseau (1780–1831), the French consul-general in Syria who visited Persia during 1807–1808, is the earliest European to gather some information on the contemporary Persian Ismailis as well as on their Imam, Shah Khalil Allah, and his place of residence in Kahak.

In 1815, Imam Shah Khalil Allah transferred his residence from Kahak to Yazd, an ancient city situated between Isfahan and Kirman on the route to Baluchistan and Sind. This decision was evidently motivated by the Imam's desire to be yet closer to his Khoja *murid*s who continued to embark on the dangerous journey to see their Imam in Persia. It was at Yazd that two years later, in 1817, the Ismaili Imam was targeted by the local Ithnaʿashari authorities and tragically lost his life in the course of a dispute between some of his *murid*s and the local shopkeepers in the bazaar. The Ismailis involved in this melee sought refuge in the Imam's residence and refused to emerge. A certain Mulla Husayn Yazdi, who was resentful of the spreading influence of the Ismailis in Yazd, now collected a mob and attacked the Imam's house. In the ensuing confrontation, Shah Khalil Allah and several of his *murid*s, including a Khoja, were murdered and the Imam's house was looted.

The reigning Qajar monarch, Fath ʿAli Shah (1797–1834), who had good relations with Shah Khalil Allah, ordered the governor of Yazd to arrest Mulla Husayn and send him and his accomplices to Tehran for punishment. The Twelver Mulla was punished physically, after a fashion, but no one was executed for the murders. Shah Khalil Allah, whose Imamate lasted twenty-five years, was taken for burial to the holy city of Najaf in Iraq, where a mausoleum was constructed for him and some of his relatives in the enclosure of Imam ʿAli's shrine.

Part Nine

The Imams in the Modern Age

Birjand ●

● Sarbisha

Naybandan ●

Khurasan

● Maybud

● Mihriz

Kubanan ●

● Kalmand

● Ravar

Zarand ●

Dasht-i Lut

● Kirman

Shahr-i Babak ● ● Rumani

Mashiz ●

● Mahan

Zaydabad ●

● Qaryat al-'Arab

● Sirjan

Kirman

Zahidan ●

● Bizinjan

● Bam

● Sayyid 'Ali Musa

● Narmashir

Dashtab ●

● Isfandaqa

PERSIA

● Sawghan

Area of
map detail

Shamil Pass ●

Bagh-i Nargis ●

● Rudan

● Bandar 'Abbas

PERSIAN
GULF

50   100   150   200
kilometres

Central and southern Persia

46

Hasan ʿAli Shah, Aga Khan I (d. 1881)

In 1817, Shah Khalil Allah was succeeded in the Ismaili Imamate by his eldest son Hasan ʿAli Shah, also known as Muhammad Hasan al-Husayni. Counted as the forty-sixth Imam, Hasan ʿAli Shah, who later acquired the title of Agha Khan, had a long and very eventful Imamate.

Born in Kahak in 1804, Hasan ʿAli Shah was thirteen years old at the time of his accession, in the aftermath of his father's murder in 1817 at Yazd. At the time, Hasan ʿAli Shah lived in Kahak with his mother, Bibi Sarkara (d. 1851). Soon after, Bibi Sarkara went to the Qajar court in Tehran seeking justice for her murdered husband. Eventually, the instigators of Imam Shah Khalil Allah's murder were punished after a fashion, and the reigning Qajar monarch, Fath ʿAli Shah (r. 1797–1834), added to the Imam's landholdings in the Mahallat area; he also gave one of his daughters, Sarv-i Jahan Khanum, in marriage to the youthful Imam. At the same time, Fath ʿAli Shah appointed the Ismaili Imam to the governorship of Qum and bestowed upon him the honorific title (*laqab*) of Agha Khan, meaning lord and master. Henceforth, Hasan ʿAli Shah became more generally known as Agha Khan Mahallati, because of his royal title and his family's deep roots in the Mahallat region, in central Persia. The title of Agha Khan has remained hereditary among Imam Hasan ʿAli Shah's successors to the Ismaili Imamate; the title was later simplified in Europe to Aga Khan.

Imam Hasan ʿAli Shah, Aga Khan I, led a tranquil life and enjoyed honour at the Qajar court until the death of Fath ʿAli Shah in 1834. In 1835, soon after his accession,

46.1 Portrait of Fath ʿAli Shah Qajar (r. 1797–1834), in watercolour on paper, painted in 1815 by the Persian artist Mihr ʿAli.

Fath ʿAli Shah's grandson and successor Muhammad Shah Qajar (r. 1834–1848) appointed the Ismaili Imam as governor of the province of Kirman, a post previously held by the Imam's grandfather, Abu'l-Hasan ʿAli (d. 1792). At the time, Kirman was in the hands of certain rebellious pretenders to the Qajar throne in addition to being constantly raided by Afghan and Baluchi bands. It was under such circumstances that Aga Khan I was quickly successful in restoring law and order to that province without receiving any financial support from the Qajar treasury. In pacifying Kirman, Aga Khan I received valuable help from the local Khurasani and ʿAta Allahi tribesmen who were among his Ismaili followers there.

Despite his services, and much to his surprise, Aga Khan I was abruptly dismissed from his governorship in 1837, less than two years after his arrival in Kirman. He was replaced by Firuz Mirza, one of Muhammad Shah Qajar's brothers. However, the Aga Khan refused to acknowledge his dismissal and withdrew with some of his forces to the citadel of the ancient city of Bam, in the province of Kirman, where he was besieged for fourteen months by government forces dispatched against him. The Aga Khan was eventually obliged to surrender and emerge from Bam. Subsequently, he spent some months in captivity in the city of Kirman. Towards the end of 1838, when Muhammad Shah had returned from his unsuccessful campaign against Herat, in Afghanistan, the Aga Khan was finally allowed to proceed to Tehran. In the aftermath of these events, the Ismaili Imam retreated to Mahallat, where he constructed a fortified residential compound for his family and numerous dependents.

Imam Hasan ʿAli Shah produced an autobiography, entitled *ʿIbrat-afza*, relating the events of his youth, his extended dealings with the Qajar regime in Persia and his eventual settlement in India. First lithographed in 1862 in Bombay, and reprinted several times in Tehran, the *ʿIbrat-afza* was critically edited and translated into English and published by The Institute of Ismaili Studies in London in 2018. This is a uniquely important primary source on the life and early career of Aga Khan I, also shedding valuable light on contemporary power politics at the Qajar court of Persia, with its strong Sufi inclinations, as well as the evolving relations between Aga Khan I and the British establishment in India.

Modern scholarship has not succeeded in identifying with any degree of certainty the root causes and intentions driving the confrontations between this Ismaili Imam and the Qajar establishment in Persia, which also coincided with the opening phase of the Anglo-Russian hegemonial rivalries in the region. The Aga Khan's dismissal from the governorship of Kirman was probably instigated also by complex rivalries for the leadership of the Niʿmat Allahi Sufi *tariqa* or order in Persia. The Ismaili Imam himself

46.2 A photograph of Aga Khan I, taken in Persia.

46.3 The walls of the residential compound of Aga Khan I in Mahallat.

46.4 Ivory handle of a dagger originally owned by Aga Khan I.

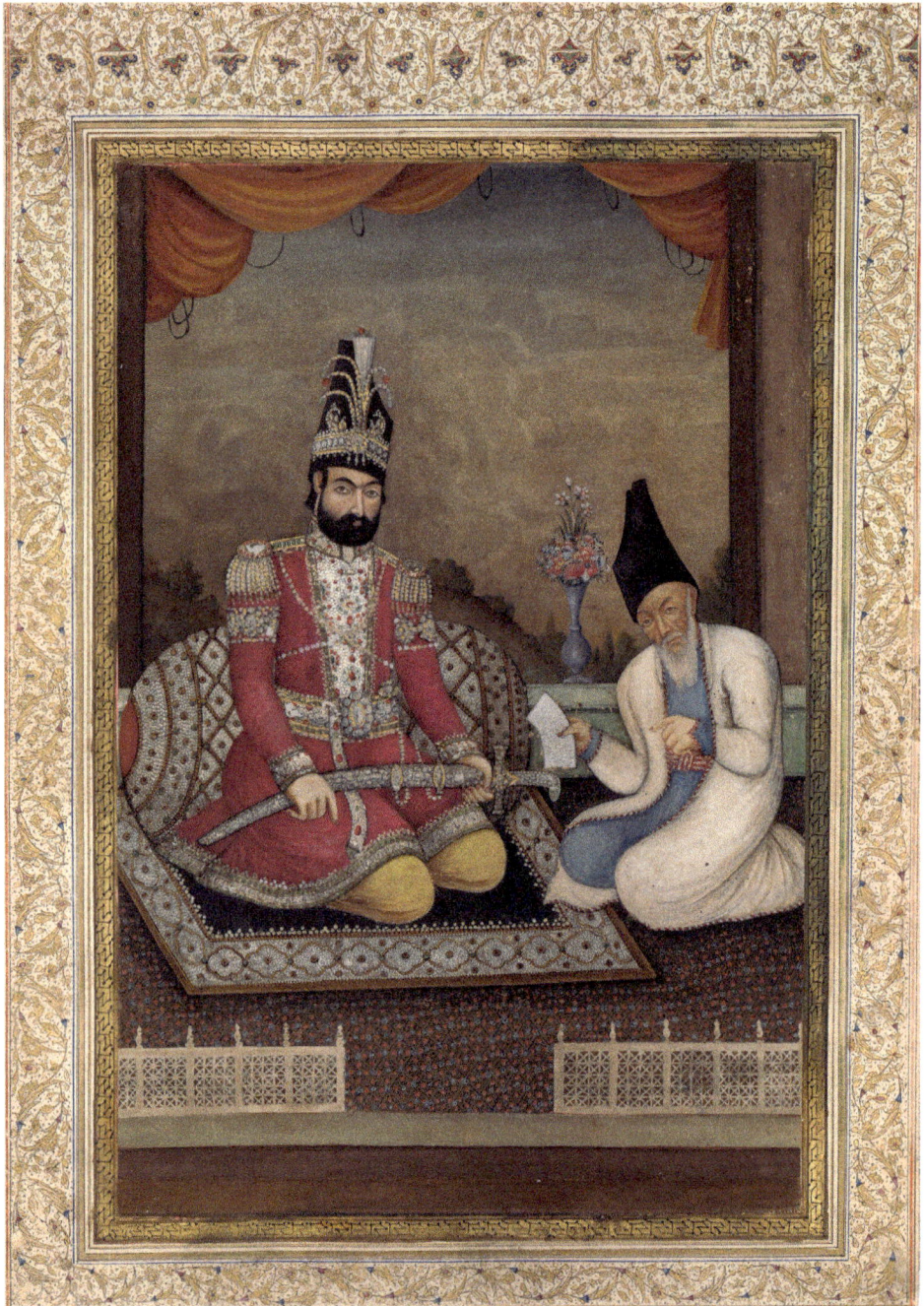

46.5 Portrait of Muhammad Shah Qajar (r. 1834–1848) and his vizier, Hajji Mirza Aqasi, painted in the 1840s.

46.6 The citadel of Bam in Kirman, photographed in the 1980s.

46.7 Aga Khan I, photographed by the Studio of Bourne and Shepherd, in India.

as well as his maternal family had close ties with this order, which witnessed incessant internal factionalism after the death in 1823 of Majdhub ʿAli Shah, the thirty-eighth master (*qutb*) of the order. The majority of the Niʿmat Allahi Sufis had recognised Zayn al-ʿAbidin Shirvani, better known by his Sufi name of Mast ʿAli Shah, as Majdhub's successor. The Ismaili Imam, too, lent his support to Mast ʿAli Shah, who earlier had enjoyed the Aga Khan's protection and hospitality at Mahallat for quite some time.

Muhammad Shah Qajar himself had Sufi inclinations. He had been initiated into the Niʿmat Allahi order, evidently by Mast ʿAli Shah, who later joined the entourage of the Qajar monarch in Tehran. However, Mast ʿAli Shah soon confronted a powerful adversary in the person of the grand vizier, Hajji Mirza Aqasi, who as a Niʿmat Allahi Sufi himself aspired to the leadership of the order. Muhammad Shah soon came under the influence of his grand vizier, who exercised absolute control over the affairs of the Persian state throughout this monarch's reign. In fact, the Qajar monarch also recognised his grand vizier as the master of the Niʿmat Allahi order, and dismissed Mast ʿAli Shah from his court. It was under such circumstances that the Aga Khan, who had continued to support the claims of Mast ʿAli Shah, aroused the enmity of the all-powerful grand vizier, who persistently intrigued against the Imam and eventually caused his dismissal from the governorship of Kirman. Nonetheless, Aga Khan I never relinquished his support for Mast ʿAli Shah, and after the latter's death in 1837 acknowledged his son Rahmat ʿAli Shah (d. 1861) as the new master of that Niʿmat Allahi branch.

In 1840, under obscure circumstances, further military confrontations took place between Aga Khan I's forces and Qajar armies in Yazd and Kirman. In these confrontations the Ismaili Imam continued to draw on the traditional support of the Khurasani and ʿAta Allahi tribesmen who were among his Persian followers. The Aga Khan himself or his younger brother, Sardar Abu'l-Hasan Khan, led the Imam's forces in a number of battles against the Qajar military. In 1841, a Qajar force of some 24,000 men inflicted a decisive defeat on the Aga Khan's much smaller army at a place on the border with Baluchistan. Thereupon, the Imam crossed the border and entered Afghanistan. He was accompanied by his brothers, other family members, many soldiers and a large retinue of servants, numbering several hundreds. This marked the end of the Persian phase of the Ismaili Imamate, which had lasted some seven centuries since the early Alamut times.

Once inside Afghanistan in 1841, Aga Khan I advanced to Qandahar, the major city in western Afghanistan, which had been occupied by an Anglo-Indian army since 1839. Henceforth, a close association developed between Aga Khan I and the British Raj, which in due course proved beneficial to the Imam's Khoja *murid*s in British India. Aspects of this association are related in the *ʿIbrat-afza* and in a variety of British

46.8 Aga Khan I, photographed by Vernon's Studios, Bombay.

46.9 Metal seal of Muhammad Hasan al-Husayni, Aga Khan I, shown mirrored.

archival documents. Subsequently, the Imam headed for Sind and established friendly relations with General Sir Charles Napier (1782–1853), the British conqueror of Sind, and provided some assistance to him. At the time, the Ismaili Imam was hoping that the British would arrange for his safe return to Persia, which remained a priority for him throughout the 1840s.

In 1845, Aga Khan I arrived in Gujarat and spent a year in Kathiawar and other towns there. These represented the first contacts between an Ismaili Imam and his communities of Khoja followers in India. In 1846, when the Imam had arrived in Bombay, the Persian government, which was still controlled by his nemesis, the grand vizier Hajji Mirza Aqasi, demanded his extradition, citing the Anglo-Persian treaty of 1814. However, the British refused to comply and only transferred the Imam's residence to Calcutta in 1847, which was farther removed from Persia. On the death of Muhammad Shah Qajar in 1848, the Aga Khan returned to Bombay and the British made one final round of renewed efforts to arrange his safe return to his homeland. All these efforts proved futile, however, and the Imam finally decided to remain in Bombay.

The modern period in the history of the Ismailis was initiated by Aga Khan I's permanent settlement in Bombay in 1848. The Imam now had more immediate reasons for retaining his close ties with the British, as substantiated by subsequent events. Most obviously he needed the support of the British Raj in establishing the seat of his Imamate in Bombay and overseeing the affairs of the substantial community of his Khoja followers in South Asia and East Africa, who were then loyal subjects of the British empire. Indeed, the Khojas had for several centuries comprised one of the most important segments of the Ismaili community. As the spiritual leader of a major Shiʿi Muslim community, Aga Khan I appreciated the protection of the British establishment in India, which strengthened his position and helped him to exercise his authority. He also received help from the British when his leadership was called into question by certain dissident members of the Khoja community. The so-called Aga Khan Case of 1866, brought before the Bombay High Court, put an end to all such challenges as the Aga Khan was formally recognised as the spiritual head of the Ismailis, with full control over all communal properties. At the same time, the distinctive religious identity of the Khojas was articulated by the Imam as 'Shia Imami Ismailis' and not as Sunnis as claimed by the dissidents, also establishing the status of Aga Khan I as the *murshid* or spiritual head of that community and heir in lineal descent to the Ismaili Imams of the Alamut period.

Aga Khan I was the first Imam of his line to set foot in India and he was most enthusiastically received by his Khoja followers there who regularly flocked to his side to pay their homage to him and receive his blessings. The Ismaili Imam now established

46.10 Mausoleum of Aga Khan I, in Hasanabad, Bombay.

elaborate headquarters and residences in Bombay, Poona and Bangalore. He attended the *jamat-khana* in Bombay on special religious occasions, also holding *durbar*s and giving audience to his followers who received his blessings. Retaining the traditional communal organisation of the Khojas, he personally appointed the *mukhi*s and *kamadia*s, the chief officers of the major Khoja *jamat*s or congregations.

Aga Khan I spent his final decades peacefully in Bombay, with seasonal stays in Poona. He maintained elaborate stables and was often seen at the Bombay racecourse. Aga Khan I's interests in horse racing and horse breeding were retained and developed much further in Europe by his successors. Hasan 'Ali Shah, Aga Khan I, the forty-sixth Ismaili Imam died, after an eventful Imamate of sixty-four years, in April 1881 (Jumada 1298 AH). He was buried in a domed mausoleum at Hasanabad in the Mazagaon district of Bombay.

47

Agha ʿAli Shah, Aga Khan II (d. 1885)

Hasan ʿAli Shah, Aga Khan I, was succeeded on his death in 1881 by his eldest son, Agha ʿAli Shah, who was his sole son by his Qajar spouse, Sarv-i Jahan Khanum (d. 1882). Agha ʿAli Shah, the forty-seventh Ismaili Imam who became known as Aga Khan II, was thus also a grandson of the Qajar monarch Fath ʿAli Shah (r. 1797–1834).

Agha ʿAli Shah was born in 1830 at Mahallat, in central Persia, where the family owned extensive properties. In 1840, at the time of Aga Khan I's final military confrontations with the Qajar establishment, the young Agha ʿAli Shah was taken together with his mother to the shrine cities of Najaf and Karbala in Iraq, where he stayed a few years and studied Arabic, Persian and Ismaili doctrines. Later, Agha ʿAli Shah returned to Persia and assumed some responsibilities there on behalf of his father. Agha ʿAli Shah and his mother eventually joined the Imam in Bombay in 1853. Thenceforth, Agha ʿAli Shah regularly visited different Khoja communities, especially in Sind and Gujarat, and dealt with their affairs. He stayed for some time in Karachi, where his future successor, Sultan Muhammad Shah, was born in 1877. Sultan Muhammad Shah's mother, Shams al-Muluk, was herself a granddaughter of Fath ʿAli Shah Qajar.

On succeeding to the Ismaili Imamate, Agha ʿAli Shah, Aga Khan II, maintained his father's friendly relations with the British, and was appointed to the Bombay Legislative Council when Sir James Fergusson (1832–1907) was the governor of Bombay. Aga Khan II had a special concern for the educational and welfare standards of the Khojas and established a number of schools for their children in Bombay and elsewhere in

47.1 Agha ʿAli Shah (right) with his father Aga Khan I (left).

47.2 Aga Khan II.

India. During his brief Imamate, Aga Khan II also increased his contacts with Ismaili communities outside India, showing a special interest in those situated in Central Asia, Burma and East Africa.

Aga Khan II was held in high regard by the Muslim population of India. He was elected president of a body called the Muhammadan National Association, and in that capacity promoted educational and philanthropic projects for the benefit of all Indian Muslims. Like his father, Aga Khan II was also closely associated with the Ni'mat Allahi Sufi *tariqa* or order. He cultivated close ties with both Rahmat Ali Shah (d. 1861), the master (*qutb*) of one of the main branches of the order, and the latter's successor, Munawwar 'Ali Shah (d. 1884), among other prominent Ni'mat Allahis.

Sultan Muhammad Shah was Aga Khan II's sole surviving son by his Qajar spouse. Both of Aga Khan II's sons by other marriages predeceased him. His eldest son, Shihab al-Din Shah, born around 1851, devoted himself to learning and composed a few treatises in Persian dealing with Ismaili doctrines; he died in 1884. Agha 'Ali Shah, Aga Khan II, was also an accomplished sportsman and hunter, particularly renowned for his tiger hunting, then a popular sport in India. He died, after an Imamate of only four years, in August 1885 (Dhu'l-Qa'da 1302 AH), and was later buried in the family mausoleum in Najaf.

48

Sultan Muhammad Shah, Aga Khan III (d. 1957)

Agha 'Ali Shah was succeeded on his death in 1885 by his sole surviving son, Sultan Muhammad (Mahomed) Shah, whose life is well documented in addition to his autobiography entitled *The Memoirs of Aga Khan: World Enough and Time*, published in 1954. Born in Karachi in 1877, he was eight years old when installed to the Ismaili Imamate in Bombay as the forty-eighth Imam. His nominal guardian was his paternal uncle, Agha Jangi Shah (d. 1896), but Sultan Muhammad Shah, better known internationally as Aga Khan III, grew up under the close supervision of his mother, Shams al-Muluk (d. 1938), a granddaughter of Fath 'Ali Shah Qajar (r. 1797–1834) who was known as Lady 'Ali Shah in the social circles of British India. Thus, both of his parents were grandchildren of that Qajar monarch of Persia.

Until the age of eighteen, as recounted in his autobiography, Aga Khan III received a rigorous education in Bombay and Poona in Arabic, Persian literature and calligraphy, as well as Ismaili doctrines. In 1898, he travelled from Bombay to Europe, which later became his chief place of residence. Aga Khan III maintained close relations with the British throughout his life. This relationship brought immense benefits to his followers in South Asia and East Africa, where they lived under British imperial rule. On his second visit to Europe, in 1900, the Aga Khan met the contemporary Qajar monarch, Muzaffar al-Din Shah (r. 1896–1907), in Paris. By then, the old animosities between the Ismaili Imams and the Qajar regime of Persia had been long forgotten.

In 1902, as a sign of the esteem in which he was held by the British, Aga Khan III was appointed by Lord Curzon, the viceroy of India, to a seat on his Legislative Council. He served in that capacity for two years in Calcutta, then the seat of British rule in India. The Ismaili Imam visited Europe again in 1904, and saw his followers in East Africa in 1905 for the second time, following his first visit there in 1898. From 1907 onwards, he visited Europe regularly every year and eventually established residences there.

In the meantime, the Ismaili Imam increasingly concerned himself with the affairs of the Muslims of India, beyond the boundaries of his own Ismaili community of followers there. As a result, he gained increasing popularity amongst the Indian Muslims and their representatives. Under such circumstances, he participated actively in the first All-India Muslim Educational Conference, held in Bombay in 1903, and served as the president of the second one, held in Delhi in 1904. In 1906, he headed the Muslim delegation that met Lord Minto at Simla, asking the viceroy to consider the Indian Muslims not as a minority religious group but as a nation within a nation whose members deserved adequate representation on the local as well as the legislative councils of India. Later in 1907, the Aga Khan played a role in the foundation of the All-India Muslim League, and served as its permanent president until he resigned from that post in 1912.

Throughout his life Aga Khan III campaigned most vigorously for the educational enhancement of his Khoja followers as well as that of other Muslims in India and elsewhere. He played a crucial role in the elevation of the Muhammadan Anglo-Oriental College at Aligarh to university status, which was finally achieved in 1912. In the same year, King George V, who was then visiting India for his coronation *durbar*, bestowed upon the Ismaili Imam the highest decoration that could be given to any Indian subject of the British empire, making him a Knight Commander of the Star of India (GCSI). During World War I, the Ismaili Imam resided in Switzerland, during which time he wrote a book entitled *India in Transition*, published in 1918, in which he expounded his ideas on the future of India.

For a decade after the end of World War I, the Aga Khan refrained from any international and Indian political activities, devoting himself exclusively to running the affairs of his Ismaili community. But in 1928, he presided over the All-India Muslim Conference held in Delhi, which put forth ideas on how independence should evolve in India. It was under the Ismaili Imam's leadership that this assembly demanded guaranteed rights for Indian Muslims within the framework of a self-governing federal India. In 1930, he led the Muslim delegation to the first Round Table Conference convened in London to discuss the future of India; Muhammad Ali Jinnah, the founder of the state of Pakistan, was one of the other members of this delegation. The Ismaili

48.1 Aga Khan III, in 1902.

48.2 A commemorative sticker celebrating the Diamond Jubilee of Aga Khan III, issued in India in 1945.

Imam also attended the second Round Table Conference, held in 1931 in London, and on this occasion had discussions with Mahatma Gandhi, the sole representative of the Congress Party of India. These conferences, lasting until 1934, marked the apex of the Aga Khan's participation in Indian politics. Meanwhile, he had served as India's delegate at successive sessions of the Assembly of the League of Nations in Geneva. Aga Khan III's involvement in international affairs culminated in his election, in 1937, as president of the League of Nations for a session.

In 1935, the Ismailis celebrated the Golden Jubilee of their Imam in Bombay and Nairobi. By then, Aga Khan III had been their Imam for half a century. The Diamond Jubilee of the Aga Khan's Imamate was celebrated, with a year's delay, in Bombay in 1946. A few months later, celebrations were also held in Dar es Salaam. The Platinum Jubilee celebrations, commemorating the seventieth anniversary of Aga Khan III's accession to the Imamate, were held during 1954–1955 in Karachi and Cairo. These jubilee celebrations and the voluntary offerings of his followers on these occasions, reflected the deep devotion of the Ismailis to their Imam. These offerings were in due course spent on projects that benefited the Ismailis and other Muslims.

In the course of his long Imamate, Aga Khan III devoted much of his time and resources to consolidating and organising the Ismaili community, especially in South

48.3 Aga Khan III, in 1953.

Asia and East Africa, where his followers are known as Khojas. He was particularly concerned with introducing socio-economic reforms that would transform his followers into a modern community with high standards of education, health and well-being. The implementation of his reforms, however, required suitable institutions and administrative organisations. The development of a new communal organisation thus became one of the Imam's major tasks.

In 1905, Aga Khan III issued a set of written rules and regulations which, in fact, represented the first constitution for the Ismaili community in East Africa. This constitution, and those issued later for other regions, also represented the personal law of the community, dealing with matters such as inheritance, marriage, divorce and so on. The constitution of 1905, initiating the Aga Khan's institutional and modernisation policies, also foresaw a new administrative organisation in the form of a hierarchy of national and local councils for the Ismailis of East Africa. Subsequently, similar constitutions, with council systems of administration and their affiliated bodies, were developed for the Ismailis of India and Pakistan.

All of the Ismaili constitutions revolved around the person of the Aga Khan as the Imam of the time, who acted as the religious and administrative head of the Ismaili community. He remained in contact with the Ismailis of different countries and guided them frequently through his *farmans* – written directives read out in the local *jamat-khanas*. Serving as another communal mechanism for introducing reforms, the *farmans* of Aga Khan III guided the Ismailis in specific directions. This Imam's modernisation policies may indeed be traced through his *farmans* and speeches on spiritual matters, education, social welfare and female emancipation, and on matters related to religious tolerance, personal conduct and so on. In particular, the education of Ismailis, both male and female, at different levels, as well as the participation of women in communal affairs, were given high priority in the Imam's reforms.

Meanwhile, Aga Khan III had concerned himself with defining and delineating the distinctive religious identity of his Ismaili followers, so as to distinguish them from the Twelver Shi'is and other religious groups, which over the centuries had served as external guises to protect the Ismailis from persecution. At the same time, he instructed his followers not to criticise other religious traditions. Aga Khan III used the religious dues and other voluntary offerings submitted to him, and the funds collected at various jubilee celebrations, to finance his modernisation policies, and create a variety of institutions with benefits accruing to the Ismailis and others. He founded and maintained a large network of schools, vocational institutions, sports and recreational clubs, dispensaries and hospitals in East Africa, the Indo-Pakistan subcontinent and

48.4 Mausoleum of Aga Khan III in Aswan, Egypt.

elsewhere. Aga Khan III was deeply concerned with alleviating poverty and helping the socially disadvantaged indigenous Muslims of East Africa. To address their needs, he founded the East African Muslim Welfare Society in the 1940s. By 1957, this institution had constructed many schools, clinics and mosques in East Africa, resulting mainly from the generosity of the Ismaili Imam.

Sir Sultan Muhammad Shah, Aga Khan III, the forty-eighth Ismaili Imam, was at the same time a successful Muslim reformer, responding to the challenges of a rapidly changing world. He made it possible for his followers, scattered in many different countries, to live in the twentieth century as a progressive community with a distinct religious identity. Aga Khan III died in his villa near Geneva on 11 July 1957, and was later buried in a permanent mausoleum at Aswan, overlooking the Nile in Egypt, the seat of his ancestors, the Fatimid Imam-caliphs. He had led the Ismailis for seventy-two years, perhaps longer than any of his predecessors. Aga Khan III was survived by two sons, Prince Aly Khan (1911–1960) and Prince Sadruddin (1933–2003), but he had designated his grandson Karim, as his successor to the Ismaili Imamate.

49

Shah Karim al-Husayni, Aga Khan IV

Sir Sultan Muhammad Shah, Aga Khan III, the forty-eighth Ismaili Imam died on 11 July 1957, in his villa near Geneva. In accordance with his last will and testament, made in 1955, Aga Khan III's grandson Prince Karim succeeded to the Imamate as the forty-ninth and present Imam, designated by his followers as Mawlana Hazar Imam. Prince Karim was the elder of the two sons of Aga Khan III's eldest son, Prince Aly Khan. Aga Khan III had explained in his last will that due to the changing circumstances of the world, it would be in the best interests of the Ismaili community for their next Imam to be a young man brought up and educated in the modern world. Consequently, he designated his grandson as his successor, in preference to either of his own sons, Prince Aly Khan (1911–1960) and Prince Sadruddin (1933–2003).

It was during the first year of Shah Karim al-Husayni, Aga Khan IV's Imamate that Queen Elizabeth II bestowed on him the title of 'His Highness', in recognition of his spiritual status. Thereafter, he has been generally designated in the Western world as His Highness Prince Karim Aga Khan. He was immediately recognised, on 11 July 1957, in Switzerland as the new Ismaili Imam, in the presence of the representatives of the Ismailis of Asia and Africa. In due course, all the Ismaili communities offered their *bay'a* or allegiance to their new twenty-year-old Imam. His father, Prince Aly Khan, who later represented Pakistan at the United Nations, lost his life in a car accident in 1960, and in 1972 he was interred in a permanent mausoleum at Salamiyya in Syria. Aga Khan IV's mother was the Hon. Joan Yarde-Buller (1908–1997), a daughter of Lord Churston.

Born on 13 December 1936 in Geneva, Aga Khan IV is the eldest son of Prince Aly Khan, whose younger son, Prince Amyn, was born in 1937. Prince Karim spent his early years in Nairobi, Kenya, before attending Le Rosey, the renowned boarding school in Switzerland, for nine years. Subsequently, he entered Harvard University, where he studied Islamic history. Upon his accession to the Imamate, the present Imam interrupted his undergraduate studies at Harvard for one year in order to visit the various Ismaili communities, during which time he was formally installed to the Imamate in a number of enthronement (*takht-nishini*) ceremonies held in Dar es Salaam, Nairobi, Kampala, Karachi and Bombay. He completed his final year of studies at Harvard during 1958–1959, receiving a Bachelor's degree in Islamic History.

The present Imam has very closely concerned himself with the affairs of the global Ismaili community that is spread throughout thirty countries around the world. Furthermore, as a major Muslim leader fully cognisant of the challenges and issues facing contemporary Muslims, he has devoted a good share of his time and resources to promoting a better understanding of Islam, not only as a religion with a set of theological doctrines but as a major world civilisation – or even a conglomerate of civilisations with their multiplicity of expressions and interpretations. To achieve these objectives Aga Khan IV has developed a multitude of initiatives, programmes and institutions of his own. By 2017, coinciding with the Diamond Jubilee or 60th anniversary of his accession to the Imamate, Aga Khan IV had indeed established impressive records of achievement in both these domains of his activities.

The present Imam has closely guided the spiritual and secular affairs of his community. He regularly visits the Ismailis in different countries of Asia, the Middle East, Africa, Europe and North America, and guides his followers also through his *farman*s or edicts. He has maintained and further developed the elaborate council system of communal administration initiated by his grandfather, extending it to several additional countries in Asia and the Middle East, such as Iran, Afghanistan, Tajikistan, Syria and the United Arab Emirates, as well as new territories in Europe, such as France and Portugal, and to the United States and Canada, in recognition of the large-scale immigration of the Ismailis from East Africa and South Asia to the West since the 1970s. The largest communities of such Ismaili expatriates are now located in Toronto, Vancouver, Moscow, London, Atlanta, Houston and a few other American cities.

The forty-eighth Imam, Sultan Muhammad Shah, issued separate constitutions for his Ismaili Khoja followers in India, Pakistan and East Africa, the last one appearing in 1954. The present Imam issued his first new constitution in 1962 for the Ismailis of East Africa, which remained valid for twenty-five years. According to this constitution, the administrative hierarchy of the region was headed, after the Imam, by a Supreme Council for Africa, an international body that directed and coordinated the activities of three Territorial Councils. The Supreme Council, with its rotating headquarters in Nairobi and other major cities of East Africa, was also empowered to function as a judicial tribunal of the second degree, following the Imam himself who represented the highest judicial authority. Under the Supreme Council, there were the three Territorial Councils in the states of Tanzania, Kenya and Uganda, with their headquarters at Dar es Salaam, Nairobi and Kampala, respectively. In each of the three East African states, there were a number of Provincial Councils charged with managing the affairs of the various districts and local *jamat*s (Arabic, *jama'a*) under their jurisdiction. A number of auxiliary bodies, such as welfare societies and women's associations, operated under the supervision of the Provincial Councils. The constitution of 1962 was much more concerned than its predecessors with matters related to marriage, divorce, guardianship, apostasy and marriage with non-Ismailis. The office holders in the council system, comprised mainly of professional individuals, did not receive any salaries.

In the meantime, the Ismaili community had retained its traditional organisational pattern in terms of local *jamat*s, each one having a *jamat-khana* where religious and social ceremonies were performed. At the *jamat* level, communal affairs have remained under the jurisdiction of a *mukhi* and a *kamadia* (pronounced *kamariya*). These functionaries officiate on various occasions, such as marriage ceremonies, funeral rites and communal prayers. They also collect the voluntary offerings to the Imam of the time.

Religious matters of general interest to the community, including especially the religious education of the Ismailis at primary and secondary levels, are the responsibility of an Ismaili Tariqah and Religious Education Board (ITREB), formerly known as the Ismailia Association, established in some twenty regions. These bodies are also responsible for the publication and distribution of literature of interest to the Ismailis, including the Imam's *farman*s and speeches. The Ismailis do not undertake any proselytising activities. There are, however, religious functionaries active within most Ismaili communities; usually called religious teachers (*mu'allim*s) and preachers (*waezeen*), they perform the vital function of instructing the Ismailis themselves in their faith and heritage. In due course, council systems with affiliated central and subordinate bodies, similar to those in East Africa, were developed for the Ismaili communities of India, Pakistan and a number of other regions.

In 1986, a new chapter was initiated in the constitutional history of the Ismailis, when the present Imam promulgated a universal document, entitled 'The Constitution of the Shia Imami Ismaili Muslims', for all his followers throughout the world. The

49.1 His Highness Prince Karim al-Husayni, Aga Khan IV, on the occasion of his accession to the Imamate, during his *takht-nishini* in Dar es Salaam, Tanzania, 1957.

49.2 Aga Khan IV, addressing members of the Ismaili community in the Bartang valley, Badakhshan, during his visit to Tajikistan in 1998.

preamble of the new constitution affirms all the fundamental Islamic beliefs and then goes on to focus on the doctrine of the Imamate, which is upheld by the Ismailis, like other Shiʿi Muslims. It also emphasises the Imam's *taʿlim*, or teaching, which guides his followers along the path (*tariqa*) of spiritual enlightenment and improved material life. This constitution was amended somewhat in 1998, but the preamble remained unchanged. Indeed, the present Imam has continuously emphasised both the *din* (religion) and the *dunya* (worldly affairs) aspects of human existence as being complementary dimensions in the well-balanced life of a Muslim.

Under the 1986 constitution, and its amendment, the council system has been established in some twenty territories. In each of these territories, a National Council directs and supervises the affairs of a network of Regional and Local Councils. At the discretion of the Imam, the jurisdiction of each National Council may be extended to regions or countries where the Ismaili communities do not yet have their own council system. The constitution of 1986 also envisages a number of additional organisations for the Ismaili territories that have National Councils. Each of these territories possesses an Ismaili Tariqah and Religious Education Board (ITREB), responsible for the provision of religious education at all levels of the community, and for research and publication of materials on various aspects of Islam and Ismaili Shiʿism. These boards are also responsible for the distribution of the primary and secondary school curricula, which are developed and published in ten languages by The Institute of Ismaili Studies in London for Ismaili pupils and students throughout the world. Since 2010, the Institute has also been responsible for designing and implementing a two-year programme for the professional training of secondary school teachers, known as the STEP Programme, in collaboration with the Institute of Education of University College London.

Furthermore, the most recent global constitution has established Grants and Review Boards in the Ismaili territories to ensure the attainment of proper standards of financial discipline and accountability by a number of institutions, such as the National Councils, the Ismaili Tariqah and Religious Boards and other central bodies which receive financial support from the Imam or the Ismaili communities. Finally, on the basis of the constitution of 1986, a number of National Conciliation and Arbitration Boards have been set up in those territories where there are National Councils. These bodies act as judicial tribunals between parties on disputes arising from commercial and other civil liability matters as well as domestic and family issues. In all matters, the utmost efforts are made to settle the disputes amicably. An International Conciliation and Arbitration Board, under the person of the Imam, acts as a judicial tribunal of the first degree, for

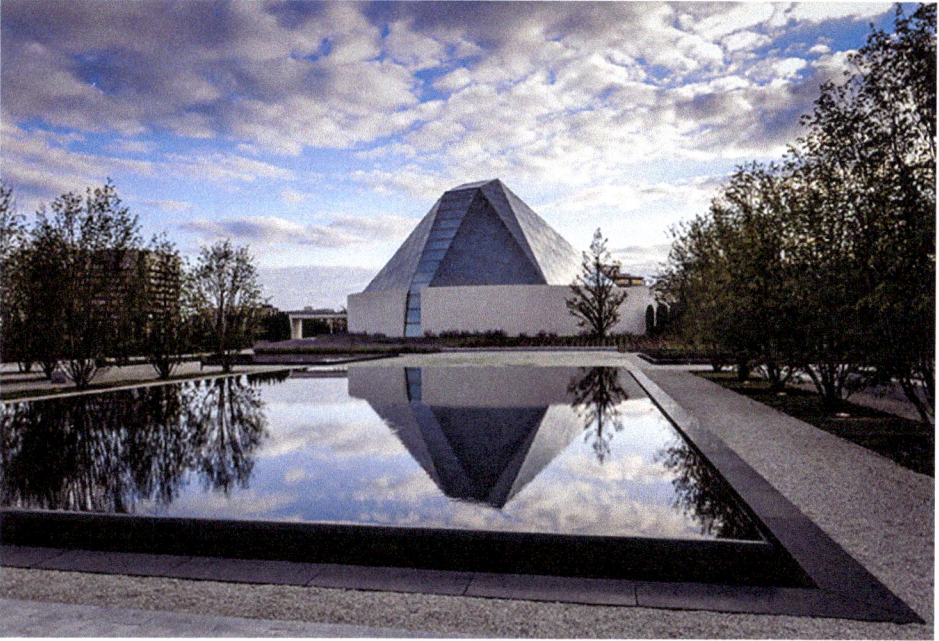

49.3 The Ismaili Centre, Toronto, Canada, designed by the renowned Indian architect Charles Correa, was inaugurated in 2014.

49.4 The Aga Khan Museum, Toronto, Canada, designed by Fumihiko Maki, was inaugurated in 2014. In front of it stands the sculpture 'Heech' (Persian, Nothing) by the Iranian artist Parviz Tanavoli.

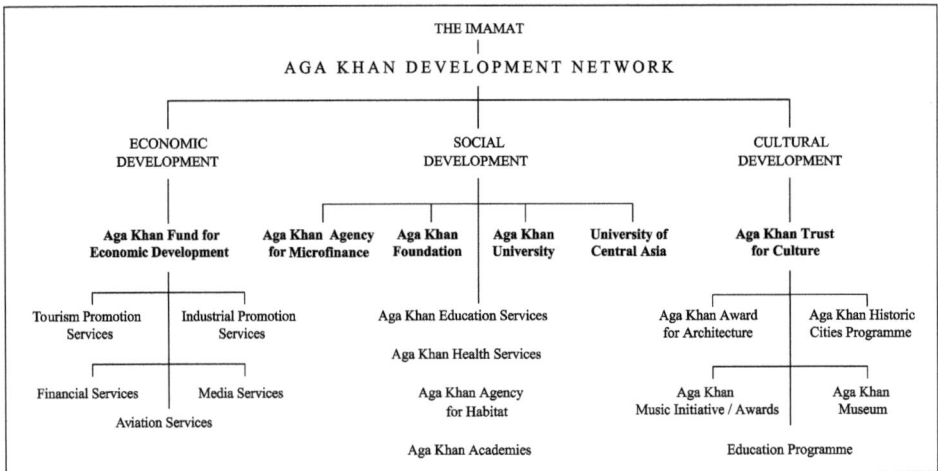

```
                              THE IMAMAT
                                  |
               AGA KHAN DEVELOPMENT NETWORK
```

Aga Khan Development Network

hearing appeals from decisions of the National Conciliation and Arbitration Boards. In all matters related to the governance of the Ismaili communities, however, the ultimate authority rests with the Imam of the time. The appointments of all the office holders in this system, as well as *mukhi*s and *kamadia*s, are strictly at the discretion of the Imam.

As noted, the present Imam has also concerned himself with a variety of social, developmental and cultural issues that are of direct benefit to the Ismailis and of broader value to other Muslims and the inhabitants of the developing countries of Asia and Africa. In these domains he has pioneered a multitude of initiatives, programmes and projects. For the implementation of these policies and programmes, and building on the foundations laid by his grandfather, Aga Khan IV has created a highly complex institutional network, which is generally referred to as the Aga Khan Development Network (AKDN).

In the area of social development, the present Imam's network has been particularly active in East Africa, Central Asia, Pakistan and India in projects for health, education and housing services as well as rural development. Many of these projects are promoted or financed through the Aga Khan Foundation (AKF) established in 1967, with its headquarters in Geneva and branches in some twenty countries. The Aga Khan Foundation collaborates with over thirty national and international organisations for the implementation of a variety of programmes in Asia, Africa, Europe and North America.

Aga Khan III launched a number of initiatives in educational reforms for the Ismailis, but the present Imam has built significantly upon that central interest of the Ismaili

49.5 The Aga Khan Centre, London, designed by Fumihiko Maki and inaugurated in 2018. The Aga Khan Centre houses The Institute of Ismaili Studies, the Aga Khan University's Institute for the Study of Muslim Civilisations, the Aga Khan Library London, and the Aga Khan Foundation, UK. It also contains a series of garden spaces that reflect the diversity of Muslim cultures around the world and in different historical ages.

Imamate and extended it to higher education and educational institutions. In this context, mention should be made of The Institute of Ismaili Studies, founded in London in 1977 for the promotion of Islamic studies in general, with special reference to Shi'i and Ismaili studies. The Institute is also in possession of the largest collection of Ismaili manuscripts, which are readily placed at the disposal of scholars worldwide. In addition to functioning as an academic institution, the Institute provides a number of initiatives and programmes for the benefit of the Ismaili community, including a Graduate Programme in Islamic Studies and Humanities (GPISH), which is now validated by the School of Oriental and African Studies, University of London. Subsequently, in 1983, the present Imam established in Karachi the Aga Khan University (AKU), with faculties of medicine, nursing and education, and an affiliated hospital, as well as the Institute for the Study of Muslim Civilisations (AKU-ISMC), set up in 2002 in London. Both the latter institution and The Institute of Ismaili Studies were relocated in 2018 to their magnificent, purpose-built, permanent premises at the Aga Khan Centre in London.

Among other initiatives of Aga Khan IV in the field of higher education, mention should be made of the University of Central Asia (UCA), set up in 2000, to foster economic and social development in the mountainous regions of Central Asia, while helping the peoples there to preserve and promote their cultural heritage. The UCA will eventually have three campuses, located in Naryn (Kyrgyzstan), Khorog (Tajikistan) and Tekeli (Kazakhstan). More recently, in 2011, the present Imam founded the Global Centre for Pluralism in Ottowa, to promote pluralistic values and practices in culturally diverse societies worldwide. As noted, Aga Khan IV has encouraged his followers to aim for a balanced spiritual and material life, and to acquire specialised education and skills, preparing them for the meritocratic world of the twenty-first century. In the economic field, too, the present Imam has launched many projects of his own. The AKDN's economic development activities, ranging from industrial promotion to media services and tourism promotion, are carried out by the Aga Khan Fund for Economic Development (AKFED) and its affiliates.

As a progressive Muslim leader, the present Ismaili Imam, as noted, has devoted much of his time and resources to promoting a better understanding of Islam as a major world civilisation with its plurality of social, intellectual and cultural traditions. In this connection, Aga Khan IV has launched a number of major innovative programmes for the preservation and regeneration of the cultural heritage of Muslim societies. The apex institution here is the Aga Khan Trust for Culture (AKTC), set up in 1988 in Geneva, for promoting awareness of the importance of the built environment in both historical and contemporary contexts, and for pursuing excellence in

49.6 The Azhar Park, Cairo. Created by the Aga Khan Trust for Culture (AKTC), the park was a gift from the present Ismaili Imam to the city of Cairo. The park's development led to an urban renewal project by AKTC in the adjacent al-Darb al-Ahmar neighbourhood.

architecture. The AKTC's mandate covers the Aga Khan Award for Architecture, founded in 1977, to enhance the understanding of Muslim cultures as expressed through architecture and to preserve the historically significant architectural heritage of Muslims; the Aga Khan Programme for Islamic Architecture, established in 1979 at Harvard University and the Massachusetts Institute of Technology (MIT), to educate architects and planners to cater for the needs of modern Muslim societies; the Aga Khan Historic Cities Programme, launched in the early 1990s to promote the conservation and restoration of buildings and public spaces in historic Muslim cities, such as Cairo where the Azhar Park was created; and the Aga Khan Museum in Toronto, inaugurated in 2014. The present Imam takes a personal and close interest in the operations of all his programmes and institutions, and regulates their activities through his secretariat at Aiglemont, near Chantilly, outside Paris. In 2015, the seat of the Ismaili Imamate was established in Lisbon, at the invitation of the Portuguese government. This move represents an example of the promotion of peace and harmony among cultures and religions. The premises of the seat, designated as Diwan, are located at the former Henrique de Mendonça Palace in Lisbon.

49.7 Aga Khan IV, delivering a speech at the Global Centre for Pluralism, Ottawa, Canada, 29 May 2014.

49.8 A view of the Aga Khan Library London, in the Aga Khan Centre. The library houses an important collection of works on the history and traditions of the Ismaili community as well as the wider Islamic world.

The present Imam, Shah Karim al-Husayni, Aga Khan IV, has successfully guided a progressive community of Shiʿi Muslims scattered globally over all the continents of the world. He has also created and directed a vast complex of institutions for the benefit of his followers and others, while concerning himself also with promoting a better understanding of Islamic civilisation in a world where Islamophobia has rapidly taken root. As a Muslim leader Aga Khan IV has indeed established a most remarkable record of achievement. In every country of Asia, the Middle East and Africa, where the Ismailis live as indigenous religious minorities and loyal citizens of their states, they enjoy exemplary standards of living, and those Ismailis who have immigrated to Western countries in Europe and North America have readily adapted to their new environments and home countries. These realities too represent an unparalleled record of success for a contemporary Muslim community. Another outstanding feature of this community is that many of its members offer their time or knowledge freely in the service and for the benefit of their co-religionists.

As we have seen in the biographies of the Ismaili Imams, summarised for the first time in this book, the Ismaili Muslims as a religious minority in many lands have

49.9 The present Ismaili Imam, Aga Khan IV, on the occasion of his Diamond Jubilee at Aiglemont, France, in 2018.

frequently experienced repression and persecution in the course of an eventful and complex history stretching back more than twelve centuries. Under such adverse circumstances, the Ismailis often resorted to extensive *taqiyya* or dissimulating practices for extended periods, disguising themselves variously as Sufis, Twelver Shiʿis, or even Sunnis. The fact that the Ismailis have emerged in modern times as a progressive Muslim community with a distinct religious identity and a strong sense of cohesion attests to the resilience of their heritage as well as to their adaptability under the capable and enlightened leadership of their last two Imams, who have led their community of *murid*s since 1885.

Glossary

Listings in this glossary are selected terms and names, chiefly of Arabic and Persian origin, frequently appearing in the book. Here pl. and lit. are the abbreviated forms for the words 'plural' and 'literally', and q.v. (*quod vide*) is used for cross-reference in the glossary.

ahl al-bayt: lit., the 'people of the house'; members of the household of the Prophet Muhammad, including especially besides the Prophet, ʿAli, Fatima, Hasan, Husayn, and their progeny. The Prophet's family is also designated as *al Muhammad*.

ʿAlids: descendants of ʿAli b. Abi Talib, cousin and son-in-law of the Prophet and also the first Shiʿi Imam. Descendants of ʿAli and Fatima, the Prophet's daughter, through their sons Hasan and Husayn are also called Hasanids and Husaynids, comprising the Fatimid ʿAlids.

ʿalim (pl., ʿulama): a scholar in Islamic religious sciences.

amir (pl., *umara*): military commander, prince; also title used by many independent rulers.

amir al-juyush: the 'commander of the armies'; a title specifically used by military viziers.

amir al-muʾminin: the 'commander of the faithful'; a title used by caliphs and Shiʿi Imams.

batin: the inward, hidden, or esoteric meaning behind the literal wording of sacred texts and religious prescriptions, notably the Qurʾan and the *shariʿa* (q.v.), in distinction from the *zahir* (q.v.).

bayʿa: recognition of authority, especially the act of swearing an oath of allegiance to a new sovereign or spiritual leader.

daʿi (pl., *duʿat*): lit., summoner; a religious missionary or propagandist, especially among the Ismailis; a high rank in the *daʿwa* (q.v.) hierarchy of the Ismailis.

daʿi al-duʿat: chief *daʿi*; the administrative head of the *daʿwa* (q.v.).

daʿwa: mission; in the religio-political sense, *daʿwa* is the invitation or call to adopt the cause of an individual or family claiming the right to the Imamate; it also refers to the hierarchy of ranks, sometimes called *hudud*, within the particular religious organisation developed for this purpose, especially among the Ismailis.

dawla: state, dynasty.

dawr: era, cycle of history.

faqih (pl., *fuqaha*): an exponent of *fiqh* or Islamic jurisprudence; a Muslim jurist in general.

farman: royal decree; written edict. For the Ismailis, it refers to any pronouncement, order or ruling made by the Imam.

Fatimids: descendants of ʿAli b. Abi Talib and Fatima, the Prophet's daughter, corresponding to Hasanid and Husaynid ʿAlids (q.v.); also the name of the Ismaili dynasty of Imam-caliphs from 909 to 1171.

ghulat (pl. of *ghali*): exaggerators, extremists; a term of disapproval for individuals accused of exaggeration (*ghuluww*) in religion and in respect to the Imams (q.v.).

ginan: a term derived from a Sanskrit word meaning contemplative or sacred knowledge, used in reference to the corpus

of the indigenous religious literature of the
Ismaili Khojas and some other communities
of South Asia. Composed in a number of
Indic languages, the hymn-like *ginan*s are
recorded mainly in the Khojki script.

hadith: a report, sometimes translated as
'tradition', relating an action or saying of the
Prophet, or the corpus of such reports
collectively, constituting one of the major
sources of Islamic law, second in
importance only to the Qur'an. For the
Shi'i Muslims, it also refers to the actions
and sayings of their Imams.

haqa'iq (pl. of *haqiqa*): truths; as a technical
term it denotes the gnostic system of
thought of the Ismailis. In this sense, the
haqa'iq are the unchangeable truths
contained in the *batin* (q.v.).

hujja: proof or the presentation of proof. The
application of the term, in the sense of the
proof of God's presence on earth, was
systematised by the early Imami Shi'is to
designate the category of prophets and
Imams. The *hujja* was also a high rank in
the Ismaili *da'wa* (q.v.) hierarchy. For the
Ismailis of different periods, the term also
generally denoted the chief representative of
the Imam when the Imam himself was not
accessible.

'ilm: knowledge, more specifically religious
knowledge. Amongst the Shi'is, it was held
that every Imam (q.v.) possessed a special
knowledge, *'ilm*, which was divinely
inspired and transmitted through the *nass*
(q.v.) of the previous Imam.

Imam: leader of a group of Muslims in prayer;
the supreme leader of the Muslim
community. The title has been particularly
used by the Shi'i Muslims in reference to
the persons recognised by them as the heads
of the Muslim community after the Prophet.
The Shi'is regard 'Ali b. Abi Talib and
certain of his descendants as such leaders,
Imams, the legitimate successors to the
Prophet. The Ismailis recognise certain
Husaynid 'Alids as their Imams,
descendants of Husayn b. 'Ali through
Isma'il b. Ja'far al-Sadiq.

kamadia: see *mukhi*.

khutba: an address or sermon delivered (by a
khatib) at the Friday midday public prayers
in the mosque; since it includes a prayer for
the ruler, mention of the ruler's name in the
khutba is a mark of sovereignty in Islam.

laqab (pl., *alqab*): honorific title, sobriquet,
nickname.

madhhab: a system or school of religious law in
Islam; in particular, it is applied to the four
main systems that arose among the Sunni
Muslims, namely, Hanafi, Maliki, Shafi'i and
Hanbali, named after the eponymous jurists
who founded them. Different Shi'i
communities have had their own *madhhab*s.
The Twelver (Ithna'ashari) Imami *madhhab*
is known as Ja'fari, named after Imam
Ja'far al-Sadiq. In Persian, the word
madhhab is also used to mean religion, a
synonym of *din*.

ma'dhun: lit., licentiate; a rank in the Ismaili
da'wa (q.v.) hierarchy below that of the *da'i*.
In the post-Fatimid period in particular,
ma'dhun was used generically by the
Ismailis in reference to the assistant of a
da'i.

Mahdi: lit., 'the rightly guided one'; the
eschatological figure in Islam; a name
applied to the restorer of true religion and
justice who, according to a widely held
Muslim belief, would appear and rule before
the end of the world. In Shi'i terminology,
the Mahdi was also designated as *qa'im*
(q.v.).

mu'allim: teacher, specifically religious teacher;
a rank in the *da'wa* (q.v.) hierarchy of the
post-Alamut Ismailis.

muhtasham: a title used commonly in reference
to the leader of the Ismailis of Quhistan, in
eastern Persia, during the Alamut period.

mukhi: a name originally used by the Ismaili
Khojas of South Asia in reference to the
head of a local Ismaili community, *jamat*
(Arabic, *jama'a*), who acted as treasurer and
also officiated on various occasions in the
local *jamat-khana*. The *mukhi*'s assistant was
called *kamadia* (pronounced *kamariya*). The
terms *mukhi* and *kamadia*, with various

pronunciations, were in time adopted by the Ismaili communities outside South Asia.

murid: disciple; specifically, disciple of a Sufi (q.v.) master; member of a Sufi order in general; also used in reference to the ordinary Ismailis in Persia and elsewhere during the post-Alamut period.

murshid: guide, Sufi master; also used in reference to the Ismaili Imams during the post-Alamut period.

nabi (pl., *anbiya*): prophet. The office of *nabi* is called *nubuwwa*.

nass: explicit designation of a successor by his predecessor, particularly relating to the Shiʿi view of succession to the Imamate, whereby each Imam (q.v.), under divine guidance, designates his successor.

pir: the Persian equivalent of the Arabic word *shaykh* in the sense of a spiritual guide, or Sufi (q.v.) master, qualified to lead disciples, *murids* (q.v.), on the mystical path, *tariqa* (q.v.), to truth, or *haqaʾiq* (q.v.); also used in reference to the Ismaili Imam and the holders of the highest ranks in the *daʿwa* (q.v.) hierarchy of the Ismailis of the post-Alamut period. It was also used in reference to the chief Ismaili *daʿi* in a certain territory, in this sense it was particularly used by the Ismaili Khojas in reference to the administrative heads of the *daʿwa* in South Asia.

qadi (pl., *qudat*): a religious judge administering Islamic law.

qadi al-qudat: chief *qadi*; the highest judiciary officer of the Fatimid state.

qaʾim: 'riser'; the eschatological figure in Islam, who is also designated as the Mahdi. In pre-Fatimid times, the Ismailis used both terms for the expected messianic Imam. After the rise of the Fatimids, the name al-Mahdi was reserved for the first Fatimid Imam-caliph, while the eschatological Imam, still expected for the future, was called the *qaʾim*. Belief in the coming of the Mahdi, or *qaʾim*, from the Prophet's household, *ahl al-bayt* (q.v.), became a central aspect of early Shiʿi teachings. In its Shiʿi use, the term denoted a member of the

ahl al-bayt who would rise and restore true Islam and justice on earth.

qiyama: Resurrection and the Last Day, when humankind would be judged and committed forever to either Paradise or Hell. In Ismaili thought, it was also used in reference to the end of any partial cycle in the history of humankind. The Ismailis of the Alamut period interpreted the *qiyama* symbolically and esoterically as the manifestation of the unveiled truth (*haqiqa*) in the spiritual reality of the current Imam (q.v.), who was also called the *qaʾim al-qiyama*.

qutb: lit., pole; in Islamic mysticism, it denotes the most perfect human being, or *al-insan al-kamil*; the head of a Sufi order, *tariqa* (q.v.).

satr: concealment, veiling; in Ismaili thought, it was used specifically in reference to a period, called *dawr al-satr*, or period of concealment, when the Imams (q.v.) were hidden from the eyes of their followers.

shah: an Iranian royal title denoting a king; it is often also added to the names of Sufi (q.v.) saints and Ismaili Imams of the post-Alamut period.

shariʿa: the divinely revealed sacred law of Islam; the whole body of rules guiding the life of a Muslim. The provisions of the *shariʿa* are worked out through the discipline of *fiqh* (q.v.).

Sufi: an exponent of Sufism (*tasawwuf*), the commonest term for that aspect of Islam that is based on the mystical life; hence, it denotes a Muslim mystic; more specifically, a member of an organised Sufi order, *tariqa* (q.v.).

sunna: custom, practice; particularly that associated with the exemplary life of the Prophet, comprising his deeds, utterances and his unspoken approval; it is embodied in *hadith* (q.v.).

tafsir: lit., explanation, commentary; particularly the commentaries on the Qurʾan; the external, philological exegesis of the Qurʾan, as distinct from *taʾwil* (q.v.).

ta'lim: teaching, instruction; in Shi'i thought, authoritative teaching in religion which could be carried out only by an Imam (q.v.) in every age after the Prophet.

taqiyya: precautionary dissimulation of one's true religious beliefs, especially in time of danger; used especially by the Ismaili and Twelver (Ithna'ashari) Shi'is.

tariqa: way, path; the mystical, spiritual path followed by Sufis (q.v.); also anyone of the organised Sufi orders. It is also used by the Ismailis in reference to their interpretation of Islam.

ta'wil: the educing of the inner meaning from the literal wording or apparent meaning of a text or ritual, religious prescription; as a technical term among the Shi'i Muslims, particularly the Ismailis, it denotes the method of educing the *batin* (q.v.) from the *zahir* (q.v.); as such it was extensively used by the Ismailis for the symbolic or esoteric interpretation of the Qur'an and the *shari'a*. Translated also as hermeneutical exegesis, *ta'wil* may be distinguished from *tafsir* (q.v.).

umma: community, any people as followers of a particular religion or prophet; in particular, the Muslims as forming a religious community.

waez (pl., *waezeen*): preacher of sermons (Arabic, *wa'iz*); particularly preachers of the Ismaili community.

wali al-'ahd: heir-designate, designated successor to a sovereign.

wasi (pl., *awsiya*): legatee; also the immediate successor to a prophet; in this sense, it was the function of the *awsiya* to interpret and explain the messages brought by prophets.

wazir: (Anglicised, vizier): a high officer of state, the equivalent of a chief minster. The power and status of the office of *wazir*, called *wizara*, varied greatly in different periods and under different Muslim dynasties.

zahir: the outward, literal or exoteric meaning of sacred texts and religious prescriptions, notably the Qur'an and the *shari'a* (q.v.), in distinction from the *batin* (q.v.).

Select Bibliography

Abbreviations

EI2   *The Encyclopaedia of Islam*, ed. H.A.R. Gibb et al. New ed., Leiden, 1954–2004.
EIR   *Encyclopaedia Iranica*, ed. E. Yarshater. London and New York, 1982—.
EIS   *Encyclopaedia Islamica*, ed. W. Madelung and F. Daftary. Leiden, 2008—.

Aga Khan I, Ḥasan ʿAlī Shāh. *The First Aga Khan: Memoirs of the 46th Ismaili Imam*, ed. and tr. D. Beben and D. Mohammad Poor. London, 2018.

Aga Khan III, Sultan Muhammad Shah. *The Memoirs of Aga Khan: World Enough and Time*. London, 1954.

—. *Aga Khan III: Selected Speeches and Writings of Sir Sultan Muhammad Shah*, ed. K.K. Aziz. London, 1997–1998.

Algar, Hamid. ʿMaḥallātī, Āghā Khānʾ, *EI2*, vol. 5, pp. 1221–1222.

Al-i Davud, Sayyid Ali. ʿAbū al-Ḥasan Khān Beglerbegī Maḥallātīʾ, *EIS*, vol. 2, pp. 29–32.

Amir-Moezzi, Mohammad Ali. *The Divine Guide in Early Shiʿism: The Sources of Esotericism in Islam*, tr. D. Streight. Albany, NY, 1994.

Amir-Moezzi, Mohammad Ali and Christian Jambet. *What is Shiʿi Islam? An Introduction*, tr. K. Casler and E. Ormsby. London and New York, 2018.

Asani, Ali S. *Ecstasy and Enlightenment: The Ismaili Devotional Literature of South Asia*. London, 2002.

Assaad, Sadik A. *The Reign of al-Hakim bi Amr Allah (386/996–411/1021): A Political Study*. Beirut, 1974.

Boivin, Michel. *La rénovation du Shîʿisme Ismaélien en Inde et au Pakistan. Dʾaprès les ecrits et les discours de Sulṭān Muḥammad Shah Aga Khan (1902–1954)*. London, 2003.

Bosworth, C. Edmund. *The New Islamic Dynasties: A Chronological and Genealogical Manual*. Edinburgh, 1996.

Brett, Michael. *The Fatimid Empire*. Edinburgh, 2017.

Canard, Marius. ʿal-ʿAzīz Biʾllāhʾ, *EI2*, vol. 1, pp. 823–825.

—. ʿFāṭimidsʾ, *EI2*, vol. 2, pp. 850–862.

Corbin, Henry. *En Islam Iranien: Aspects spirituels et philosophiques*. Paris, 1971–1972.

Cortese, Delia and Simonetta Calderini. *Women and the Fatimids in the World of Islam*. Edinburgh, 2006.

Dachraoui, Farhat. ʿal-Ḳāʾimʾ, *EI2*, vol. 4, pp. 458–460.

—. ʿal-Manṣūr Biʾllāhʾ, *EI2*, vol. 6, pp. 434–435.

—. ʿal-Muʿizz li-Dīn Allāhʾ, *EI2*, vol. 7, pp. 485–489.

Daftary, Farhad. *The Ismāʿīlīs: Their History and Doctrines*. Cambridge, 1990; 2nd ed., Cambridge, 2007.

—. *The Assassin Legends: Myths of the Ismaʿilis*. London, 1994.

—. 'Ḥasan-i Ṣabbāḥ and the Origins of the Nizārī Ismaʿili Movement', in F. Daftary, ed., *Mediaeval Ismaʿili History and Thought*. Cambridge, 1996, pp. 181–204; reprinted in F. Daftary, *Ismailis in Medieval Muslim Societies*. London, 2005, pp. 124–148.

—. *A Short History of the Ismailis: Traditions of a Muslim Community*. Edinburgh, 1998.

—. 'Ismāʿīlī-Sufi Relations in Early Post-Alamūt and Safavid Persia', in Leonard Lewisohn and David Morgan, ed., *The Heritage of Sufism*: Volume III, *Late Classical Persianate Sufism (1501–1750)*. Oxford, 1999, pp. 275–289.

—. *Ismaili Literature: A Bibliography of Sources and Studies*. London, 2004.

— (ed.) *A Modern History of the Ismailis*. London, 2011.

—. *Historical Dictionary of the Ismailis*. Lanham and Toronto, 2012.

—. *A History of Shiʿi Islam*. London, 2013.

—. 'The Fatimid Caliphs: Rise and Fall', in Assadullah Souren Melikian-Chirvani, ed., *The World of the Fatimids*. Toronto, London and Munich, 2018, pp. 20–43.

—. 'Dāʿī', *EIR*, vol. 6, pp. 590–593.

—. 'Esmāʿīl b. Jaʿfar al-Ṣādeq', *EIR*, vol. 8, pp. 625–626.

—. 'Ḥākem be-Amr-Allāh', *EIR*, vol. 11, pp. 572–573.

—. 'Ḥasan II', *EIR*, vol. 12, pp. 24–25.

—. 'Ḥasan Ṣabbāḥ', *EIR*, vol. 12, pp. 34–37.

—. 'Jalāl-al-Din Ḥasan III', *EIR*, vol. 14, pp. 403–404.

—. 'Kahak', *EIR*, vol. 15, pp. 349–350.

—. 'Nūr al-Dīn Muḥammad II', *EI2*, vol. 8, pp. 133–134.

—. 'Rāshid al-Dīn Sinān', *EI2*, vol. 8, pp. 442–443.

—. Rukn al-Dīn Khurshāh', *EI2*, vol. 8, pp. 598–599

—. 'Shams al-Dīn Muḥammad', *EI2*, vol. 9, pp. 295–296.

—. 'Muḥammad III b. Ḥasan, ʿAlāʾ al-Dīn', *EI2*, vol. 12, Supplement, pp. 632–633.

—. 'Muḥammad b. Ismāʿil al-Maymūn', *EI2*, vol. 12, Supplement, pp. 634–635.

—. 'ʿAbd Allāh b. Maymūn al-Qaddāḥ', *EIS*, vol. 1, pp. 167–169.

—. 'Aga Khan', in *The Princeton Encyclopedia of Islamic Political Thought*, ed. G. Bowering. Princeton, 2013, pp. 22–23.

— et al. 'Ismaʿilism', *EIR*, vol. 14, pp. 172–212.

Daftary, Farhad and J.H. Kramers. 'Salamiyya', *EI2*, vol. 8, pp. 921–923.

Daftary, Farhad and D.S. Richards. 'Fāṭimid Dynasty', in *The Oxford Encyclopaedia of the Islamic World*, ed. John L. Esposito. New York, 2009, vol. 2, pp. 229–232.

Daftary, Farhad and Zulfikar Hirji. *The Ismailis: An Illustrated History*. London, 2008.

Department of History, Centre for the Great Islamic Encyclopaedia. 'Aga Khan', *EIS*, vol. 3, pp. 153–165.

Dumasia, Naoroji M. *The Aga Khan and His Ancestors: A Biographical and Historical Sketch*. Bombay, 1939; reprinted, New Delhi, 2008.

Eboo Jamal, Nadia. *Surviving the Mongols: Nizārī Quhistānī and the Continuity of Ismaili Traditions in Persia*. London, 2002.

Esposito, John L. (ed.) *The Oxford Dictionary of Islam*. Oxford, 2003.

Frischauer, Willi. *The Aga Khans*. London, 1970.

Gleave, Robert, et al. 'Jaʿfar al-Ṣādeq', *EIR*, vol. 14, pp. 349–366.

Habibi Mazaheri, Masʿud. 'Aḥmad b. ʿAbd Allāh al-Mastūr', *EIS*, vol. 3, pp. 215–218.

Halm, Heinz. *The Empire of the Mahdi: The Rise of the Fatimids*, tr. M. Bonner. Leiden, 1996.

—. *The Fatimids and their Traditions of Learning*. London, 1997.

—. *Die Kalifen von Kairo. Die Fatimiden in Ägypten 973–1074*. Munich, 2003.

—. *Shiʿism*, tr. J. Watson and M. Hill. 2nd ed., Edinburgh, 2004.

—. 'Sitt al-Mulk', *EI2*, vol. 9, pp. 685–686.

Hamdan, Hussein and Aram Vardanyan. 'Ismaili Coins from the Alamut Period', in Peter Willey, *Eagle's Nest: Ismaili Castles in Iran and Syria*. London, 2005, pp. 288–307.

Ḥasan-i Maḥmūd-i Kātib. *Haft bāb*, ed. and tr. S. J. Badakhchani as *Spiritual Resurrection in Shiʿi Islam: An Early Ismaili Treatise on the Doctrine of Qiyāmat*. London, 2017.

Hodgson, Marshall G. S. 'The Ismāʿīlī State', in *The Cambridge History of Iran*: Volume 5, *The Saljuq and Mongol Periods*, ed. John A. Boyle. Cambridge, 1968, pp. 422–482.

Idrīs ʿImād al-Dīn b. al-Ḥasan. *ʿUyun al-akhbār wa-funūn al-āthār*, ed. A. Chleilat et al. Damascus, 2007–2014.

Ivanow, Wladimir. 'Tombs of Some Persian Ismaili Imams', *Journal of the Bombay Branch of the Royal Asiatic Society*, New Series, 14 (1938), pp. 49–62.

—. *Alamut and Lamasar: Two Mediaeval Ismaili Strongholds in Iran*. Tehran, 1960.

—. 'A Forgotten Branch of the Ismailis', *Journal of the Royal Asiatic Society* (1938), pp. 57–79.

—. *Ismaili Literature: A Bibliographical Survey*. Tehran, 1963.

Jafri, S. Husain M. *Origins and Early development of Shīʿa Islam*. London, 1979.

Juwaynī, ʿAlāʾ al-Dīn ʿAṭā-Malik. *Taʾrīkh-i jahān-gushā*, ed. M. Qazvīnī. Leiden and London, 1912–1937. English trans., *The History of World-Conqueror*, tr. John A. Boyle. Manchester, 1958.

Kāshānī, Abu'l-Qāsim ʿAbd Allāh b. ʿAlī. *Zubdat al-tawārīkh: bakhsh-i Fāṭimiyān va Nizāriyān*, ed. M. T. Dānishpazhūh. 2nd ed., Tehran, 1987.

Khākī Khurāsānī, Imām Qulī. *Dīwān*, ed. W. Ivanow. Bombay, 1933.

Kohlberg, Etan (ed.) *Shīʿism*. Aldershot, Hants, 2003.

—. 'Zayn al-ʿĀbidīn', *EI2*, vol. 11, pp. 481–483.

Lakhani, M. Ali. *Faith and Ethics: The Vision of the Ismaili Imamat*. London, 2017.

Lalani, Arzina R. *Early Shīʿī Thought: The Teachings of Imam Muḥammad al-Bāqir*. London, 2000.

Landolt, Hermann, S. Sheikh and K. Kassam (ed.) *An Anthology of Ismaili Literature: A Shiʿi Vision of Islam*. London, 2008.

Lane-Poole, Stanley. *The Mohammadan Dynasties: Chronological and Genealogical Tables with Historical Introductions*. Westminster, 1894.

Lewisohn, Leonard. 'An Introduction to the History of Modern Persian Sufism, Part I: The Niʿmatullāhī Order: Persecution, Revival and Schism', *Bulletin of the School of Oriental and African Studies*, 41 (2003), pp. 439–453.

—. 'Sufism and Ismāʿīlī Doctrine in the Persian Poetry of Nizārī Quhistānī (645-721/1247-1321)', *Iran, Journal of the British Institute of Persian Studies*, 41 (2003), pp. 229–251.

Madelung, Wilferd. *The Succession to Muḥammad: A Study of the Early Caliphate*. Cambridge, 1997.

—. *Studies in Medieval Shiʿism*, ed. S. Schmidtke. Farnham, Surrey, 2012.

—. 'ʿAlī b. al-Ḥosayn', *EIR*, vol. 1, pp. 849–850.

—. 'al-Baqer, Abū Jaʿfar Moḥammad', *EIR*, vol. 3, pp. 725–726.

—. 'Ismāʿīliyya', *EI2*, vol. 4, pp. 198–206.

—. 'Shīʿa', *EI2*, vol. 9, pp. 420–424.

— et al. 'Ḥosayn b. ʿAlī', *EIR*, vol. 12, pp. 493–506.

Mājid, ʿAbd al-Munʿim. *al-Imām al-Mustanṣir bi'llāh al-Fāṭimī*. Cairo, 1961.

al-Maqrīzī, Taqī al-Dīn Aḥmad b. ʿAlī. *Ittiʿāẓ al-ḥunafāʾ*, ed. Ayman F. Sayyid. Damascus, 2010.

Maʿṣūm ʿAlī Shāh, Muḥammad Maʿṣūm Shīrāzī. *Ṭarāʾiq al-ḥaqāʾiq*, ed. M. J. Maḥjūb. Tehran, 1339–1345 Sh./1960–1966.

Melikian-Chirvani, Assadullah Souren (ed.) *The World of the Fatimids*. Toronto, London and Munich, 2018.

Mirza, Nasseh Ahmad. *Syrian Ismailism: The Ever Living Line of the Imamate, AD 1100–1260*. Richmond, Surrey, 1997.

Momen, Moojan. *An Introduction to Shiʿi Islam*. New Haven, 1985.

al-Mufīd, Muḥammad b. Muḥammad. *Kitāb al-Irshād: The Book of Guidance into the Lives of the Twelve Imams*, tr. I.K.A. Howard. London, 1981.

Mustanṣir biʾllāh. *Pandiyāt-i javānmardī*, ed. and tr. W. Ivanow. Leiden, 1953.

Nanji, Azim. *The Nizārī Ismāʿīlī Tradition in the Indo-Pakistan Subcontinent*. Delmar, NY, 1978.

Poonawala, Ismaili K. *Biobibliography of Ismāʿīlī Literature*. Malibu, CA, 1977.

Poonawala, Ismail K. and E. Kohlberg. 'ʿAlī b. Abī Ṭāleb', *EIR*, vol. 1, pp. 838–848.

Pourjavady, Nasrollah and Peter L. Wilson. 'Ismāʿīlīs and Niʿmātullāhīs', *Studia Islamica*, 41 (1975), pp. 113–135.

Rashīd al-Dīn, Faḍl Allāh b. ʿImād al-Dawla. *Jāmiʿ al-tawārīkh: taʾrīkh-i Ismāʿīliyān*, ed. M. Rawshan. Tehran, 2008.

Ruthven, Malise. 'The Aga Khan Development Network and Institutions', in F. Daftary, ed., *A Modern History of the Ismailis*. London, 2011, pp. 189–220.

Rypka, Jan. *History of Iranian Literature*, ed. K. Jahn. Dordrecht, 1968.

Samiʿi, Majid. 'Anjudān', *EIS*, vol. 3, pp. 731–734.

Sayyid, Ayman F. *al-Dawla al-Fāṭimiyya fī Miṣr: tafsīr jadīd*. 2nd ed., Cairo, 2000.

Shackle, Christopher, and Z. Moir. *Ismaili Hymns from South Asia: An Introduction to the Ginans*. London, 1992.

Shah-Kazemi, Reza. *Justice and Remembrance: Introducing the Spirituality of Imam ʿAli*. London, 2006.

Shah-Kazemi, Reza, et al. 'ʿAlī b. Abī Ṭālib', *EIS*, vol. 3, pp. 477–582.

Shihāb al-Dīn Shāh al-Ḥusaynī. *Khiṭābāt-i ʿāliya*, ed. H. Ujāqī. Bombay, 1963.

Sutūda, Manūchihr. *Qilāʿ-i Ismāʿīliyya*. Tehran, 1345 Sh./1966.

Thomson, Kirsten. *Politics and Power in Late Fatimid Egypt: The Reign of Caliph al-Mustanṣir*. London, 2016.

al-Ṭūsī, Khwāja Naṣīr al-Dīn Muḥammad. *Rawḍa-yi taslīm*, ed. and tr. S. J. Badakhchani as *Paradise of Submission: A Medieval Treatise on Ismaili Thought*. London, 2005.

Vazīrī, Aḥmad ʿAlī Khān. *Taʾrīkh-i Kirmān*, ed. M. T. Bāstānī Pārīzī. 2nd ed., Tehran, 1352 Sh./1973.

Vellani, Shams. *People of Faith: Essays on a Historical and Contemporary Profile of the Ismailis*. London, 2020.

Virani, Shafique N. *The Ismailis in the Middle Ages*. Oxford, 2007.

Walker, Paul E. 'The Ismāʿīlī Daʿwa and the Fāṭimid Caliphate', in M. W. Daly, ed., *The Cambridge History of Egypt*: Volume I, *Islamic Egypt, 640–1517*, ed. Carl F. Petry. Cambridge, 1998, pp. 120–150, 557–560.

—. *Caliph of Cairo: Al-Hakim bi-Amr Allah, 996–1021*. Cairo and New York, 2009.

—. *Exploring an Islamic Empire: Fatimid History and its Sources*. London, 2002.

—. *Fatimid History and Ismaili Doctrine*. Aldershot, Hampshire, 2008.

—. 'Institute of Ismaili Studies', *EIR*, vol. 13, pp. 164–166.

Willey, Peter. *Eagle's Nest: Ismaili Castles in Iran and Syria*. London, 2005.

Zambaur, Eduard K.M. von. *Manuel de généalogie et de chronologie pour l'histoire de l'Islam*. Hannover, 1927; repr. Osnabrück, 1976.

Picture credits

Aga Khan Museum, Toronto 2.3. 12.3, 17.3, 18.3, 28.2, 26.1; Alamut Cultural Base 23.4, 27.3; Alamy 45.1; Arthur M. Sackler Gallery, Smithsonian Institution, Washington, DC 5.2, 28.3, 32.6, 35.2, 35.3; Basilica di San Marco, Venice 15.3; Bibliothèque nationale de France 27.2; Bodleian Library 11.3, 20.6; Bridgeman Images 44.4; Brooklyn Museum 46.1; Dallas Museum of Art/Ira Schrank 3.1; Daniel Demeter/Syria Photo Guide 8.1, 24.1, 24.2, 24.3; Edmund Sumner 49.9; F. Daftary Collection 18.6, 28.1, 32.1, 32.3, 37.1, 37.2, 40.1, 40.2, 40.3, 44.1, 44.2, 44.3, 46.2, 46.3, 46.6, 46.7, 46.9, 47.1, 47.2; GCP 49.4, Harvard Art Museums 2.1, 46.4; IIS, Janis Esots 20.1; IIS, R. Harris 11.4, 14.3, 18.4; IIS, Naushin Shariff 16.4, 16.5; ISCU 8.2, 11.1, 11.2, 11.5, 12.1, 12.2, 13.1, 13.2, 14.1, 14.2, 14.4, 15.1, 15.2, 16.1, 16.2, 16.6, 17.1, 17.2, 18.1, 18.2, 18.5, 19.1, 19.2, 20.4, 20.5, 23.1, 23.2, 26.2, 26.3, 26.4, 26.5, 32.2, 32.4, 32.5, 35.1, 46.10, 48.2; Istanbul University Library 1.3; John Sturrock 49.7; Kareem Ibrahim 49.3; Karim Jivraj 20.2, 20.3, 23.6, 27.4; Library of Congress Prints and Photographs Division 5.1; Marc Ryckaert (MJJR) 48.4; Mehdi Rafiei 23.5; Metropolitan Museum of Art 17.4, 29.1, 46.5; Enayat Meghani c/o ITREB Pakistan, and Mohamed Keshavjee, 46.8; Süleymaniye Library, Istanbul 9.1; Musée du Louvre 15.4; Museum of Islamic Art, Cairo 16.3; National Library of Russia 4.1; National Portrait Gallery 48.1, 48.3; Nicolas Tikhomiroff 49.1; Sameer Noorani 46.11; Public domain 2.2, 23.3; Shutterstock 49.6; Sotheby's 12.4; TAJAN 3.2; The British Library Board 1.1; Topkapı Palace Museum, Istanbul, 1.2; V&A 41.1; Världskultur Museern 17.5; Vazir Karsan 49.5; Virginia Museum of Fine Arts 27.1; Zahur Ramji 49.2, 49.8.

Maps and graphics by R. Harris, except the AKDN organogram.

Every effort has been made to trace copyright holders and to obtain their permission for the use of copyright material. The publisher apologises for any errors or omissions in the above list and would be grateful if notified of any corrections that should be incorporated in future reprints or editions of this book.

Index

bay'a (oath of allegiance) 24, 29, 225
Berbers 3, 60, 69, 70, 73, 75, 81, 93, 103, 118;
 see also Kutama; Sanhaja; Zanata
al-Bharuchi, Hasan b. Nuh 46
Bibi Sarkara, mother of Aga Khan I 14, 195, 201
Birjand, in southern Khurasan 149
Bohras 46
Bombay (Mumbai) 15–16, 163, 202, 208, 209–11, 213, 217–18, 220, 226
Brethren of Purity *see* Ikhwan al-Safa
Britain, British 15–16, 202, 210–11, 213, 217–18
Buluggin, founder of the Zirid dynasty of Ifriqiya 75, 90
Burhan I Nizam Shah 173
Buyids (Buwayhids), of Persia and Iraq 5, 32, 83, 90–1
Buzurg-Umid, Kiya, lord of Alamut 118, 120, 125, 127
Byzantines 3, 71, 73, 79, 81, 89

Cairo (al-Qahira) 4, 6–8, 79, 83–4, 89, 93–7, 99–100, 103–6, 111–12, 117–18, 122, 220, 235
Calcutta 15, 210, 217
caliphate xi, 2–4, 6–7, 10, 24, 27–28, 29, 33, 44, 50, 53, 60, 65, 67, 70–1, 73, 79, 84, 87, 91, 93–5, 100, 103, 111–12
Canada 18, 226
Carmatians *see* Qarmatis
Caspian Sea 121
Central Asia 3, 5, 10–11, 17–18, 38, 85, 94, 104, 136, 141, 147–8, 157, 166, 178, 185, 213, 234
Christians, Christianity 5, 54, 90, 95
concealed Imams xii, 51–60, 66, 117–23
Copts, Christian community in Egypt 5, 90
cosmology 50
Crusaders 8, 134
cyclical history 50

Da'a'im al-Islam, of al-Qadi al-Nu'man 4, 85–6
da'i (summoner) 2–6, 8, 10–12, 50, 53–5, 58, 65–7, 69–70, 83–5, 90, 94–5, 100, 104–5, 108–9, 117, 120, 125–6, 134, 141, 149, 166–7, 178
da'i al-du'at (chief *da'i*) 6, 85, 104

Damascus (Dimashq) 33, 37, 89
Dar al-'Ilm (Dar al-Hikma), Cairo 5, 94
Dar es Salaam, in Tanzania 220, 226–7
al-Darazi, Muhammad b. Isma'il, Druze leader 94
dassondh (tithe) 186
da'wa (Persian, *da'wat*) 2–9, 11–13, 52, 54, 60, 65–6, 84, 87, 90, 93–4, 100, 104–5, 109, 112, 125, 135, 143, 147, 157, 162, 166–7, 175, 177–8, 185–6
 early Ismaili 2–4, 53, 55, 57–8, 60, 65–6, 73, 79, 83, 109, 111
 Fatimid 4, 6–7, 71, 79, 84, 87, 109
 Nizari 6–9, 105, 112–13, 118, 122, 131, 141, 148, 181
al-da'wa al-hadiya (the rightly guiding mission) 2, 52
dawla (state, dynasty) 3, 87
dawr, adwar (cycle/s, era/s) 50
dawr al-satr (period of concealment) 2, 8, 49, 51, 53, 125
 for pre-Fatimid Ismailis 49, 53
 for Nizaris 57, 118, 122
Day of Judgement 9, 125; *see also* qiyama; eschatology; Paradise
Day of Resurrection *see* qiyama
Daylam, Daylaman, region in northern Persia 120
Deccan, in India 13, 173, 193
Delhi 218
Dhu'l-Faqar 'Ali, Ismaili Imam 175–8
didar, visiting the Imams 14, 183
Druze (Druses) 95–6

East Africa xii, 1, 16–17, 211, 213, 217, 220, 222–3, 226–7, 232
education 16–19, 105, 213, 216–18, 220, 222–3, 227, 230, 234
Egypt, Egyptians xii, 4, 6–10, 17, 32, 66–7, 69, 71, 73, 81, 83, 86, 89, 91, 93, 100, 103–4, 112, 117–18, 122, 223
Epistles of the Brethren of Purity *see* Rasa'il Ikhwan al-Safa
eschatology 50; *see also* qiyama
esoteric interpretation *see* ta'wil
Europe, Europeans xii, 1, 8, 14, 16, 71, 134, 196, 201, 211, 217–18, 226